Cases in
Government Succession Planning

*Action-Oriented Strategies for Public-Sector
Human Capital Management, Workforce Planning,
Succession Planning, and Talent Management*

Edited by

William J. Rothwell
Workforce Education and Development
Pennsylvania State University
305A Keller Building
University Park, PA 16802
Phone: 814-863-2581
Fax: 814-863-7532
E-mail: wjr9@psu.edu

James Alexander
710 Roeder Road
Silver Spring, MD 20910
Phone: 301-578-1695
E-mail:
halex8420874@yahoo.com

Mark Bernhard
Director
Continuing and Professional Education
702 University City Boulevard (0364)
Virginia Tech University
Blacksburg, VA 24061
540-231-4682
540-231-9886 (Fax)
E-mail: mcb7@vt.edu

HRD Press • Amherst • Massachusetts

Published by: HRD Press, Inc.
                22 Amherst Road
                Amherst, Massachusetts 01002
                1-800-822-2801 (U.S. and Canada)
                1-413-253-3488
                1-413-253-3490 (fax)
                http://www.hrdpress.com

ISBN: 978-1-59996-154-5

Editorial services by Suzanne Bay
Production services by Anctil Virtual Office
Cover design by Eileen Klockars

Dedication

William J. Rothwell dedicates this book to his wife Marcelina and his daughter Candice. They are the inspiration of his life.

James Alexander dedicates this book to his family, and especially to Prudence for her ongoing support and encouragement.

Mark Bernhard would like to dedicate this book to his wife, Laura, and his three children: Sam, Amy, and Jake. They are the light of his life and make everything else possible.

Acknowledgments

The authors would like to thank Larry Bienati and Jim Graber for their professional contributions to this book, which have broadened its scope immeasurably.

CONTENTS

INTRODUCTION

Succession planning is an important part of overall public- and private-sector planning, but government succession planning is somewhat unique. Government employers do have many things in common with their counterparts in private-sector and not-for-profit enterprises, but they also face some unique challenges that private-sector managers and not-for-profit managers do not. "Government" is not one entity, but many, and there are differences among international governments, U.S. and state governments, and local government entities. "Local" government can refer to a country government, a municipal government, a township, a village, a school system, water and sewer departments, public health departments, volunteer political action groups, and even waste management and mosquito abatement districts! Many of these governmental entities do not ever use the same terms to discuss succession. (What's the difference, for instance, between *replacement planning, succession planning, workforce planning, strategic human capital management,* and *talent management*?)

But let's treat first things first in this introduction. What is the need for this book, what is its purpose, and for whom is it written? What are some key definitions? How does government succession practice differ from practices in other settings? What are some key concepts for readers to bear in mind as they examine the cases in this book? What key pitfalls should be avoided? This introduction will cover these issues.

The Need for the Book

Almost everyone knows that the government workforce is aging, but few people realize that this problem is actually global in scope and not restricted to the U.S. Indeed, governments outside the U.S.—including United Nations agencies—face a wave of retirements that will complicate and even threaten their future effectiveness.

Why should we all care about this problem? If we want to receive government services (or are dependent on them), we *should* care. If business leaders rely on government to provide essential services, then they *must* care. After all, it is tough to live and work in a society where roads and bridges are crumbling, schools are dysfunctional, prisons are not well staffed, and other government services are not being efficiently and effectively provided. Society cannot bear it if government does not work.

The Rockefeller Institute of Government performed a public-sector workforce analysis that was published by the IBM Endowment for the Business of Government. "Life After Civil Service Reform: The Texas, Georgia, and Florida Experiences" reported that:

— Nearly half of all government workers (local, state, and federal) are 45 years old or older, compared with just over 31 percent for the private sector.

— From 1994 to 2001, the percentage of older workers in the government workforce showed greater increases for those years than the percentage of older workers in the private sector.

— Nationally, 50 percent of government jobs are in occupations requiring specialized training, education, and job skills, compared to just 29 percent in the private sector.

— The number of workers age 25 to 44—prime recruitment fodder for government—is expected to drop by three million from 1998 to 2008. This suggests that the competition for workers just coming into their professional stride is going to get increasingly fierce.

Max Stier, author of *The Future of the Public Workforce: Issues, Challenges, and Actions Needed,* an issue paper written for the American Society for Public Administration, says that compounding the usual difficulties for government and good public administration are several other workforce-related issues:

— Despite the impact on the national psyche of the 9/11/2001 attacks, public trust in government continues to be relatively low. While the general public might appreciate the work of public employees more that they did all through 2001, government is still not seen as an employer of choice by most of the highly skilled (and sought after) members of the national labor pool.

— While a growing number of some of the most experienced and dedicated public employees are preparing to retire from or otherwise leave public service, many government jurisdictions, including the federal government, are discovering that due to years of downsizing and tight budgets, the employee "bench strength" in many organizations at the mid-career level is quite low. Recruitment for public service jobs needs to focus at all levels: entry level, mid-level, and senior level. Many government organizations still focus primarily, if not exclusively, at the entry level.

— The poor image of government as an employer needs to be addressed not only through a better public relations campaign, but also by ensuring that government truly is a model employer with a world-class workplace.

— The challenges that governments are being asked to address and the size of national populations looking to the government for services is growing, requiring it not only to replace departing employees, but to replace them, in many cases, with higher-skilled employees.

— Many government organizations still operate on the model of a "cradle to grave" workforce that will spend their entire careers within government. There is evidence that the percentage of high-performing employees who will actually do that is rapidly declining.

— Government organizations, therefore, need to adjust their workforce planning, employee benefit policies, recruitment and retention practices, and so on.

— Government civil service laws, rules, and procedures were developed to promote and protect public service values such as merit-based hiring, advancement and removal, fairness and equity, non-partisanship, and diversity. However, over time many of those laws, rules, and procedural safeguards have become outdated or so encrusted with successive layers of "refinements," additions, and new requirements that they now often hinder rather than help government organizations in their quest to recruit, retain, and motivate a quality workforce.

— Criticisms of some civil service system weaknesses, though sometimes justified, can also unintentionally lead to cures that are worse than the illness.

— Movement to an "at will" system for hiring and termination purposes without some procedural safeguards against undue partisan political interference could have serious consequences for a government and the public it serves.

The purpose of this book

This book is not intended to provide best-practice examples. For one thing, it is tough to find information about government succession planning and related topics. This book is intended to provide examples of how various governmental entities have met the succession planning challenge. Case studies describe real people doing real things, and that is our purpose. We want to describe how real managers in real governmental agencies at different levels of government and in different settings addressed the succession challenge. It is intended to be a primer on government succession planning, human capital management, talent management, and workforce planning.

The audience for the book

This book is written for government leaders, government human resource professionals, and students interested in government careers.

Key terms

It is important to explain how we are defining key terms in the book, such as these:

Short-term replacement planning. What should be done when individuals in important positions are temporarily out sick or on vacation? Who is in charge? Short-term replacement planning addresses these questions. It allows an organization to continue functioning even when individuals in important positions are away from the organization.

Long-term replacement planning. What should be done in the event of the sudden death, extended disability, or other long-term loss of individuals in key positions? Long-term replacement planning facilitates organizational decision making by identifying who can be appointed to the position on an acting basis or on a permanent basis.

Succession planning. Not to be confused with replacement planning, succession planning focuses on building the organization's internal bench strength so that individuals who are interested in promotion are given a chance to become qualified through systematic development. In short, succession planning does not guarantee promotions; it is about planning how you will prepare individuals to be qualified for promotions.

Technical succession planning. While traditional succession planning tends to focus on vertical promotion (that is, up the chain-of-command), technical succession planning focuses on preserving institutional memory. Individuals with much experience might possess special technical knowledge or institutional memory that is valuable to the organization. Technical succession planning is thus about passing on this kind of wisdom from one "generation" of workers to the successors in the next generation. Some might say that this wisdom is the same as knowledge or intellectual capital, but it really is not: technical succession planning is all about isolating, distilling, and passing on special knowledge about the organization, its products, its services, and its customers in practical ways.

Workforce planning. Workforce planning is broader (bigger) than succession planning. While traditional succession planning focuses on leadership continuity, workforce planning asks how well the collective talents and skills of individuals in the organization match up to the strategic plan and objectives of the organization. State government agencies often talk about their succession plans in terms of workforce planning.

Human capital management. Human capital management is broader (bigger) than workforce planning. It focuses on integrating all aspects of human resource management to ensure that the right kind of people are recruited, selected, compensated, appraised, and developed to meet the agency's present and future needs. U.S. government agencies often refer to people planning as "strategic human capital management."

Talent management. Talent management, sometimes a term in search of a meaning, refers here to the integrated application of approaches to recruiting, retaining, and developing the best people in a way consistent with organizational needs.

Job competencies. A competency is a set of related skills that leads to successful or best performance. *General competencies* are the sets of related skills that are or should be shared across a group of individuals at the same level on the organization chart. *Technical/functional competencies* are the special technical competencies essential to performing in one function or department. Competencies are foundational to succession planning, workforce planning, human capital management, and talent management because they permit decision makers to pinpoint what is needed by people to perform at a given level or in a department or function.

How is government succession different from other sectors?

Government succession shares more in common with private and not-for-profit organizations than many would care to admit, but there are a few important differences worth discussing.

First, in democratic governments, succession at the highest levels is usually a function of elections. Unlike businesses, government agencies are headed up by individuals who are either elected by the people or are appointed by those who are elected. Voters are the ultimate judges of qualifications and merit to serve in leadership.

Second, in democratic governments, succession is subject to law—sometimes in the form of a written civil service code that has the force of law. Succession can also be affected by collective-bargaining agreements that prohibit replacement planning that would identify successors before a vacancy occurs. There is generally no prohibition from developing people who are interested in being promoted and trying to qualify. Most civil service systems require all job vacancies to be posted and all applicants to be considered on the basis of their ability to do the job.

Third, government agencies may well differ from private organizations regarding the support that will be critical to future success. In business, it is a truism to say that the CEO is the chief stakeholder and sponsor and that without the CEO's support, no succession planning program will have any hope of succeeding. It is, after all, the CEO who can hold everyone accountable for identifying and developing successors.

In most government settings, however, the senior-most officials are generally short-timers who rely on the public or on elected officials for their jobs. While that has the advantage of making government responsive to voters, it may also mean that senior-level officials are not as interested as they could be in long-term efforts to groom individuals in their agencies. By contrast, senior career officials possess the most institutional memory and are often the agency's opinion leaders because of their superior knowledge of agency constituents, laws affecting the agency, and past successes and failures. Hence, in government, the key stakeholders of succession programs are the senior-most career officials. Their support is critical. Their immediate supervisors, however, must at least provide some support by approving budget requests and other efforts intended to build agency bench strength.

Fourth and finally, government agencies under collective bargaining agreements might find it difficult to prevent promotions based on seniority or other previously-agreed-upon factors. That complicates efforts to select candidates based on past performance or merit, or make decisions based on who can perform the job. Consequently, performance management systems that are designed to identify people who do their present jobs well might not be used as much as they should to make promotion or other employment-related decisions.

Summarizing key concepts

A model of some kind is essential to help conceptualize and communicate key concepts about succession planning or related programs. A model is, of course, a simplified representation of something more complex: Good models point to what should be done or what results should be achieved in a step-by-step fashion, yet are still flexible enough in application to allow for decision-maker preferences, cultural differences, or other factors.

Many models have been offered to guide succession planning and related programs in governmental settings. Some models are simple; others are quite complex. The same basic model can be used to guide succession planning, but additional steps must be included if the goal is to integrate recruitment, selection, development, retention, and other key HR strategies.

One popular approach is to characterize succession and related issues by addressing several important questions raised in Rothwell, 2005; Rothwell, Jackson, Knight, and Lindholm, 2005; and Rothwell and Kazanas.

1. What is the agency's mission, and what measurable objectives are to be achieved in a specific time period?

2. How many and what kind of people does the agency possess now?

3. How many and what kind of people will be needed over time to achieve the agency's mission and realize its strategic objectives?

4. What changes in people over time are expected? (Examples would include projecting expected retirements and other predictable changes in the number and type of people available.)

5. What gaps exist now and are expected over time in matching the number and types of people needed with those who are working in the agency?

6. What action steps can be taken to narrow the gaps?

7. How will the relative success of the action steps be evaluated?

By answering these questions, managers and HR officials are able to estimate when and how to manage recruitment, selection, development, and other efforts so as to fit the number and kinds of workers needed with the number and kinds of workers available.

A different model is needed for technical succession planning, where the focus of attention shifts from people to specialized technical knowledge/institutional memory. HR professionals and agency managers should:

1. Become committed to the need for technical succession planning.

2. Identify the key processes of the agency.

3. Pinpoint what special knowledge is possessed by individuals.

4. Identify which individuals are most at risk for retiring or otherwise leaving the agency.

5. Find ways to distill the knowledge.

6. Transmit the knowledge to successors or other people.

7. Evaluate the results of knowledge hand-offs.

What key pitfalls should be avoided?

Every succession planning or related effort will have its key pitfalls. It is worth listing and describing some of them. How your agency deals with them is often a creative and continuing challenge.

Pitfall #1: The "like me" bias. There is a well-known bias in selection systems for individuals to pick people like themselves. This is called the *"like me" bias.* Every human being regards the world from his or her own filters, and those filters are based on "who we are." If we feel that we are good, we will be naturally inclined to seek out people who are like us. There is only one problem with this thinking: If leaders clone themselves, they might be doing the organization a disservice, because the kind of leader the organization needs if it is to succeed in the future might be different from the kind of leader it needs today.

Steps must be taken to ensure that no one person identifies his or her successors. It is an organizational matter, and should command attention from other managers as well as those who head up a department, a division, or even an organization.

Pitfall #2: The "like us" bias. The "like me" bias is related to the "like us" bias. We humans tend to select those we feel comfortable with. For that reason, concerns about "fitting in" may eliminate best-choice candidates. Sometimes it is best to have people who do not fit in. Breakthrough thinking and quantum leaps in organizational productivity generally come from diverse rather than homogeneous workforces.

Pitfall #3: Past performance will always guarantee future success. There is a natural temptation to regard promotions as rewards for past success or past loyalty, but there is danger in that thinking. Success at one level does not guarantee success at higher levels on an organization's chain of command. Think of this simple analogy: How do we know that someone can successfully ride a bicycle if we have only seen them ride a tricycle? It does not naturally follow that being able to ride a tricycle means that every individual can also ride a bicycle. A better approach is to conduct some form of *potential assessment,* a systematic and relatively objective process in which individuals being considered for promotion are given tryouts to see how well they can perform at a higher level of responsibility.

Summary

As you read the cases that follow in this book, take notes on what you believe will or will not work in your own organization. But bear a few important points in mind from this introduction, and note how special terms are used by the organizations in each case study.

- There are differences in the way public-sector and private-sector entities set up and describe their programs.

- Models should guide action. On what basis is a program designed and carried out? How are the issues described in this introduction addressed in each case?

- Pitfalls should be identified and avoided. In each case study, see if pitfalls were identified. What steps, if any, were taken to avoid the common pitfalls?

- Look for lessons learned. What lessons can be summarized from the cases? How can they be used in your unique agency setting?

William J. Rothwell
James Alexander
Mark Bernhard

OVERVIEW

This book focuses on government succession planning, human capital management, workforce planning, and talent management. It is organized into four main sections.

Part I presents five case studies from international settings. Part II, focused on the Federal government of the U.S., includes seven cases. Part III centers on state government agencies in the U.S., and consists of five case studies. Part IV centers on succession practices in local governments of the U. S. Several cases have been written specifically for this book. Other cases are republished from other sources—with permission, of course, from the copyright holders. But all the cases share a common focus on government succession planning and related issues.

The book concludes with an Appendix that contains a planning checklist; a list of Web sites linking you to valuable information on talent management, succession planning, and human capital management; and the Table of Contents for the CD ROM that accompanies the book, as well as a list of Recommended Resources and brief biosketches of the book's three editors. The CD-ROM provides readers with many resources on succession planning from case authors and public sources to assist those responsible for succession planning and related practices at the government level.

WORKFORCE PLANNING: THE BACKGROUND

$\mathbf{O}$nly a relatively few agencies within federal, state, and local governments have addressed the problem of what they will do when key people retire or otherwise leave their current positions, taking valuable leadership, management, and technical expertise with them. It is critical that such agencies and departments create specific plans to address such manpower gaps and shortages if they are to remain effective in the near and long term.

It is natural to wonder how government is faring with succession and work-force planning. The most detailed study of that issue was conducted in January of 2004 by the International Personnel Management Association. We are including a summary report about the study prepared by IPMA as a framework for the cases included in this book.

A checklist for agency workforce planning from the U.S. Office of Personnel Management has been included in the Appendix to help assist agencies in their planning efforts.

Results of a 2004 Survey on Workforce Planning Conducted by the International Personnel Management Association

In a January 2004 survey of IPMA-HR members about their workforce planning activities, 97 organizations responded out of a population of 5,700 members. Only 36 respondents (37%) reported that their organization had a workforce planning process that includes defining staffing requirements (both staffing levels and competencies), identifying current staff availability, projecting future staff availability, and calculating specific differences between staffing supply and demand. Sixty-one respondents (63%) said that they did not have a workforce planning process in place.

Background Table 1-1

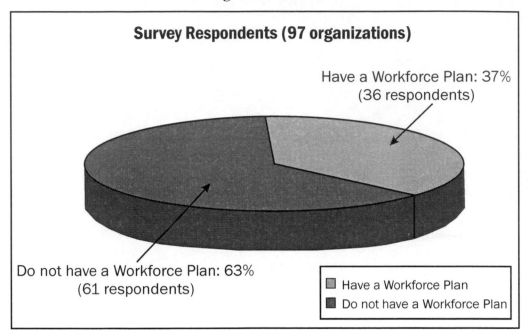

Survey Respondents (97 organizations)

Have a Workforce Plan: 37%
(36 respondents)

Do not have a Workforce Plan: 63%
(61 respondents)

☐ Have a Workforce Plan
■ Do not have a Workforce Plan

In an effort to explain the low response rate to the survey, a random sample of the 359 members who responded to the demographics section of the survey but did not respond to the workforce planning questions were contacted via telephone. They explained that they did not have a workforce plan or process in place, so they did not respond to the Workforce Planning Survey section.

These findings are really not surprising to people familiar with government succession and workforce planning when viewed in light of other studies in both the private and public sector. The U.S. General Accounting office in its reports *High-Risk Series: An Update,* GAO-01-263 (January 2001) and *High-Risk Series: An Update,* GAO-03-119 (January 2003) identified strategic human capital management as a government-wide high-risk area, after finding that the lack of attention to strategic human capital management had created a risk to the federal government's ability to serve the American public effectively. A poll was also conducted by the Society of Human Resource Management (SHRM) in December 2003, in which respondents were asked at what levels their organizations had succession plans in place. An astonishing 60.5 percent responded "We do not have any succession plans."

The results of the IPMA-HR survey clearly indicate that strategic workforce planning is still a relatively new concept or practice for many of the organizations. Of those who indicated that they did have a workforce plan in place, 21% of organizations reported that they had a plan developed that was less than two years old. Nine percent had a plan that was between 2 to 5 years old, and only 6 % said they had a plan in place for more than five years.

This was further highlighted when respondents were asked to indicate the status regarding the development of their workforce plan (i.e., a product that the organization uses to identify and address the staffing implications of its organizational strategies and plans).

- We currently have a work plan: 21.6 %
- We are in the process of developing a plan: 18.6 %
- We are planning on developing a plan: 26.8%
- We have no immediate plans to develop a plan: 30.9 %

Those agencies that indicated they were in the process of developing a workforce plan were in varied stages of development. For some, there was no definitive time frame, while others indicated they would have one by June–July, 2004, by 2005, or within the year. A few agencies indicated that they were in the very early stages of development and were hopeful by late spring of 2005 that they would, by then, have developed a workforce plan. For those who indicated that they plan on developing a workforce plan in the future, the responses were similar: work will begin in 2–3 months; within the next 6 months; in 1–2 years; in 2005; hopefully in the next year; indefinite time frame; or it is still in the discussion phase.

For those who responded that they have no immediate plans to develop a workforce plan, the responses are interesting and a bit alarming in light of several current trends: the increasing challenge for agencies to deploy the right skills in the right places; the growing number of employees who are eligible for retirement and the fact that agencies are finding it difficult to fill certain mission-critical jobs; rapidly evolving technology; and the dramatic shifts in the age and composition of the overall population, which can exacerbate the problem.

Some of the reasons cited by those with no immediate plans to develop a workforce plan were:

"This has not been a priority with city management to date."

"Our firm is small and we only hire senior/seasoned HR professionals."

"It's not that it would not be great to have one, but we just don't have the staff to create one at this time."

"It is not considered a high profile concern of management."

"Time and manpower availability."

"Developing a workforce plan has not been viewed as a pressing issue. We have always 'gotten by' with dealing with replacements or backfilling as the need arises. We are facing huge budget shortfalls imposed upon us by our state's inability to balance the budget."

"With the exception of a few specialized positions, staffing vacant positions is not difficult. We are focusing on the development of leaders for future key positions."

"The city manager is currently looking at a Strategic Plan, including performance measures and benchmarking for the entire city first, and all our attention has been to work on that."

"As an organization, we are currently occupied with staff reductions and a budget crisis."

"Due to our small size, we have not done this in a formal way in the past (from what I can tell), but we are growing and I can see a need for a more-formal program to handle our continued growth."

"The HR function has provided a proposal for workforce planning to the Executive Staff for their consideration, but it was never approved for HR to proceed with developing anything. We are planning to re-submit a proposal in the near future."

"Over the past decade, it has not been difficult for the City to find qualified pools to fill most of the City's positions. However, we realize that this will change as the local and regional demographics change, so we are considering succession planning."

"Due to budget restrictions, we cannot plan for the future at this time."

"There have been other fires to put out, first. Top management has not seen the need for any assessment."

"Normal recruitment/retention efforts are expected to maintain an effective workforce."

Workforce Planning Process and Alignment with Organization Strategic Plan

For those agencies with a workforce planning process, 39% indicated that their process was aligned with their organization's strategic plan, while only 6 % said it was not aligned. However, 13% percent of the agencies whose workforce planning process was not currently aligned with their organization's strategic plan said it would be aligned in the future.

In addition, 40 percent indicated that their workforce planning process was aligned with their organization's budget process, while 18 percent said it was not aligned to the budget process.

Workforce Planning Staff Size

The full-time equivalent staffing of workforce planning operations tends to range from:

0–1 for 20 percent of the respondents

2–10 for 31 percent of the respondents

11–25 for 2 percent of the respondents

51 or more for 5 percent of the respondents

Workforce Plan Elements

Respondents who had a workforce plan in place indicated that several elements were or will be included in their plan. Respondents were asked to select all elements that applied.

Background Table 1-2

Workforce Plan Elements	Percentage
Training and development	50.5%
Recruitment	49.5%
Classification	48.5%
Competencies	48.5%
Selection and Staffing	48.5%
Succession Planning	46.4%
Diversity	44.3%
Internal Forecasting (estimates internal supply and demand; labor costs; growth rates; organizational efficiency, and revenue)	42.3%

Background Table 1-3

Workforce Plan Elements	Percentage
Retention	40.2%
Compensation	38.1%
External Forecasting—forecasts of industry and other external supply and demand trends; competitor assessment (i.e., compensation, benefits surveys)	30.9%
Performance	
Skill Gap Analysis	29.9%
Detailed Statistical Demographics	27.8%
	23.7%
Benefits	
Work/Life Issues	23.7%
Reporting	19.6%
Redeployment	17.5%
Budgeting	15.5%
	1%

Workforce Planning Automated Systems

Respondents indicated that they use various automated systems in their work-force planning process. The use of an agency database was most frequently cited.

- Agency database—34%

- Commercial database (e.g. Peoplesoft, MS Access, SAP, Oracle)—18.6%

- Other types of systems are being used (development of own software, PRISM Statewide Payroll and Human Resources System (SPAHRS).

- Mississippi Executive Resource Library and Information Network (MERLIN);

- Submitting surveys to other localities;

- The Commonwealth of Virginia's database—5.2 %

Also, twenty-one percent (21%) indicated that their workforce planning system is part of an integrated human resource management system. Thirty-six percent (36%) said workforce planning is not part of an integrated human resource management system.

Background Table 1-4

New Programs/Strategies Implemented as a Result of Workforce Planning Analysis	
Programs/Strategies	**Percentage (%)**
Recruitment	18.6
Retention	24.7
Competencies	14.4
Reduction in Force (RIF)	10.3
Early Retirement	9.3
Improved Benefits	8.2
Redeployment Programs	7.2
Privatization	5.2
HR Development Programs	1.0
Downsizing/Rightsizing	1.0

Other programs indicated by respondents: development of career paths; pay/ salary study; reorganizations and furloughs; succession planning; training assessment, and skills gap mitigation.

When asked if their organization is taking any steps to transfer knowledge from its experienced workers to less-experienced workers, 45 percent said yes and 20 percent said no.

Ways Various Agencies Are Transferring Knowledge

— Written procedures where possible and train various staff in different departments as a back up to critical functions

— Implementation of strategies such as mentoring, on-the-job training, job shadowing, job previews, and promotional readiness evaluations

— Allowing double-fill of some positions temporarily, creating specialized positions that will move into highly specialized professional positions after being mentored

— Central HR staff working with County departments to build career paths and ladders that provide training to current county workforce, in order to prepare for upcoming retirements. Also, the County is embarking on the development of a succession plan.

— Company-wide leadership/management and skills training programs

— Creating and updating desk manuals on a regular basis; identifying job functions; mentoring through identification of employees eligible to fill key positions within the organization; cross-training

— Cross training, internships, mentoring, and delegation of key projects

— Developed a training program in knowledge-transfer tools and techniques for agency managers. Agencies are using these as appropriate for their environment. The information is also available on the workforce and succession management Web site that is supported.

— Developing communities of practice, central repositories for long-term employee knowledge before retirement, and other similar initiatives

— Documentation of current processes; documentation of historical data; training; mentoring

— Every employee has a trained back-up person

— Identification of cross-training opportunities, promotional opportunities, special project opportunities, and re-assignment opportunities

---

(continued)

Ways Various Agencies Are Transferring Knowledge *(concluded)*

— Knowledge management is a new concept to the organization and is done informally. We are in the process of tapping into developing more-thorough programs/processes around knowledge management. Existing programs include supervisory training.

— Knowledge transfer occurs in a variety of forms, such as formalized on-the-job training, informal and formal mentoring relationships, documentation of policies and procedures, and in select agencies through knowledge management programs

— Identification of training courses for future advancement

— Overlap with new hires and retirees. Return of retirees for special projects and assistance. Improved documentation of systems and procedures.

— Debriefing of departing employees to gain insight into their institutional knowledge

— Person-to-person knowledge transfer on an individual basis and through programs offered by the Human Resource Development Institute. The Institute, a division of the centralized State Department of Personnel, offers a variety of training programs and seminars.

— Serving as mentors and/or trainers, coming back after retirement, and working alongside less-experienced employees

— Skill gap analysis, evaluation of potential retirements, and taking steps to transfer that knowledge to those interested. Providing training to employees related to knowledge needed. Mentoring.

— Succession planning programs developed and implemented by line agencies

— Succession planning. Mentoring. Hiring replacement employees while employee is still working.

— The County is beginning to create a generic plan that agencies can follow to develop a department-specific Succession Plan, which will include KSA-gap analysis and practices to overcome

— Use of senior experienced workers as mentors to newer employees, use of ISO process to document procedures for employees to use, use of project management plans and quality assurance plans after action reviews, and lessons learned to transfer knowledge

— The creation of a Knowledge Management Committee that has developed some recommendations to capture organizational knowledge

— The development of focus group meetings to inform employees and encourage their participation

Barriers preventing production of complete and timely workforce plans

It is important to note the barriers respondents said are preventing organizations from producing complete and timely workforce plans. The U.S. General Accounting Office in its December, 2003 report *Effective Strategic Workforce Planning* identified numerous lessons and strategies that can help agencies successfully implement strategic workforce plans based on the human capital experiences of leading organizations. These lessons and strategies include ensuring that top management sets the overall direction and goals of workforce planning; involving employees and other stakeholders in developing and implementing future workforce strategies; establishing a communication strategy to create shared expectations, promote transparency, and report progress; educating managers and employees on the availability and use of flexibilities; streamlining and improving administrative processes; and building transparency and accountability into the system.

In the IPMA-HR survey, several barriers to producing complete and timely workforce plans were cited by respondents:

Background Table 1-5

Barriers to Production of Complete and Timely Workforce Plans	
Barriers	**Percentage**
Preoccupation with short-term activities	39.2%
Insufficient staffing to work on this	34.0%
Lack of funding	25.8%
Lack of executive support	18.0%
Restrictive merit system rules on hiring, etc.	13.4%
Insufficient marketing effort	6.2%
Lack of executive support	14.4%
Lack of confidence in planning techniques	6.2%
Insufficient marketing effort	2.1%
Resistance to change	1.0%

Other barriers cited by respondents:

"Agencies' uncertainty of what to do. There is no current overall mandate to conduct workforce planning, although it is encouraged by the Governor's Office. There is no alignment with the budget process."

"Change in administration has put a halt on the process."

"Fiscal constraints to support new initiatives."

"Focus on short-term needs and results due to use of annual, individual performance objectives for senior executives and biannual rotation of commanders."

"There is support from the mayor, but certain department heads refuse to believe they could structure their departments differently or lose any employees."

"Plans are completed too late to be useful."

"We have not yet implemented workforce planning formally. A potential barrier would be lack of resources dedicated to workforce planning efforts."

"We have received funds for HR initiatives linked to WP, but more funding would enable more comprehensive programs."

Succession Planning

It is interesting to note that of the 97 respondents to the workforce planning survey, 39 percent of the organizations are actively involved in succession planning, but 40 percent are not. Twenty people did not respond to that item. Thirty-two percent (32%) indicated that succession planning was part of their workforce plan, while 8 % said it was not part of their workforce plan.

Benefits or Positive Outcomes Realized by Organizations as a Result of Their Workforce Planning Process

For those organizations that have a workforce planning process, there have been some positive outcomes. Benefits described by some agencies include these:

Benefits of Workforce Planning

— A raised awareness of the imminent mass retirements resulting from the baby boom generation. Organized thoughts and procedures via a flexible system that was well received. Development of a program and instructional materials for line-department staff.

— A heightened level of importance of the workforce planning function by the newly created workforce planning office at the central HR level that is dedicated to assisting agencies with the workforce planning process.

— A leadership academy has been initiated to prepare future leaders.

— Ability to see where retirements are happening, and planning for those. Also seeing what efficiencies can be found by restructuring departments, taking advantage of vacancies; and successful redeployment of displaced employees.

— Anecdotally, departments that have engaged in workforce planning efforts have found themselves prepared to deal with large-scale retirements and turnover in their workforce, as well as a reminder of the value and utility in making sound job-related selections.

— Has assisted in retention when employees realize management is interested in their career advancement and training necessary to achieve their career goals. Enables management to better forecast budgets and tie staffing and competencies with strategic planning.

— A thorough look at recruitment/staffing processes inside of HR. However, the workforce plan was recently implemented, so tangible outcomes have not yet been seen.

— Budget and vacancy management planning.

— Demand areas have been identified. Reallocation of workforce has occurred in some areas. Awareness at the executive level for workforce planning is increasing.

— Employees (top to bottom) are held accountable for their actions, and each person sees how their actions affect the other. The process is set up to reflect goals and points for accomplishing specific goals.

Part I

INTERNATIONAL CASE STUDIES

What are governmental entities other than those in the U.S. doing about succession planning? The cases in this section provide clues about that, as well as global perspective. The cases we have selected do not necessarily represent "best practice," but they are representative of common practice in some locales. The international case studies presented here come from Canada (Cases 1 and 2), Australia (Case 3), and Europe (Cases 4 and 5).

Undoubtedly, one volume could be written on international examples alone. But they are difficult to find, and it is harder still to get people to agree to be interviewed or have the results published. One researcher for this book contacted an Asian government (which will not be named) and asked high-level officials if they would be willing to be interviewed to have a case appear in this book. The response: "In this country, government succession planning is a *military* top secret." In another example, the ambassador for one EU nation was interviewed over dinner in Europe. It became quickly apparent to the interviewer that no effort had been established by that government to bring an objective approach to succession planning: All decisions about succession in that government are made only when vacancies become available, and personnel selections are made solely on the basis of political affiliation and individual popularity. That case does not appear here, since it would only be an embarrassment to the government whose official was so blunt in his description of the process.

Still, it is worth reading the cases in this section to gain a global perspective on how some governments around the world are addressing succession planning.

The cases presented in Part I are:

Permission has been granted by each agency to use the case information for this book.

SUCCESSION PRACTICES AT THE BUSINESS DEVELOPMENT BANK OF CANADA

> *Case Introduction:* This case study on succession planning at the Business Development Bank of Canada, a financial institution wholly owned by the Government of Canada, is presented in interview format.
>
> **Interviewer:**   Ying-Hsiu Liu
>
> **Interviewees:** Mary Karamanos
> Senior Vice President of Human Resources
> Business Development Bank of Canada
>
> Cécile Cournoyer
> Director of Talent Management and Leadership
> Business Development Bank of Canada

Ying-Hsiu Liu: **There must have been a lot of changes within the three years since we last spoke.**

Mary Karamanos: Yes, there have been. For the most part, I think that our evolution is continuing. The last time we spoke, I didn't have a director. Cécile is our director of talent management and leadership development.

Cécile Cournoyer: And there was no talent management section, as well.

Karamanos: We are continuing to place very high importance on the work related to talent and succession, as many organizations are. I think we have taken some steps, and it shows our commitment to what it is we are doing for the organization.

Liu: **The board and the president must believe your performance is good, because you can now add the talent management.**

Karamanos: Yes. I would say that is a fair statement.

Liu:	**How does your agency define succession management, workforce planning, human capital management, and leadership development?**
Karamanos:	We define *succession management* as an ongoing process whereby we are continuously evaluating our talents—our assets in our organization—and assessing where they are in their development and what gaps we have identified that need to be addressed in order to prepare them for the next step in their career progression. It is a process that is taken very seriously in the organization. I am happy to say that while it is important, we do more than just talk about corporate succession; we do it. This notion of succession management permeates the entire organization. Our field operational groups also have a get-together on an ongoing basis to discuss staff talent, their development, and their readiness to assume new or changing roles in the organization.
Cournoyer:	So it's truly, as Mary said, an all-encompassing program or activity or process. We structure it a bit differently when it comes to key and critical positions, for obvious reasons. When we say "critical," we're talking about those very specific more-senior positions, but no matter where you are in the organization, we do a formal process every other year and the career-management process every other year. For every employee, it is from top to bottom, and goes up to the top. Every year we look at succession for the key and critical positions. As Mary indicated when you first spoke, this goes all the way to the board of directors, who are very interested in finding out what's going on. They want to have the assurance that we know where our gaps are and that we have a pool of people internally, and that we are working on readying these people and know when it is more appropriate to recruit externally as well.
Liu:	**What is the purpose of your agency's succession management program, and what led to the perceived need for it?**
Karamanos:	The purpose obviously is to ensure that we have the talent necessary to meet our needs. We are a bank. We are only as good as the people we have ready to serve our clients. We are a development bank, so even more important is that we pride ourselves for having

more of a personal relationship with the clients. So we need to have the right talents who are well trained, who are developed, and who understand the organization more than just the role that they fulfill everyday, because they are representative of the BDC in the marketplace. The purpose of the succession planning management is to make sure that we have that talent ready when the need arises. Sometimes succession works at a pace you don't anticipate. We go through the exercise and we actually look at our populations—we look at people in key positions—and more or less to assess when that person might be retiring or might be moving on to another job. We start to ask questions about the time frame and when we will need to start developing the people behind. Is there only one person who can take over, or do we have the luxury of having more than one person—a pool of talents at that time to draw from? So the purpose is always to have a very fluid and ongoing document that gives you some opportunities to plan ahead and gives you some flexibility . . . At least this gives management the opportunity to reflect very seriously on what the impact is if one person leaves, because it is a domino effect.

Liu: **Exactly. I also remember you mentioned that succession planning is also a question of time—that it takes a lot of time to prepare and develop talent. I also noticed that BDC is a growing organization, yet some senior managers might be going to retire. How do you address these two issues?**

Karamanos: Those are the issues that we consider and discuss very openly as a management team. You are absolutely right. There are also a couple other issues that I could add to that mix, but let us talk about those you raise: The issue of demographics and the baby boomers who are in the last phase of their careers—and that could be people who have just left the organization. For us, they actually started retiring last year on a more frequent basis, so we are right in the heat of it. Let's put a few other interesting factors into the mix, such as the very hot and dynamic labor market. What work is going on? If you have talented people sitting there who do not feel that they are being challenged, maximized, moving up, inspired, and challenged in the organization, someone else could come and take them away! So succession management is clearly important to us. We have actually integrated succession planning into our talent-management strategy for the last three years since you and I last spoke. I think we have made some very significant progress in what Cécile talked to earlier—how we access our talent; our regional succession or career-management process; and how we develop our talent from two perspectives: from a technique perspective so they can become more proficient and better technically, but also from a leadership perspective, because the higher up you go in the organization, you tend to need less on the technical side but much more breadth in terms of leadership capabilities. That's where succession really fits in: it's the final outcome of all these smaller strategies that we have under the umbrella of talent management.

Liu: **Three years ago, when we last spoke, you didn't have talent management. How did the subject of talent management come up, and how did you implement it? How does talent management work with career management, performance management, and even succession planning management?**

Karamanos: Talent management is probably the broader label we put on a couple of processes that need to work together. Cécile talked about them earlier when she introduced herself and gave you a list of a number of areas she looks after. Under talent management, we look at two very important areas: recruitment and selection of talents; and performance management. How do we assess the performance of our talent, of our labor, and of our workforce? Under career management the discussion we have with them on an ongoing basis is about their career aspirations, where they want to go, and how we can help support them in getting there. We look at what an employee's career aspiration is and actually work on a development plan with her or him so that she can get the proper learning activities, coaching activities, and mentoring that will enable the individual to get to the next step that she or he identifies. Leadership development sits in here, because we have so many managerial roles in an organization. So we have raised awareness of what leaders need to be doing, and in the last year and half, we have updated our leadership competencies. We have been going coast to coast in Canada and talking to all our employees about leadership competencies. We use these competencies to form the basis of something that we are very, very proud to have developed: a transitional leadership program. What that program is designed to do is to effectively support an individual's development before they take a leadership position. We train them on what they need to be doing as a leader, so that when they are selected for their first leadership role, they have had some training, some learning, and some development by the time they have to be responsible for people. Now this is a fundamental change, because in the past we always promoted people based on how they performed in their job. This is important—we never want to discount that. However, if I am performing in my job as an individual contributor, I am also responsible for more than myself. When I moved into my first-level leadership role, I then had to get performance *from other people.* How did I make that transition? We developed this program shortly after you and I spoke in 2003 and created the architecture around how this would work.

Cournoyer: It is actually an evolution of our President's Leadership Forum, which was very focused and included maybe ten participants. It was a very good program, but it was not enough to have just targeted just ten people a year. So we asked how we could incorporate more leaders. This is how we moved into the transitional leadership program.

Karamanos: It is not so novel that you won't see it elsewhere in companies, but we are very happy to have been able to get it up and running in a relatively short period of time. And I think we are already starting to see results.

Cournoyer: And as of this fall, there have been and will be close to 200 leaders who are part of the process. There were 15 in the pilot, and since then, 50 people have been part of the process. We added 35. We call them "practicing" leaders—first-level managers, with a little bit more experience who are involved in the process in the summer and in the fall. We add all our senior leaders—over 70 people, including our vice presidents from across the country, based on the premise that leadership must be developed in everybody.

Karamanos: I think we made some significant inroads since we last spoke. Going back to your question about talent management, we see all of this under—for lack of a better word—talent management. You know what? When we went out there and talked to our employees about our talent management, they understood that we are committed to this.

Liu: **What measurable goals or objectives, if any, help to provide direction to your agency's succession-management program?**

Cournoyer: I guess like a lot of organizations, metrics and measures are something that we struggle with and something that we really want to be better at. One thing that we started doing, as Mary mentioned, is quarterly reviews. We look at progress, if there has been any improvement, is there anything being done with an employee. In fact, we found that the higher in the organization the individual is, the less that is done formally to move them to other positions. We sort of assume that it's simply going to be okay . . . Whatever the level is, people need to see the strengths and the gaps and understand that something has to be done about it . . .

The Board wants to see that the program is delivering results, so we cannot say that there has been no improvement. We must have metrics also.

Liu: **What groups are targeted for participation in the program? Why were they selected?**

Cournoyer: We actually include everybody. The process will be slightly different, depending on where we are looking. However, the process starts with career management. Every employee in the organization—no matter what level or where they are in the field or the head office—is asked what their strengths and areas of development and career goals are . . . We have area discussions with branch management and senior vice leaders and talk about development potential: *Is this realistic? And can we move this person to the next level? What is the strength of this and the strength of that?* People actually challenge one another during these meetings. The managers have to get back to the employees and tell them what they need to do in order to move up to a higher level. Not everybody does it consistently, but we are getting better at it. These are difficult conversations sometimes. The development discussions move up corporately. We then look at vice presidents, and we even look at senior vice president and executive vice presidents. We call it a "corporate review," where we look at key and critical positions and what we have and what we don't have. This gives us a really clear picture of where the gaps are . . . We are moving farther away from a more traditional succession planning process, where you have a job and you have names of people who are next in line. We try to think more in terms of a pool, and now we have various people targeted for several positions . . . We are not looking at developing one person for one specific position, but rather for something more global. We are for strengthening the strengths and bridging the gaps.

Liu: **Does your agency use job competencies, defined as characteristics that describe successful performance, as a key foundation for the succession program? If so, explain how. If not, explain what the key foundation is for the program.**

Cournoyer: We have reviewed competencies and revised models for leaders and for individual contributors. When we did the last formal succession management exercise, we did not talk specifically about competencies. However, because competencies are the foundation of the transitional leadership program and help us see which people have gaps and which people who have strengths, it will definitely become more and more embedded in the process. It is going to take some time to learn how we can bring the competencies to the forefront as we do with succession management.

Karamanos: We are continuously working on that, but I think that we also have to lay a very extensive foundation in terms of our competency work.

Cournoyer: It used to be really about performance, but now it is about performance AND leadership development. The link between leadership development and succession is so close.

Liu:	**How is individual job performance assessed?**
Cournoyer:	There is one formal review at the end of the fiscal year. Also, there is a mid-year review that is less formal. Actually, in some of our branches it is a quarterly review. Typically, the employee is asked to provide us with input as to their contributions during the year. It is a factual request, not something long. It's to make sure that we don't forget anything and that we get the employees' insights. This is shared with the manager. Based on that input, comments from clients, client-satisfaction results, engagement results, and obviously achievement of a numerical target or project achievement, the manager prepares an assessment and assigns ratings to a number of key objectives or responsibility areas. Then the manager writes a narrative to support those ratings which is shared with the second-level manager of the employee.

Then we take it up a notch. We have what we call a performance management process (PACT) and a PACT review committee. Let's take a region, such as Ontario: You have a senior VP of Ontario, and you have maybe 20 areas within that region. Each branch manager, the HR people, and the senior VP will be part of all the PACT meetings. They will review all the assessments for consistency and ask if the narrative matches the rating. If they are not consistent, people will challenge one another on their criteria. The senior VP and the HR person know what is happening in the other regions, so it is really a big effort—quite an undertaking. It requires a lot of time and energy, but performance management is done consistently every year to ensure as much fairness as possible . . . I have people comment on this. Some regions invite employees to participate in some of the discussions. People are incredibly impressed at how the process unfolds on a yearly basis. Obviously, the informal quarterly meeting is not as comprehensive, but it ensures that there are no surprises at the end of the year.

Liu: **How do you assess your employees' readiness for promotion?**

Karamanos: We have a talent review that we conduct at the top every four months—three times a year. In the field, we do them every quarter, and management gets together as a team and has discussions about talent in their respective area. We assess individual readiness for promotion based on overall performance, and sometimes based on how they perform on special assignments or projects that they have been working on, as well as anything else that has been of a developmental nature or what we call their PDP or professional development plan. And if they've been involved in the transitional leadership program—a new component. For example, we did a regional pilot with our first-level leaders: 15 people. Not practicing leaders, but people who had been identified as potential leaders of the future, or new leaders who had been in the job for six months. Five were not leaders, and all five have since been promoted. We used the transitional leadership program to assess them because we did a full-day competency assessment. We use those assessments to then work on a developmental plan. And also at this level of leadership we assess curriculum—courses or modules that the employee will participate in . . . The results of their competencies gives us a read on whether or not someone is going to have difficulties with, say, delegation. If an individual is going to have difficulty leading people or giving constructive feedback, we then have to be able to provide them with the type of learning activities to prepare them. In fact, what we have tried now is to measure the effectiveness compared to that of before. The individual usually feels better equipped having been exposed through class activities and coaching to things they will encounter as a new leader. You've in fact taken away the shock factor of being a leader for the first time. So, we're very excited about having done this. We've already seen people appointed to leadership positions and being better equipped to take on the new challenges. I think they've been better accepted by their team and by employees they manage as a result of this, because the program is not an easy program. I think that people understand that we have high standards for performance and we are very much keeping a high bar in terms of the caliber of leadership we want to develop for the organization.

Liu: **You mentioned a full-day competency assessment. Did you use any evaluation form? And how did you assess competency?**

Karamanos: It is a set of psychometric testing, which is complemented by role play and simulations. It is done externally, but we developed it with the help of experts in the field of psychometrics testing. We have included role-play simulations that will really open the participants' eyes to situations that they could encounter in the jobs. We do that in the first of part the program. The psychologist who has done the assessment meets privately with the individual and briefs them on how they performed; where are their areas of strength and which ones can be leveraged; and what areas of development need to be addressed. Then they arrange a three-way meeting with the participant, the leader, and the manager. Managers have the opportunity to see the outcome of their employees' participation and can help to coach them, guide them, and support them in their development, because the development plan is very important. We believe the managerial role is so critical in this process, so we actually developed a one-day program to help them be better coaches. So the managers will not do anything with the employees unless they themselves have gone through a program to improve their coaching skills. We have achieved ownership on both sides: the ownership from the employees, and the ownership from the managers.

Liu: **How is individual developmental planning carried out, if at all? For instance, does your agency use an individual development plan?**

Karamanos: Yes. Cécile has mentioned that it is part of our career management process. Virtually every employee, bank-wide, does what we call a PDP (personal development plan). With the introduction of our transitional leadership program, I can tell you that the development plan is getting even better. We have I think made some very good progress in terms of identifying developmental opportunities for people: internal courses, external courses, and so on.

Cournoyer: And replacing one manager during a vacation or another manager in another location. We are getting better at all these things.

Karamanos: I think we are more creative than we used to be. We even will fly someone from one part of the country to another for their stage. It could be two weeks, it could be a month, it could be three months. I think we are doing a very good job in this area, and we are also doing a better job in terms of defining specific objectives. For example, to measure the effectiveness of one's stage, the developmental opportunity you want is to very clearly outline what the objectives are at the beginning: What do we want this employee to be experiencing or to be part of or exposed to so they understand how to handle the real situation when they are in that role? I would say the bank does this quite well. They also do it across disciplines. For example, we might take a business-development account manager and put him or her into the credit department for a period of time, and then bring them back. Why is that important? Because they actually see what their colleagues in credit have to do when business development brings in potential clients. How do you assess the client's file? What due diligence has to be done? I think it is important to expose them to so much more than just their job. And we hear very positive comments about that.

Cournoyer: I guess we are answering the next question as we go along, because we do many focus groups for development. We have action learning projects and choose people from across the country, depending on the scope of the project or its purpose. We want to take advantage of that as we get to the next stage in the transitional leadership development program.

Karamanos: Something we don't talk about too much as an organization is the investment we make every year, dollar-wise, in learning activities both internal and external. It far exceeds the benchmark in the general industry, and even in the financial sectors. We spend a little over four percent of our payroll on learning and development.

Liu: **What activities such as training, executive coaching, job rotation, and so forth are used to build individual competence? How are those planned?**

Karamanos: I would say they are all done, and then a few other things that we can add to that, such as being involved in a project team, task forces, focus groups. The discussion that the managers have with each employee every year is when fundamental processes are discussed. That's where the manager will make suggestions. Sometimes employees tell them that the next time a development activity is offered, they would like to be involved. Those developmental discussions—not talking about performance, but just development, on its own—they enable the manager and the employee to develop a really sound professional developmental plan. Managers talk with one another about shipping people from one area to another area to develop them. One of them might say "I think your employee would really benefit from something in this department. Why don't we arrange to have them spend a month or two weeks here?" You have to be flexible and open. But you have to time this so it does not hinder your business. You also want to make the experience measurable, with objectives, and exciting for the employees.

Liu: **What is the budget for the succession planning program, if you know it? How is the succession program evaluated? What measures or metrics are used to assess success?**

Karamanos: The actual succession planning program does not really have its own budget. The activities we use to develop people for succession purposes are really the budget we use, and they all come under different areas, such as talent management and leadership development. That's the way we approach this. We know that we are spending significant dollars. As I mentioned before, about four percent of our payroll is being spent on the development of people. All these dollars go toward a better succession planning process.

Liu: **So what's the budget for leadership development or talent management?**

Karamanos: I would say a little over a million dollars this year will be devoted to leadership development, the transitional leadership program, and other talent management activities related to the external coaching and sometimes mentoring. I would say that's about it.

Liu:	**Is one million for both programs, or just for leadership development?**
Karamanos:	It's all for leadership development, because coaching is also part of leadership development.
Liu:	**How about talent management? Is there any specific budget for talent management?**
Karamanos:	Not really. Talent management is like a branding that we use to support a process like career management. It's an investment of people's time—it's not a budget. The other budget you might want to know about is our learning budget. We spend about three million dollars on that. Learning is the outcome of talent management and succession.

We are making significant progress, and we are very pleased to share our ongoing progress in this area. We are committed to talent throughout the organization, and we would be happy to send you some information from our presentation about some of the work we have done in the last two or three years since we last spoke. If you have other questions, please feel free to call us. To summarize, succession is at the top of our mind at our senior management level and top of mind at the board level. It is something that we go out and talk to our employees about throughout the organization, so everyone understands what the challenges are from HR's perspective. They see first-hand the commitment we have to ensure that we have the talent to continue our growth and to continue to have our prosperity.

Liu:	**Do you mind sharing with me the challenges that you face in talent management?**
Karamanos:	Ensuring that we are maybe one step ahead, from a succession perspective. We want to be sure we have thought through all the possible scenarios—that would be a challenge. The other challenge is continuously finding ways to stimulate our accelerated pool of talent—the future leaders of tomorrow. There is also another challenge: an external one. As a crown corporation government agency in a very commercial environment of banking, we also have to retain talent.

Contact Information

Interviewer: Ying-Hsiu Liu
                       University of Illinois Global Campus (Instructional Design)
                       E-mail: abateaching@gmail.com

Interviewees: Mary Karamanos
                       Senior Vice President for Human Resources
                       Business Development Bank of Canada
                       5 Place Ville Marie, Suite 400
                       Montreal, Quebec, H3B5E7
                       Canada
                       Phone: 877-232-2269
                       E-mail: Mary.Karamanos@bdc.ca

                       Cecile Cournoyer
                       Director, Talent Management and Leadership Development
                       Business Development Bank of Canada
                       5 Place Ville Marie, Suite 400
                       Montreal, Quebec, H3B5E7
                       Canada
                       Phone: 877-232-2269
                       E-mail: Cecile.Cournoyer@bdc.ca

THE NOVA SCOTIA GOVERNMENT SUCCESSION MANAGEMENT MODEL

Case Introduction: This case study on succession planning efforts by the Government of Nova Scotia is presented in interview format. Additional information about the Nova Scotia Leadership Continuity Program follows the interview.

Interviewer: Heather E. McKinney

Interviewees: Kenya Macfadyen, Senior Consultant
HR Planning and Succession Management
Nova Scotia Public Service Commission

Valerie Hearn, Acting Director
HR Innovation and Growth
Nova Scotia Public Service Commission

Kate Martin, Director of Human Resources
Nova Scotia Department of Community Services

Sharon Cox
Human Resources Initiative Coordinator
Nova Scotia Environment and
Labour Department

Sandra Jackson, Executive Office
Insurance Review Board
Nova Scotia Department of Finance

Heather McKinney: **How does your agency define succession management, workforce planning, human capital management, and leadership development?**

Valerie Hearn: From the corporate perspective, we see it as a structured approach that focuses on identifying and developing talent. And while we see it as a structured approach, we also like it to be flexible with implementation so that departments can think about their needs, culture, and readiness and adapt the process to fit that. So really our goal is to create an environment for people to develop their skills in preparation for future possibilities so the workplace will be well positioned for whatever lies ahead. So this means we don't focus just on the leadership roles, but we focus on the development of all our employees, particularly the professional and technical roles. For example, we have strategies in place for finance, HR, IT, and policy.

McKinney: **Moving on to the second part of question 1, what about workplace planning, if that is applicable?**

We are actually in the process of defining "workforce planning" corporately, but basically we see it, as many do, as ensuring that we have the right people with the right skills in the right places at the right time. And we are going to be positioning it as a framework for managers, to help them make workforce decisions based on an organization's mission, strategic plan, budgetary resources, and a set of desired workforce competencies. So it's really about managing the movement of employees in, out, and within an organization, and we also look at all aspects of HR activities regarding attraction and retention.

McKinney: **And how does HR interact with your plans and ideas? Is it a smooth relationship there, in terms of getting your ideas implemented?**

Hearn: Pretty well. Maybe I can pass that over to Kate and Sharon in terms of how they found implementation within their own department.

Kate Martin: Community Services was one of the pilot departments for government. We are a very large department with about 2,000 employees, which includes agency employees that are funded by the department of community services. But the department would not necessarily be the employer, so there are certain complexities with implementing succession planning within an organization like Community Services. We were one of the first departments that piloted it, and I think once we had a common understanding in terms of what succession planning was and we developed a methodology and an operational plan to deliver succession planning within the department, things went quite smoothly. But those initial talks up front are what is key and critical, and certainly there has to be a common understanding of the roles and responsibilities of the public service commission and the line departments. We felt that it was the Public Service Commission's role to develop the program piece, and we would operationalize that within our line organization.

Sharon Cox: I can echo the same things that Kate is describing. Our department, Nova Scotia Environment and Labour (NSEL), saw succession management in the same way in that there was a program, plan, or a model developed so that we would take and mold that to the unique needs and requirements of the Department of Environment and Labour. We are not as large a department as Community Services. We are about 450–460 employees large, but we have very distinct operational units within the department that have distinct needs in and of themselves, so we needed to take that model and develop what was useful and what was going to address the needs of our employees in Management and Operations. And I think that when we looked at succession management, as Valerie mentioned earlier, we wanted to take that to a different level and present that to employees more so in a different context, such that we had actually renamed our process and gave it that uniqueness by calling it "career planning." We saw that this was not just to feed the leadership pipeline; it was more to develop everybody on an upwards as well as a lateral level.

McKinney: **How does your agency define leadership development?**

Kenya Macfadyen: That is a good question. I don't feel that we have a way we define leadership development, but we do quite an extensive amount of work around leadership development.

McKinney: **Okay. Even if you do not have a formalized stamp-of-approval definition, how would you describe it, for example, if you were training someone? In their coaching, how would you describe leadership development?**

Hearn: That is really difficult to say, because we have not really put any words into place other than that we are developing leaders. We have a leadership competency model. We have eight competencies that we use to define the roles and responsibilities and the behaviors that we expect from our leaders. We also have leadership development programming where we target the supervisory level, the middle management, and the executive level, so again we provide formalized leadership modules based on the leadership competencies to help them develop those competencies.

Martin: As a line department, we would feed into the program that the Public Service Commission (PSC) has. From a line department perspective, what we have established is a structure for training and development within the Department of Community Services whereby in the regions where most of our employees reside, we have regional training committees, and those training committees are used to approve and consider persons who are participating in both succession planning and career development initiatives and recommending and prioritizing individuals for training and development that would be offered from a leadership perspective through the PSC. If the training is extensive and very costly (for example, if it is a master's degree program that we would want an employee to complete at an educational institution) or we wish to send them on a three week leadership program outside the province, we have what is called a "provincial steering committee" to which those four regional training committees report. The provincial steering committee is chaired by the Assistant Deputy Minister and it is intended to be strategic in that we know the department's business plan. We know what the skills required are in terms of the various program areas to deliver our programs, so it is that committee that puts the stamp of approval on the high level and the costly training and development. As well, we are able to look at the big picture across the department and get a perspective on many aspects of leadership, training, and development.

McKinney: **Correct me if this is wrong, but it sounds as if the processes are definitely in place for training in terms of leadership development and strategies. Maybe a paragraph definition has not been put together yet, but the processes are in place.**

Hearn: Yes. If departments aren't using a structure similar to mine, they are certainly using something along those same lines that would go into decision making.

Cox: We have tried to heavily incorporate a process within our identification of leadership. And so the objective being out of this is that we feed into some of the corporate programs on leadership development. This process helps us identify the skill development that is needed and the skill development that is already there, and helps us decide how we can provide those types of opportunities that will retain employees who are ready to move on to something else or into the leadership development pipeline. So we've really tried to operationalize the model by identifying that talent pool that will feed into those programs.

McKinney: **To identify the talent pool, do you use subjective and objective data, such as Myers-Briggs for objective personality information, with other open-ended, subjective types of assessment? I am trying to understand what different types of indicators and career pathing tools you currently use, and when.**

Cox: At the line department level, as we go through this talent development process, we basically are in the infancy stage, I guess, and will improve upon this as resources and tools are developed. But we go through a self-identification and career-pathing process, where they are given some instruction on how they can do some career exploration and self-discovery in terms of what type of career path they want to be on. Then they also link up their strengths that are already in place, as well as their development opportunities that they might want to work on. And basically that information feeds into a talent review process where we marry those two things and then we decide what types of opportunities we can provide for them within the department. But we do not employ, right at that specific process, any type of structured models. I would say that would occur if we identify them to move on to one of the more formal leadership programs. This would be a more integral process in identification.

McKinney: **What is the purpose of your agency's succession-management program, and what led to the perceived need for it?**

Hearn: From a corporate perspective, not unlike many, many other organizations, we are facing a potential-retirement group, and we certainly found the need for making sure that we had the right skills and competencies in place. We have also found it difficult to fill certain positions in the past, and we are expecting for it to become even more difficult in the future. This is why, again, we are looking at strategies for some of the professional areas, such as HR, IT, finance, and policy.

The PSC is a small agency, the central agency, but we felt the need to do succession management within our own department, so we developed the tools and the process for corporate use to provide to departments. But we also piloted the tools and the process within our own small department, to make sure that the tools and processes would work, and then to make sure that they would be passed on to the departments. We are going through our own succession-management process, because we've had quite a bit of turnover within our own department. Again, because we are primarily HR, it is difficult to find experienced people to replace people as they move out.

One of the things that we found when we did our own pilot was that within the PSC, we were all what we call MCP (Management Compensation Program) employees. This means we are not a bargaining unit: we are all considered management employees. That made it somewhat easy for us to test the tools as we went through the process, but it also made us very aware that we needed to make adaptations as we provide these tools to the departments. Kate and Sharon can probably talk to you more about this.

Martin: In Community Services, we found some real gaps. It is a department that is going through tremendous change. There are legislative changes and huge program changes by way of technology and policy. Every program in the department is going through quite a bit of change at various levels and on various fronts. There are huge cultural considerations there, and change management issues as well. So there are all kinds of factors that Community Services is facing because of the state of flux the department is in at this point in time. But what we are noticing are heavy retirements. People actually are going out the door quicker than ever and they are not just saying it; they are doing it.

Then they are being hired back by the government on a contract basis to help with the gaps that have been created. We've had that discussion, and we are really concerned about that as a line organization. I can see plugging those gaps through that method for a few months, but we need to support staff, and we need to start giving them those opportunities to develop, and we really need to be careful and cautious about hiring on a contract basis with ex-employees. I am not unsupportive of that, but I do see a pattern emerging, and I think it is at a cost to our own employees. I really think we're missing opportunities there. There are huge gaps between the people who either are retiring or who can retire within the next five years, and the folks who are at the next up-and-coming level. I think it is because the baby boomers have probably been in these jobs for so long, and they have had a lot of opportunities.

And there are other groups, for whatever reason, whom we have not focused sufficiently on, particularly in the HR community. I am seeing huge gaps between the directors, the managers, and the HR consultants. We are attempting to deal with those gaps through what we call an HR strategy, where we have looked at the competencies and are basically trying to build on those and build on our HR capacities.

But that's just one functional area. I'm sure the same could be said across various program areas in any organization, but I am only speaking to that from my own perspective because that is my area. We have had difficulty in recruiting for senior positions. We have recruited nationally. We've had some situations that really have not worked out and the fit has not been appropriate. Sometimes that is because of the readiness of the people whom we have put into these positions. So we do need to do a much better job of preparing people, and really *focus*.

Sandra Jackson: Just to let you know what happened at the Department of Environment and Labour—and what led us on the path of looking into succession management models: I think it is pretty well acknowledged that for a number of years—and I think that the research shows this—we and other public-sector organizations are probably more impacted by the retirements than the private-sector industries. In the looming retirements, we do have some very technical-type positions that are becoming more and more difficult to fill. One example: At the Department of Environment and Labour we have a lot of technical staff whom the department has trained to a certain level of expertise. Those individuals are actually able to go out on their own into the private sector and make a lot more money that they can within the public sector. So it is becoming more difficult for the department to retain those people and to attract people into those technical levels.

Several years ago, our department had a number of pockets of divisions where some of these problems were starting to be acknowledged and attempts were being made to try to address some of the looming shortages and loss of knowledge that would be happening with retirements. It was really the results of a corporate-wide survey done by the PSC in 2004 that really hammered home to the senior management in the department that this was something that needed to be acted on sooner rather than later. We were all behind the eight ball, and needed to start looking at what we would do in the face of looming retirement.

I know that by 2010, 50% of our management rank can retire—that is a huge loss in corporate knowledge. We needed to start looking at what we could do to get people ready to take on those new roles. And acknowledgment started to creep up into senior management that we had a number of different types of positions that were difficult to fill, either because of technical reasons or because of regional reasons. Positions are difficult to fill because they are in more remote locations, and people do not want to relocate to those areas and take on the position. The department recognized that it needed to take some of these initiatives and attempts that had been started in some of the divisions and actually take it to another departmental level and create a process for starting to address some of these issues.

Martin: Another thing: There is a huge increase in public expectation of government from a client-service perspective. The public wants us to be held accountable as well, and it is very difficult to deliver on that front. We find ourselves with gaps that create huge liabilities for government. We definitely have a pressing need in Community Services to get on with developing our future leaders within the department.

Hearn: Another reason why the PSC wanted to get into the succession management process as well is because the PCS had undergone a restructuring a number of years ago. We had new employees in the organization. We are fairly small—around 60–65 people most of the time—and the employee survey results, as well as focus groups that we had after the survey results, indicated that the employees within the PSC wanted the senior management team to know who they were. They wanted them to know the skills and the competencies that they could bring to their role, and also what they wanted to do for their future career paths. So there was a real need for employees to have senior management basically know who they were. The process that we had designed and implemented we made sure was very transparent, based on very open, honest discussions between the managers and their direct reports, so that the senior management team did know who the people were.

Cox: I have to add to what Valerie said, because I think that is a very important and not so obvious part of succession management, when we are all talking around the table about retirement stats driving this process as well as filling critical positions. We don't want to forget what Valerie has brought up already: the fact that there are employees within the organization who want to be seen and who want to have the opportunity to showcase their talent. This gives them that opportunity to do that, because it is not all about attraction and recruitment—it is about retention as well. So we want to give them the opportunity to develop their skills, but also to develop an inventory for the organization so we know what kinds of skills are out there and so that when they have these types of critical decisions, they are quite aware of what those skills are within their own organization. We don't want them to panic. They should evaluate the kinds of opportunities they have from within.

McKinney: **When you share that the person wants management to get to know who they are, does that mean on a professional and personal level? And where is that data stored in HR? Is it in a common place where anyone in HR and/or the government can access that pool to see what talents currently exist within? Or is it only a select few who can access this database?**

Hearn: I will talk from the PSC perspective. We went through a process where the individuals met with their managers to talk about their future career goals, what their strengths were, where they wanted to develop, et cetera, and we used a tool called a "talent potential matrix" so that it provided some structure for those conversations to take place. It was purely professional, more so than personal, and we wanted to recognize as well that we are not looking at development for people who want to advance up to a more senior level, but we also want to identify people who want to perhaps move somewhere further down the line in the future, as well as people who were very happy doing what they do but still want to continually be challenged and have the opportunities to develop in their current positions. So that's how the matrix formed the conversations between the managers and their employees. As we did talent reviews in the PSC, that information was rolled out to the most senior level on the management team, where it was stored on a spreadsheet. We do not have a database at this point in time. It's always a hope for the future, but we do have a spreadsheet that provides the basic information for each employee within the PSC: their name, a manager, strengths, development areas, general ideas of their performance: achieving or exceeding, not achieving all their expectations, all to what their talent level potential matrix rating was. Is it someone who needs to be advanced right away because they want to? If we do not find something to facilitate that advancement, is there a retention risk? We want to know whether or not they are a growth employee and are looking for future development and future roles, we want to know about mastery and if they want to stay where they are. What can be done to capitalize on their talent and make sure they are kept challenged and happy in their role? So this is the kind of information that we store within a spreadsheet and use as part of the talent review process. The senior management team flags the retention risks and any areas of concern, especially around critical roles. We also identify critical roles and identify very high-level action items that should be addressed.

McKinney: **Does everyone have access to the spreadsheet, where you can go to update your people accordingly? Or is that information sent to someone who is the "spreadsheet master," who has permission to update the spreadsheet? How do you handle document version control?**

Hearn: The spreadsheet has not been updated. It is kept by the commissioner and by the HR person assigned to the particular group. It has not been updated since the talent review took place, approximately a year ago now. The plan is for the senior management team to revisit it. We have it in our plan in the next few months to go through this process again so individuals can update their own career-development plan. We have a lot of new people within the PSC who need to be known by the senior management team, and we also need to revisit and make sure that action plans are being put into place with individuals and then actioned. So *no,* the spreadsheet is currently not updated on an ongoing basis, but rather on a yearly basis at this point.

Martin: We use a similar tool in Community Services. Valerie's organization is quite a bit smaller than Community Services. In our department, we went through the talent review process and utilized that tool in terms of determining where the gaps were, the stages of readiness for staff, the strengths, weaknesses, a heavy emphasis on opportunities, and this was all tied into their career plan. We considered retention risks, and the tool has a section that addresses action plans. Those action plans are as a result of the talent review session. What we did was, we gave each of the managers, directors, and various management levels within the organization structure a copy of the talent review spreadsheet and the report on succession management initiatives for their direct reports. And all of that is tied into their performance management plan. There is a heavy onus on Community Services managers to oversee the development of staff and to ensure that the action plans agreed to at the talent review sessions are actually followed through over the next year. We have a process in place whereby we do this annually, and it is rolled up to the deputy-executive committee level. It also ties into the provincial training committee structure as well, so we definitely review this on an ongoing basis. Managers will be having career discussions tied into discussions along the performance management piece. In the provincial government, we are heavily unionized in terms of the workforce, so we definitely have the process and use the tool, which I think is excellent. And we have made managers accountable for seeing that their staff develop in accordance with that plan.

McKinney: **What measurable goals or objectives, if any, help to provide direction to your agency's succession management program?**

Hearn: In terms of the PSC implementing the pilot, tools, and so on, the key to this whole process are the career development workshops for both the employees and for the managers of teams. We encouraged the managers of teams to participate in both workshops. What those workshops primarily did was to make sure that people understood what the succession management process was all about, how to think about their career and develop their career development plan within those workshops to provide management with the tools to have those good discussions that their direct reports need for planning their career, et cetera. So our goal is to have a very high percentage of employees within the PSC attend workshops, and we were really hopeful that we would get 75% participation. We ended up with 92% in the month of August, which was just way beyond our expectations. We were really pleased, and we had all of the executives and senior leaders participate in the workshops as well, so we were very, very pleased with those results.

Martin: If communicated properly (and communication is the operative word—I could say it three times, it is that important)—what we have to have is an understanding of what succession planning is throughout the organization. Managers need to understand it—they don't. Without the training and the communication, we have pre-meetings with managers in order to get buy-in. It ties into their readiness. It is a whole cultural piece for managers. It's new. They don't have time for it. These are operational people who have everybody knocking at their door. And here's another HR person coming to town.

They already have found it difficult to follow through with the performance management expectations, so in Community Services, what we did seven years ago was a lot of training around performance management. We set expectations. We put new tools and new processes in place to the point where it is mandatory that managers complete performance management documents and have the performance management process in place in the department. It definitely requires a monthly report, and if you have an outstanding performance evaluation in Community Services, you do not want to be on that list. So that was an effective way of ensuring that we have a process followed.

So now that it is well established, we are coming along with succession planning. It is hugely time consuming. But at the end of the day, in our department we went out to the four regions, we met with the regional management team, we met with the managers individually, and we discussed their staff. We helped them understand succession planning. We then had coaching and mentoring workshops for managers. Then all staff managers and unionized employees were required to attend career planning sessions.

We had fifty training sessions, and it was time consuming. The fruit of that came out in the final talent review discussions that took place and in the subsequent months during the spring and early summer. Because succession planning starts years ahead of time, to get the buy-in of managers and to have real and true succession planning the communication piece is critical.

We use the term "preferred employer" or the new term "the 21st century employer." To achieve that, a number of human resource programs are married together. We certainly have an extensive employee survey initiative, and we know where our weaknesses and our strengths lie in each of the separate departments of government. We have other programs, such as employee recognition and flexible work options for employees. In Community Services, we have been able to say that succession planning is just another program on the plate that we can offer. So it kind of ties into government's direction and future direction, as far as the workforce is concerned.

McKinney: **The options that you shared, such as flexible hours: have they surfaced through climate surveys, where the employees expressed an interest?**

Martin: It came out in many forms, and started a number of years ago. Since our workforce is unionized, it also came out of part of the collective agreement. And there are some flexible group benefits for staff, such as the modified work week—a flexible work program that is available when operational requirements can be met by the staff in government departments.

Cox: We had similar experiences to those of Kate. I think it is very important to reiterate how important communication is. Cultural change is a really slow process, and it takes a really long time to get there, so it is going to take a long time to really embrace these kinds of concepts. And as Kate said, managers and senior leaders in our department—they saw it from a higher level as a very important initiative to take. But a lot of people are very fearful of the amount of work that it is going to take to be successful, and the challenge is in getting them to embrace that hard work up front to get to that easy end. This becomes part of your culture, and it becomes easy to do when you do the hard work up front. You have to invest that time in order to get the additional benefits, if you are going to succeed. But there is always a lot of work up front, and everybody knows how much work they have on their plate . . .

I think the other fear is that if managers and senior leaders are going to do something, they want to do it well. They don't want staff to lose confidence in the fact that they are taking this on. They want to be able to project that they are trying to do a good job at being good leaders and providing that type of support to employees—not wanting to go too fast, but at the same time wanting to see results. So it is sort of a mixed bag when you try to put it all together. You are looking at a long time before you see the actual results of the hard work that you put in. And also, I think there is concern from the current leadership in the organization—maybe they are looking at being displaced if they buy into this too much. I don't know if that was necessarily a large concern, because I think what was interesting is that people realized that with the type of labor market that we have today and the generational differences, it is not too surprising that the younger, future leaders in today's labor market do not want that additional responsibility. So it's kind of a wake up call that somebody else does not necessarily want your job. So there's other types of values that the workforce has today. Maybe being in a leadership role that may have impacts on lifestyle and flexibility is not one of them. And that's another challenge when you talk about succession planning: How you are going to fill that pipeline based on the differences. So there's a lot of realizations as we went along here, and reasons why we needed to do it and discover along the way the best ways to do it.

Martin: But in the end, what this ended up evolving into was a wonderful opportunity. Managers were in on the talent reviews, and it became obvious that they really did want to support staff. They were appreciative of the fact that HR created the time and set that time aside that allowed them to think about their staff and to assist and support their staff through the talent review process. And in the end, it was very, very positive. In my opinion, they bought into it completely. We also had a deputy minister who had this as a priority in the Department of Community Services. She had it in the departmental business plan for executive planning. She took it to the committee, which is basically her "kitchen cabinet," and they were told that it is a priority for them. It was also put on the regional management agendas. So all the way around, from the management perspective in Community Services, it was clear that this was a priority *and* an HR priority on an ongoing basis. The deputy minister was passionate in her commitment to succession planning. It was a regular item on her executive planning agenda, so that push and support from the very top, on a consistent basis, really went a long way in making it successful to the degree that it has been.

Cox: That is true. The most important aspect of this is senior management support in championing the process and the value of this process, and staying behind it and not losing steam the whole way through. Sticking with it right through until you see the results. I think that is certainly what we've found in our department: We had terrific support from senior management. As much as they had fears, they stuck with it and kept with it and made the experience really successful. Certainly so far. In phase one, we have had an excellent participation rate in the career planning workshops—approximately ninety-two percent, and that is in large part due to the commitment in senior management to make it work.

McKinney: **Regarding the new generation, you mentioned the flex hours and schedules. What values have you found or that have been expressed to you that are important to them in the workforce that maybe you didn't think of before, since you mentioned that is has been a wake-up call on some fronts?**

Cox: In our department, similar to what Kate describes in their department, we saw succession management as one component among a variety of initiatives to engage our employees, to attract new employees, and to retain the ones we have. And this succession management program is part of a four-pronged approach. We looked at what was being said in the employee survey regarding what employees wanted: A healthy workplace, recognizing diversity, the need for balance, and wanting to be recognized and rewarded—those types of things that the new generation of employees are looking for when they select an organization to work for. So we wanted to create some programming that would be two-pronged: benefit our current employees, and build a recruitment/retention strategy around having a better chance at attracting people to our organization. So like you said, flex hours certainly is something that people are interested in. Through collective agreement, we kind of already had those things in place.

What we need in order to move forward is consistency in application, and knowing when it is operationally feasible to be able to afford to give those things to people. And also I think that people are looking for a healthy place to come to work to, as well as a place that recognizes the contribution that they are putting in. So we are seeking to do these types of things. There's a broad range beyond that in terms of what attracts new employees to an organization, but certainly there's a shift toward trying to address the personal needs of each employee, as opposed to just looking at the career needs of the employees . . .

Martin: The younger employees are very well qualified and very committed, and they want interesting work. So if you have employer branding, I think that is important. I think we need to revisit the notion of a career in the public service being an honorable one, and do a little more marketing on that front. Government is a very interesting place to work—there are diverse careers. Our employment covers occupational areas, and I try to explain this to my kids. Now some of the lights have come on, and they ask questions. Some of their friends have an interest in a career with the public service; family is extremely important to them, as are values and a lifestyle that will provide interesting work. As my daughter said, "I want to be able to coach a hockey team and do all of these things, too. If I become such and such, I will not have that flexibility." So those are some of the things that I think that young people are considering.

McKinney: **What groups are targeted for participation in the program? Why were they selected?**

Hearn: From the corporate perspective, we are hoping that all employees can be included in the process at some point. There are issues with unionized employees, which Sharon and Kate can address better than I. For the PSC pilot that I was involved in, all of the employees within our department are what we call NPP, so they are not unionized. They were all included, and we looked at all roles, all levels, et cetera.

Martin: In Community Services, we have implemented succession planning in what we are calling a phased approach. Phase one is the management group, and I think across the group we had approximately 120 managers whom we met with. They received training, and so on. Then, in phase two, we are moving into the bargaining unit employees, and that is a much larger group. So basically, we are not only capturing all of the employees in our organization, we are capturing some employees who are in funded agencies in the department.

Jackson: The approach we used in Environment and Labour is very similar to the one Kate just mentioned. We call it a process, not a program, because a program indicates that there is a start and end date, and we see this as an ongoing process that gets integrated into the culture of the department. We are certainly doing phased implementation and rollout of the process. All of our staff are targeted for the initiative, but we have rolled out a phased approach to make the numbers a little more manageable.

Phase one will provide some learnings from our initial rollout that we can take to the second stage. In our first phase, which operated through the spring of 2006, we had all of our management class and all of our administrative support staff, who are not in the bargaining units. But we also wanted to include some bargaining unit staff in our first phase so that we could get some learning from that; we included three different divisions in addition to our management staff. We had all of the staff within the policy, information, and business services divisions, which were smaller divisions, and we had a large group of technical staff.

Our inspector specialist IIIs, who are regional, gave us a regional flavor to the first phase we were doing. They are a bargaining unit and are also a very large, cohesive group, so we could learn some things from the talent review that we were doing instead of just doing talent review at one or two stages and rolling that up to senior management. We were able to do talent review with inspector specialist IIIs who were members of a different level. We learned how that process worked through all of those levels, so we were able to take some learning from the process and apply them to the second phase. We are in the phase of going throughout the province.

McKinney: **Does your agency use job competencies, defined as characteristics that describe successful performance, as a key foundation for the succession program? If so, explain how. If not, explain what you consider to be a key foundation for the program.**

Hearn: From the corporate perspective, we definitely use competencies, but we call them "leadership" competencies, and there are eight. So all of the non-unionized employees in government have the leadership competencies as part of the management process, and use them as the basis for discussion around succession management.

Martin: In Community Services, we use the eight leadership competencies as well. In certain sectors, such as in the HR area, we are conducting a separate HR strategy, where competencies have been identified for non-management positions as well.

Cox: In our learning and experience providing the workshops, we do the same process. Bargaining units have objectives too; they are not competencies, but they are called objectives or standards for performance appraisal purposes. They are individual to each job or person, as opposed to a generic set of eight competencies that the management staff would use. When we are looking at development opportunities (development from an upward perspective as opposed to a lateral perspective), we encourage that bargaining unit staff to use those eight competencies when they strive for development. If they are looking for upward mobility and they want to move into the management and leadership ranks, those are the types of competencies they are going to want to possess. We encourage them to put their developmental goals into the form of the competencies that are used by MCP (and again, I am speaking in terms of the bargaining unit staff). We encourage them to do that and to use the performance-management system as the foundational approach to talking about career development. Employees need to be strongly grounded in their field before they can develop beyond their current role.

McKinney: **How is individual job performance assessed?**

Hearn: From the corporate perspective, it would be through the performance management system that we have in place. All Management Compensation Program employees (a non-unionized program) are expected to go through a performance management process on an annual basis. Its key components, the leadership management competencies, are also assessed individually, and the manager assesses their performance as well.

Martin: We have an established performance management system that is similar to the one at the PSC, including leadership competencies.

McKinney: **How is individual preparedness for promotion assessed?**

Hearn: From the corporate perspective, as part of and in preparation for the talent review process, the introduction of that talent potential matrix is done so that we can look at people's potential based on three different categories: whether or not they are ready for advancement and want to advance; whether or not they want to advance (and development will take some time, so it is further into the future); and mastery, which is considered development in their current role.

Martin: Talent review in Community Services is very similar to the PSC. We use the matrix tool, as well.

Cox: I concur. We do the same in environment and labour. And one more point to add on is that when we look at how they are assessed for promotion, our objective by the end of the day . . . is that they are competition-ready. It does not qualify them to have that promotion—they still have to go through a competitive process. Our aim here is to make our employees marketable and competition-ready, so that they are ready to go when that opportunity arises.

Hearn: I'd like to add that from a corporate management perspective, we have always wanted to make this a very transparent process—one where managers and employees equally engage. We encourage the employees and the managers to sit down and discuss the career goals of the individual and come to an agreement as to where they fall within that talent matrix.

McKinney: **How is individual developmental planning carried out, if at all? For instance, does your agency use an Individual Development Plan?**

Hearn: From a corporate perspective, we have introduced a comprehensive career development plan that was developed over two years ago through another program that we provided. We are encouraging managers to incorporate this career development plan within the performance management process. We want to get managers away from thinking of development only as training toward actually thinking of the future goals and aspirations and the potential of the employees, and look at ways of integrating their career goals with their everyday work. In addition to the career development plan, we have a guide based on self-management, sort of something we expect people to take themselves through. We also provide corporate training in the area of career development, and this is something we have introduced this year. We look at the career management cycle and process, and provide modular training to employees on such things as how to understand what they value and work with and where they want to go. It is a whole self-assessment piece. Another module gives some tools, such as the Myers-Briggs, to help them understand where they want to go as well. Career development planning and résumé and interviewing tips have been packaged into modular training that is now available to all employees through our corporate training calendar. One of the things that is really important is that we are in the process of developing a workshop for managers to help managers understand how they can support the development of their direct reports as well.

McKinney:	**Does development training mostly occur in groups, or is it done individually?**
Hearn:	They go through the training in a group fashion.
Cox:	We tweek the model as we go, but we have found that it is important to do the training up front for managers and employees who need skill development. They need to know up front what the expectations are, and managers need to know about the tools and resources that are available. Even after we had the workshops, we ended up needing to carry that momentum forward and do one-on-one career development counseling. Some people need that extra bit of push or help in terms of how to use the tools and resources if they did not get this in group training. They also need to prepare for the talent-review process because we had that tiered level and there was a rollout process . . .We did mini-prep sessions with each of the management teams to demystify the process, because sometimes the managers are not sure how to run these meetings. We let them know what information should be covered in the meetings and help them prepare and run smooth and efficient facilitation because they all have a lot of employees going through this process, which can take a lot of time. It is important to provide that administrative and organizational support up front. We added some things to the process, and get great support from the Public Service Commission
Martin:	We did have great support from the PSC. They were our partners in this initiative. All of the staff at Community Services will have completed a career development program by the time succession management is implemented. As well, early on after the performance-management training, staff did receive training on how to do an individual development plan, so for those who want to do an individual development plan, that is certainly available. In terms of the HR team, each consultant is assigned to a region or a division and they provide a lot of support and advice to the managers and staff as required. We also did, before the talent reviews, what we refer to as "mini-prep" sessions, where we went out and met with managers in advance of the formal talent review.

I have to say, it paid great dividends in the end. We need to remember that confidentiality was a key component of this piece, as was not construing these talent review sessions in any way with performance management or with any type of punitive action (which can often be misunderstood by staff, especially when HR is involved). Because often in the past, when HR would come into the field, it was not because something was going really well, but because something was not going well. We are starting to turn that around and shift that thinking, with very positive results.

Hearn: In terms of prepping the manager, when we did the talent review meeting with the senior manager at the PSC, we were essentially the very first department to go through this. That was one of the things that we did not do. That was a great learning because although we provided workshops on how to have the discussions and fill in the forms and have all of that kinds of work done ahead of time, when the senior-manager team came together after the very first talent review, there were some who were not as well prepared as they could have been. I'll be completely frank here—most likely this was because they had never participated in a management review process like that, and were not quite sure of what they should bring to the table. That made it a little bit more of a difficult session to facilitate. We did have a second rollout where, again, we did learn from the first one. People were much better prepared and the facilitator was much more aware of what she needed to do, so it went much more smoothly. I think that having a prep session for managers who are participating in a review session is really, really key.

McKinney: **What activities such as training, executive coaching, job rotations, and so forth are used to build individual competence? How are those planned?**

Hearn: We do have leadership programming in place. Formalized, modular training for at least three levels of leadership is offered to employees. It is planned within the PSC, and we have employees across government attending these sessions. Recently, we created a program called the Leadership Continuity Program, and maybe we can speak more about that off line because it is a quite extensive program. Basically, it is a program that focuses on building talent pools of leaders and providing accelerated development. It has been in place for three years, and includes about 175 participants at three levels of leadership. At the executive level, what we were able to do with the PSC was to provide funding to departments that will allow their participants at the executive level to move out and into another role in another department in order to gain the development that they required. Again, it is quite a comprehensive program, so if you want more information on this program, I would be happy to provide that to you.

McKinney: ***Yes, I will take you up on that offer. Thank you.***

Martin: In Community Services, we certainly use the Leadership Continuity Program that Valerie speaks of. We also, where necessary, use external professional consultants—not frequently, but in certain circumstances. If someone retires while we are waiting to fill the position, we would bring someone up to act in that position for up to six months. We do job rotation, particularly in Community Services, because there are so many strategic and departmental initiatives and projects going on that there are many opportunities for special and project assignments and project leads. I think government funded about 75 staff members over a period of time to complete a Masters in Public Administration program, and that was a significant investment in terms of the Government of Nova Scotia commitment. I think it goes as far back as 2001, which was the first graduating group of those 75 staff members.

Cox: Also, I wanted to speak to the succession management model and the talent review process within that model. What came out of that for us in terms of the leadership development program is that there never was really any process to identify which individuals would be put forth to go into those programs. The benefit of having gone through a succession management model and the talent review that is built into it is that we had the opportunity to review those people who were ready or who needed that type of training. So it was a very good training-identification exercise for us to be able to identify how we would be able to employ a process to readily identify people when we needed to and at the appropriate time.

We heard around the table with various levels of management that there is a secondary spin-off of this process: It was a really valuable team-building exercise, with exposure to skills in other divisions that they never really knew existed. It gave them an opportunity to see those skills across the department, and opened up their view of the type of talent pool they had for some of the opportunities they were thinking about. They had a narrow scope on which individuals they thought could do the work, and came to the conclusion that there was a bigger pool out there than they really knew about.

We are identifying some developmental opportunities up front, but we are still trying to work through an ongoing process—I guess an inventory of developmental opportunities that we could have ready . . . rather than just send them off to formalized training, we want to be able to find those opportunities within the organization that they might be able to do in their current role. So we are working on that in terms of the kind of training we want to provide and the skill development and formal training we can do.

Hearn: We do have a number of tools available to all employees for development that are based on the competency model that we have in place. For example, we have recently integrated the 360° feedback process that assesses leadership competencies, as well as development guidelines by the same vendor that provide a huge number of activities and ideas . . . We do have tools available to all employees as they wish to access them.

McKinney: **What is the budget for the succession planning program? How is the succession program evaluated? What measures or metrics are used to assess success?**

Hearn: Within the PSC, we do have corporate budget associated with succession management. It is quite small at this point in time, and it is undergoing evaluation. We are looking to see how we can use it differently in the future, but right now we have a total of 10 full-time equivalencies—basically positions with a total of approximately $800,000 in associated salary. Five of those positions are used for the Leadership Continuity program, and the other five are to be able to provide corporate initiatives for people who need to get corporate things done across government. For example, we have a big focus on diversity, so we have used one of those positions to have someone work on developing the diversity programming across government. That is considered a succession management position and approach. Again, as I say, we are closing down the leadership continuity program, and are certainly looking at other ways of using that money and FTE's for the future.

Martin: In Community Services, there is not really a dedicated budget for succession planning, but we do need a driver, and HR development "owns" succession planning, if you will, in the sense that it is dedicated to making sure the training is provided and keeping the program pieces moving. The accountability at the end of the day rests with managers, who must make sure that it all takes place. I think through our structure, our training budgets, and our committees, there are training dollars associated and are linked right into each of the regions (as does the head office steering committee). So in an indirect way, in this department, succession planning is funded.

McKinney: **How are these succession planning programs evaluated?**

Martin: That is a piece of work that I think we are getting to. I think the metric piece and the measurement piece are the next steps in the evaluation, and will be in consideration with the PSC. We are not there yet, because the program is just too new.

Cox: I am going to add the experience from environment and labour in this area, as well. As you have heard from the others, it is mainly concentrated in the staffing budget right now. We have an individual unit or branch within the department that does provide core and job-specific training, but they do not necessarily provide more of that corporate HR training that we would find under succession management in terms of our career development or coaching. We do have a small dedicated budget to do that, but the budget is shared with a number of those other HR initiatives that the department is rolling out around healthy workplaces and recognition and diversity. We are sharing that budget in terms of making succession management a part of those processes. We can measure success and evaluate progress from our experience over time with the process. Looking at measures or metrics, we have not developed formal measures around that area. I guess that I can speak for us all right now when I say that we look for higher-level results of our employee survey. In terms of whether or not we are being effective and making a difference, I guess from more of a quantitative source rather than a qualitative source, that's what we need to look toward to expand our evaluation methods around that.

McKinney: **How do I refer to community service, environment, and labor? Are they each their own department? And how does this relate to the Public Service Commission?**

Cox: Yes. Department of Environment and Labour, Department of Community Services.

Hearn: The PSC is what we call a central agency. We provide support and program development to the departments.

Cox: We are all working together for the Nova Scotia Government Succession Planning Model.

Q & A's About the Leadership Continuity Program

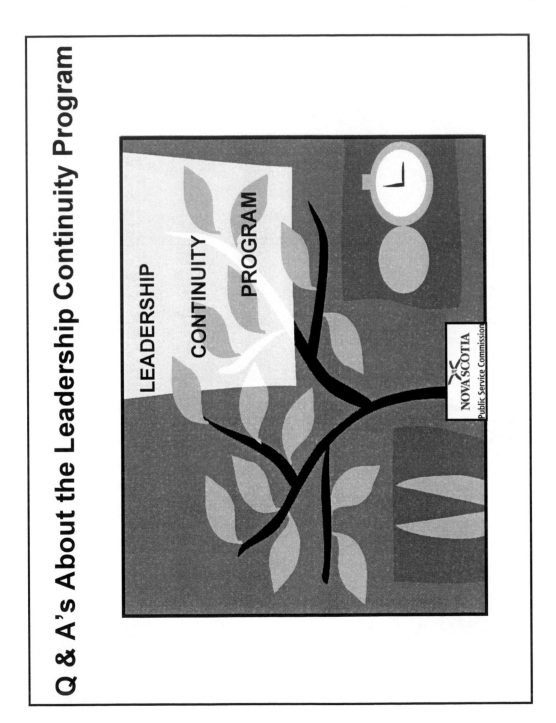

LEADERSHIP CONTINUITY PROGRAM

What is the Leadership Continuity Program?

The LCP is a corporate succession management program that has been developed by the Public Service Commission to ensure leadership continuity across government. It provides the tools and process for individuals who currently demonstrate leadership skills and competencies and want to **accelerate** their development and achieve their career goals.

The LCP takes an integrated and structured approach in identifying and closing competency gaps for our future leaders.

The objective of the LCP is to create a pool of future leaders that will achieve leadership continuity for the government. This is achieved by providing **accelerated development and learning** that is focused on portable skills and leadership competencies. The development is tailored to match individual and business needs and skills are gained through training, projects and work experience.

The philosophy of the program is one of transparency, honest and integrity with diversity and the fair hiring policy as its foundation.

The policy of the program includes the following key principles:

- ➤ individuals are responsible for their own career development
- ➤ there is no stigma for not applying or deciding to opt out
- ➤ the pros and cons are laid out to potential candidates
- ➤ staying in the pool is not guaranteed—new participants are invited on a regular basis, and poor performers are directed to alternate career development tools
- ➤ there is no guarantee of a promotion, and
- ➤ vacated positions are posted and open to all employees

What benefits does this program provide for me and the organization?

From an organizational perspective, this program helps address critical HR issues related to demographics. The demographics indicate that we will be facing a shortage in skilled professionals and leaders. For example, 57% of our management employees are eligible to retire over the next five years. The LCP is a succession management strategy that will help develop the leadership capacity that we will need in the near future.

LEADERSHIP CONTINUITY PROGRAM

Who is eligible to participate in the LCP?

This program is designed for individuals who have demonstrated the desire, commitment and potential to move into supervisory, mid-manager and senior manager roles in the near future. There are certain criteria that need to be met to become a participant, such as performance appraisal results, behavioural flexibility, etc. Your HR representative can provide you with more details.

In addition to meeting the criteria, there is a screening process that is required as the program has a limited number of positions each year.

How do I apply for the LCP?

All employees will be notified through their normal means of communication from the HR community that applications for this program are being invited. If you are interested, it is strongly recommended that you discuss your interest with your manager to ensure that you meet the criteria and that this is the most beneficial program for you. More details on the process are provided in the application kit available on the website www.gov.ns.ca/psc/lcp.

From an individual perspective, there are many benefits to be gained from participating in this program. For example, you will have:

∨ support from your manager, HR Director and Deputy Minister to develop and reach your career goals

∨ the opportunity to receive objective 3rd party feedback on your leadership competencies to identify areas for development

∨ development plans customized for your development needs

∨ the opportunity to be in a group of people with the same goals and interests in career development, and

∨ the tools and processes that will allow you to reach your career goals/milestones more quickly than you might have otherwise

How is this program different than the Career Assignment Program and Executive Career Assignment Program?

The CAP and ECAP process requires two assessments (one at the beginning and one at the end of the program) and involves a pre-qualification process. These programs also involve secondments into different work areas for varying lengths of time, e.g., one or two years.

LEADERSHIP CONTINUITY PROGRAM

How will working in a regional office affect my ability to participate in the LCP?

The location of your office should not have any adverse affect on your participation. It is expected that most of your development is going to occur while you are in your current job. If it is required that you participate in a project or take on a responsibility that involves managing people in other locations, there are many ways to work "virtually" through our technology, ability to teleconference, use internet and email tools, etc.

What exactly would I be doing in the LCP?

The first step you will take in the program is to undergo an assessment of your leadership competencies. The assessments are done by the Federal Government's Assessment Centre in Halifax. Those going into the supervisory and mid-manager levels will undergo a one-day assessment; for those in the senior manager level, it is a two-day process.

This assessment provides you with an opportunity to receive actionable feedback provided by an objective 3rd party. The results are yours and we recommend you share them with your manager to help you with the next step in the program.

The second step involves using the results of your assessment and working with your manager (with

support from your HR representative) to create your own development plan. The development plan is there to guide you in

- maximizing your potential
- gaining a global perspective
- tailoring assignments
- targeting formal training opportunities as required, and
- identifying and achieving key job challenges required for future roles

As your plan will be customized to your development needs, there is no set time frame for your participation in the LCP. However, as the development is to be accelerated, the time frame should not exceed three years.

We ask that you also submit a copy of your development plan to the Public Service Commission as we are accountable for the program and required to report on the development plans as a measure of the programs progress and success.

TIP: As you progress through the program it is important that you understand what the leadership competencies are and how you need to demonstrate them. These competencies (as defined in our performance management system) form the foundation of this program and are also integrated in the other HR programs and processes such as recruitment, performance

LEADERSHIP CONTINUITY PROGRAM

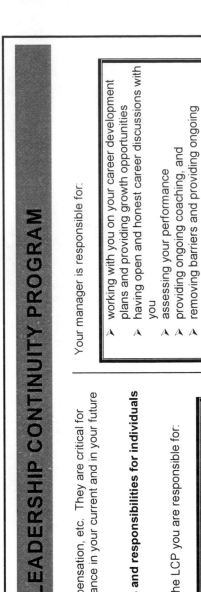

management, compensation, etc. They are critical for successful performance in your current and in your future roles.

What are the roles and responsibilities for individuals in the LCP?

As a participant in the LCP you are responsible for:

➢ your own career development and management
➢ participating fully in coaching and feedback sessions with your manager and others as appropriate
➢ being open to, and acting on, feedback
➢ leaving your comfort zone as required for development
➢ proactively seeking out projects, assignments, etc., that will provide you with development opportunities
➢ creating your own development plan, and
➢ monitoring and managing your progress

Your manager is responsible for:

➢ working with you on your career development plans and providing growth opportunities
➢ having open and honest career discussions with you
➢ assessing your performance
➢ providing ongoing coaching, and
➢ removing barriers and providing ongoing support

In addition, your HR representative will support you and your manager through the program and development planning. The Public Service Commission will provide the tools, processes and support to the departments' HR teams and senior manager participants.

What should I do if I feel my manager is not supporting me with my development?

A key requirement for participation in this program is the support of your manager, HR Director and Deputy Minister. They would have recommended you as a participant, therefore if you feel you aren't getting the support, the first thing you need to do is meet with your manager to discuss your concerns. S/he may not be completely aware of your development needs, or there may be some issues within the department that are creating difficulties/barriers that you aren't aware of. If

LEADERSHIP CONTINUITY PROGRAM

you are unable to resolve the problem in your meeting, then you have an option of approaching your HR representative. S/he may be able to provide some alternatives or suggest other approaches.

Will I be moving to other departments or changing jobs within my own department?

Typically, at the supervisory and mid-manager level, you will remain in your current role with the objective of taking on new and challenging projects, assignments, etc., aimed at developing your leadership competencies. However, as your development plans are customized, there may be a need and/or opportunity to take on another role within or external to your department—this would be determined and facilitated by your manager and/or HR representative.

At the senior manager level, there may be a greater need for movement within or across departments. This will be determined on an individual basis in consultation with your manager, HR representative and the Public Service Commission.

What happens if I am not successful or want to leave the program?

It is important to remember that this program is focused on developing your leadership skills and competencies. You have been accepted into this program because you have demonstrated your potential as well as your

willingness to learn. You can expect some instances or projects/assignments that will call upon skills you have not yet developed--do the best you can in these cases and don't be afraid to ask for help. As long as you are maintaining your performance levels in the areas for which you are responsible and are demonstrating the willingness and motivation to do well in those areas in which you are still learning, you will be encouraged to continue with the program.

If you are finding the accelerated approach to development is not the best approach for you and your performance in other areas is suffering as a result, you and your manager may decide that you should discontinue in this program. This does not mean however, that your overall development should discontinue as well; instead it means that you can use the career development tools available and focus on developing at your own speed.

Where can I get more information on this program?

You can find more details on the program by going to: www.gov.ns.ca/psc/lcp.

Contact Information

Interviewer: Heather E. McKinney
Senior Manager of Organization Development
Pennsylvania State University
Phone: 814-696-0809

Interviewees: Kenya MacFadyen, Acting Senior Consultant
HR Planning and Succession Management
Nova Scotia Public Service Commission
Phone: 902-424-2706

Valerie Hearn, Acting Director for Innovation and Growth
Nova Scotia Public Service Commission
Phone: 902-424-3177
E-mail: hearnvx@gov.ns.ca

Kate Martin, Director of Human Resources
Department of Community Services
Human Resources Division
5675 Spring Garden Road
P.O. Box 696, Halifax, Nova Scotia
Phone: 902-424-2751
Fax: 902-424-0152
E-mail: martincf@gov.ns.ca

Sharon Cox, Manager
Human Resources Initiatives
Department of Environment and Labour
Government of Nova Scotia
Phone: 902-424-8052
E-mail: coxst@gov.ns.ca

Sandra Jackson, Executive Office
Nova Scotia Insurance Review Board, Department of Finance
5151 Terminal Road, 2nd Floor
P.O. Box 2251
Halifax, Nova Scotia B3J 3C8
Phone: 902-424-6978
Fax: 902-428-5781

This e-mail address should be used for inquiries regarding Novia Scotia's succession planning efforts: succession@gov.ns.ca

FOUR AGENCY EXAMPLES FROM THE GOVERNMENT OF AUSTRALIA

> *Case Introduction:* This is actually a series of four short case studies from Australia. They were first published elsewhere.

Agency Case Study 1

Description of the Agency

This is a small agency with around 150 employees and an operating budget of approximately $15m. All activities are based in one location in the city. The HR manager reports to the director of Corporate Services.

The Business Issues

Over the next 1–2 years, this agency will be making major changes to the way it delivers its current services. The agency will be streamlining all processing and technical operations using new systems and technology, and possibly outsourcing some activities. The business focus will be on responsiveness to customers and efficiency. The agency is also considering introducing new products and services.

These changes are necessary if the agency is to provide a service which is competitive by industry standards and meets the increasing expectations of customers. At the same time, this agency faces continuing uncertainty due to possible changes in legislation and Government direction.

What the Agency Wanted to Achieve Using the Framework

The HR manager wanted to use to framework to determine the critical HR management strategies required to support the business direction. This was to involve both managers and HR staff to achieve an organizational position.

The HR manager believed the current HR management agenda (based on the HR management initiatives in the agency's strategic direction) did not adequately reflect the real business issues. There was a long list of HR projects which were not prioritized.

The HR manager also wants to use the external consultant to obtain the views of the CEO, directors, and managers on what HR issues they saw as important.

This exercise was timely, as the agency was about to review its strategic direction and the CEO had just been appointed.

Methodology

Planning meeting. An initial planning meeting was held with the HR manager and the consultant to agree on the methodology, and to brief the external consultant on the agency and its approach to the management of human resources. The methodology was deliberately low key and designed to build alliances and a partnership between human resources and managers, resulting in a joint commitment to tackle the most important people issues.

Assessment. The consultant met with the HR staff to assess the current situation, using the framework as the basis. Relevant documentation was also provided to the consultant, such as business plans, HR policies, and the recent Organization Diagnostic Survey.

The consultant interviewed the CEO and each director to obtain their views on the key business issues facing the agency and the degree of alignment between the HR and these issues. Again, the framework provided the basis for discussion. The consultant also held two focus groups with third-level managers.

The Office of the Public Sector Standards Commissioner had recently completed an audit of the agency, which covered most of the issues relating to external reporting.

Analysis. A written report was prepared by the consultant for the HR manager. The report summarized the business issues and highlighted the gaps in alignment, using the framework as a basis.

Action planning. A half-day workshop was held with two directors and the two senior HR staff, facilitated by the consultant.

During this workshop, the group considered the report and reviewed the current approach to HR management. The group then agreed on the critical business issues and the HR implications. There was agreement that the way people issues were managed could "make or break" the success of the business strategy.

The group agreed on five HR strategies which would be the focus for 1998/99. A one-page summary of the business issues and HR strategies was prepared. This enabled managers to immediately see the alignment and the links between the different strategies.

This led to refocusing the Enterprise and Workplace Agreements to ensure the improvement strategies align with the HR strategy and facilitate the business direction.

The HR manager met with the CEO to discuss the action plan. A meeting was held with the executive team and the HR strategies were agreed to in principle. These strategies are at present being considered in a review of the agency's strategic direction.

The intention is for the executive team to agree on an implementation plan, which will involve HR and business managers taking joint responsibility for the implementation of the strategies. Changes are currently being made to the HR structure and the role of the HR manager to ensure the successful implementation of the HR strategy.

The HR manager now attends executive team meetings whenever HR issues are on the agenda.

Comments

The timing of this exercise was important. The business issues were clear and there was recognition of the need for major organizational change. The HR manager now has a capable team ready to work on the HR strategy.

The framework was a useful assessment tool and a way of communicating a broader role for HRs and how HRs can contribute to the success of the agency.

The exercise enabled HR to be seen as forward-looking strategic thinkers who are preparing the agency to successfully implement its business strategy.

This moves away from the reactive, policing, and problem-solving perception of HRs. It was also valuable for the agency to have an independent assessment of its HR approach.

Agency Case Study 2

Description of the Agency

This agency is one of the larger public-sector agencies, with approximately 900 employees and an operating budget of approximately $386m. The agency has a diverse range of operations that are spread over several metropolitan and country locations. The HR manager reports to the director of Corporate Services.

The Business Issues

In the last two years, this agency has doubled in size with the transfer of functions from another agency.

There will continue to be changes to the Department's services and business processes during the next year. This will streamline services using technology and make them more accessible to customers. Some services will be integrated and provided from one centre. The agency also intends to test services on the market for competitiveness.

These changes will impact on the structure and work practices in business units and will require changes to job roles and new skills. There will also be a need for strong leadership at all levels through the change process.

The agency is about to introduce a business planning process to support the strategic direction.

What the Agency Wanted to Achieve Using the Framework

The HR manager wanted to use to framework to obtain feedback from key stakeholders on what their business issues were and whether the current HR strategy would meet their needs.

This would provide a strategic focus and complement feedback from recent workshops where customers were asked to comment on HR services.

The exercise was timely, as the HR manager was about to revise the HR structure and prepare the HR business plan for the next 12 months.

Methodology

Planning meeting. An initial planning meeting was held with the HR manager and the HR team to agree on the purpose of the exercise, discuss the framework and its elements, and decide on process.

Assessment. The emphasis in the methodology was on interviews with HR staff and a representative of the senior management team in each division, as well as a review of documentation.

Analysis and Action Planning. A written report prepared by the consultant was in two sections. One was an assessment based on the issues prompts. The second provided a summary of each division: its business issues, the workforce implications, and comments on the current HR approach.

A presentation was made to the HR manager and the executive director of Corporate Services. A second presentation was made to the HR team.

During these sessions, the current HR strategy was discussed. The feedback from the CEO, directors, and managers was very positive about the current HR approach, particularly relating to performance management, training and development, and leadership. The feedback provided the HR team with a summary of the main workforce-related issues requiring attention over the next year.

The main gap in alignment related to resourcing and the need for flexibility. The HR manager and team were well aware of this situation and had already considered options.

Comments

Again, the timing of this exercise was important. Over the last twelve months, the HR manager had concentrated on improving systems and streamlining HR processes, using technology. This has freed up staff and positions, which can now be directed toward higher-value activities.

The HR team is now in a position to work more closely with business units to address their specific needs. The structure is currently being changed to provide an HR consultancy service to each program area. This will be supported by on-line access to HR information and services.

Agency Case Study 3

Description of the Agency

This is a small agency, with around 80 full time staff and an operating budget of $6 million. Most staff are located within the city, with a regional office in the north of the state. The HR manager reports to the director of Corporate Services

The Business Issues

The agency is undergoing significant change. A recent government review has signaled potential major changes in the way services are delivered, structured, and organized. The nature of work could change, affecting operating hours and support services within the agency.

What the Agency Wanted to Achieve Using the Framework

One of the senior line managers wanted to use the framework to review the "current state" of HR practice within the agency and also evaluate the extent of alignment between the HR function and the organization's business requirements. He also wished to gauge the current organizational climate in relation to the major changes that were occurring.

Methodology

Planning Meeting. An initial meeting was held between the senior line manager, the CEO, and the consultant to both brief the CEO and agree upon the methodology. A small "steering group" consisting of the line manager, the HR manager, and the consultant was formed to select individuals to be interviewed and to manage the process.

Assessment. The consultant met with middle and senior managers to assess the current situation, using the framework as the basis for information gathering. Relevant documentation was also provided to the consultant: the annual report, strategic plan, enterprise agreements, government review papers, etc.

The questions in the framework were used selectively, depending on the individuals (e.g., questions of strategy and business issues were asked of the Chief Executive Officer and senior line managers, whereas specific HR issues were addressed to Corporate Services and Human Resources).

Analysis. A written report was prepared by the consultant for the HR manager and the senior line manager. The report summarized the business issues and highlighted the gaps in alignment. Because the organization does not have a large HR department and therefore a large pool of resources, the consultant provided an extensive list of suggested actions (based on best-practice materials) to provide additional support and guidance to the agency.

Some of the significant findings that emerged:

- The need for the agency to more clearly articulate its strategic direction and its change agenda, and be able to communicate this to its staff.

- The need to re-position human resources to provide greater strategic support for the agency.

- The need for workforce planning to ensure that the agency has the right number and mix of personnel to meet the needs of its changing strategic direction.

Action Planning. A discussion was held between the HR manager, senior line manager, and the consultant to identify the critical issues. It was agreed that the priority issues were to identify the critical strategic outcomes and the change agenda. This was seen as a prerequisite to realigning HR to business strategy.

It was agreed that the consultant would conduct a mini-workshop with the senior managers to overview the assessment outcomes and to assist them in identifying the critical change issues that needed to be addressed, and ways of communicating them to staff. This would then provide the HR manager with the basis for beginning to address some of the other issues outlined in the report.

Comments

This exercise has raised the issue of timing and organizational readiness when undertaking a strategic HR analysis. In some ways, it may have been more helpful to undertake the exercise once the uncertainty affecting the organization's future (which to a large extent is governed by factors external to the agency) was at least partly resolved.

The exercise has been helpful, however, in acting as a catalyst to highlight the change-management issues facing the agency. It has also assisted the agency in identifying some of the key areas of HR practice needing attention.

Agency Case Study 4

Description of the Agency

The organization is a medium-sized agency, with approximately 700 employees and an operating budget of approximately $70 million. Its services are located in a metropolitan regional centre, and there is a presence in the Asian region.

The agency prides itself in its progressive approach to customer service and commitment to training.

The HR manager reports to the director of Corporate Services.

The Business Issues

The agency is undergoing significant changes in legislation, technology, and structure through its shift to the funder-purchaser-provider model and an output-based management approach.

These changes are necessary for it to remain competitive in an industry where high standards are expected by customers and there is potential competition through external providers.

What the Agency Wanted to Achieve Using the Framework

The agency prides itself in adopting best practices in its operations, and was keen to trial the framework to ensure that its HR practices are aligned to organizational strategy. Additionally, the organization has a relatively new HR manager, who is keen to ensure that the HR function is strategically positioned within the agency. It was the HR manager's intention to use this analysis as the basis for developing a Divisional Human Resource Plan.

The exercise was timely, given the shift toward the funder-purchaser-provider model. Two of the executive positions have recently been filled, including that of strategic planning director.

Methodology

Planning Meeting. An initial meeting was held with the HR manager to identify how the project would be approached and who should be interviewed. The organization has a medium-sized HR branch with highly experienced staff, and it was deemed essential to gain their support and commitment from the beginning. They were subsequently briefed on the project, its rationale, and the process that would occur.

Assessment. The consultant conducted an individual interview with the Chief Executive Officer to ascertain the strategic and business issues facing the organization, the critical HR issues facing the organization, and his assessment of the HR function. All of this was done using the Strategic HR Framework.

The HR manager was interviewed to obtain an assessment of the HR function.

Key documents were reviewed, including the Annual Report, recent review reports, enterprise agreements, details of the Structural Realignment of Service Delivery activities, and Public Sector Compliance reports.

Analysis. A written report was prepared by the consultant for the HR manager. The report summarized the business issues, highlighted the gaps in alignment, and made recommendations of suggested actions that could occur to address these gaps.

Some of the major findings were:

- There are no strategic or operational plans in place.
- Performance and productivity indicators need to be more aligned throughout the agency.
- The organization needs a more diverse, outward looking approach to recruitment.
- There is an immediate need for workforce and succession planning to assure the necessary skills to meet the needs of the future.
- Performance management processes need to be established to reflect an output-based team approach.

Action Planning. A three-hour workshop was held with a mix of directors, middle managers, and HR staff. The aims of the workshop were to:

- Agree on the critical business-related issues facing the organization.
- Agree on the critical HR priorities.
- Agree on a model for HR and business managers to work together.

This workshop agreed on the priority areas to be addressed by the HR group (on behalf of the organization) over the next twelve months. The priorities included:

- Establishing a HR vision
- The need for more strategic information
- Recruitment and diversity issues
- Establishing service agreements with HR
- Identifying overhead costs of HR
- Developing a performance management system that reflects output-based management and team requirements
- Working with the executive to manage the change and communication processes
- Dealing with the potential loss of intellectual capital and knowledge

Comments

Agency case study 4 is regarded as leading edge in many of its people-management practices, and this exercise has helped refine many of its processes for strategic purpose.

One of the critical issues to emerge was the need to link HR strategy and information to the organization's strategy and information requirements.

The workshop with senior managers and the chief executive proved invaluable in improving the business partnership between senior management and HR. It also confirmed the strategic contribution HR can make to business success.

CAMBRIDGESHIRE (UK) COUNTY COUNCIL SUCCESSION PLANNING

Case Introduction: This is actually a brief case study from the UK. First published elsewhere, it describes how a local government approached the succession planning challenge.

Succession planning has recently been implemented by the council as a means of developing existing talent and producing a larger pool of viable internal candidates for strategic management positions (director and above).

The aim is to eventually embed the process throughout the organization, so that all managers regard preparing their staff for internal career enhancement as an intrinsic part of their role.

Background

Cambridgeshire is the fastest-growing county in the UK, with a total population of 553,600 in 2000. The county council is the largest employer in Cambridgeshire, with around 6,000 full-time-equivalent staff. The council has a majority-Conservative administration. The council had been experiencing difficulties in filling vacancies at the strategic-management level, particularly in financial services.

By conducting an internal audit to analyze the proportion of senior managers appointed internally, the council discovered this to be low compared to other employers.

In addition, there were perceptions among some employees that the council did not consider internal candidates for recruitment to senior posts.

Key Challenges

A separate risk audit identified that the council's failure to recruit to key posts was resulting in potentially serious risk for both the organization and service users. It was established that the current structure of some teams did not lend itself to the automatic identification of managerial successors.

When the council decided to employ succession planning as a means of addressing this problem, it consulted staff. During the process of discussion, it was discovered that some had concerns about the equal-opportunities aspects. However, on balance, employees were satisfied that the council's proposed approach would be fair and that the system would not promote the favored few.

We felt that the best way of tackling any negative preconceptions was to identify potential successors for strategic leader posts, and develop them into viable candidates.

The aims behind succession planning are to improve the coherence and consistency of our services, as well as to become a council that offers long-term career prospects and staff development. By focusing on the high-profile strategic management positions, we were seeking to send out a powerful message to the whole organization about the importance of employee development, while at the same time address the authority's specific recruitment difficulties at this level.

The project had the support of key strategic sponsors, including the chief executive, the chairman of the Appointments Committee, the director of HR, and the Organizational Development manager.

There were no externally-set time pressures to deliver on succession planning. However, we were working to our own timetable, which is informed by a pressing need to standardize succession planning across the organization.

What the Council Did

Every director is now asked to nominate individuals they are actively developing as people with the potential to be either their own successor or successor to a similar position within the organization. Members of staff may also nominate themselves onto the scheme. An early question the authority faced was whether to develop employees for specific posts, or for a pool of posts. The authority is keen to break down silos and to develop a pool of talent for posts across the organization, while increasing the candidates' breadth of experience and widening the opportunities open to them. However, the authority also recognizes that it employs a considerable number of professionals who wish to follow a career in their chosen profession. The guidance produced on succession planning therefore encourages managers to consider their staff for posts across the organization, but also recognizes that progression within the directorate will be the preferred career path of some.

Equal opportunities have emerged as a key theme of Cambridgeshire's succession plan. Marian Mair, who is organizational development manager, is driving succession planning in the council and has worked hard to promote the message within the authority that a well-developed succession-planning scheme can offer valuable development opportunities to individuals and improve business continuity.

The scheme has been favorably mentioned in external inspections, and employees have given positive feedback about the development opportunities offered.

Of the 40 participants who began the scheme in 2003, 20 are now in more-senior posts within the organization, and there are more women on the strategic leadership team than ever before.

The changes have been transformational, based on a clear need and targeted objectives.

Key Outcomes

The appraisal process has been greatly strengthened with the introduction of succession planning. Once the selection to the succession planning scheme has been endorsed, the line manager and the nominee agree on a personal development plan, focusing on areas where assessment indicated that the nominee needed development in order to carry out a more-senior role. Corporate and operational HR offer support for this process (if required). These development plans can include delegation of challenging tasks or assignments to potential successors, planned deputizing, secondments, shadowing, mentoring, job rotation, lateral movement, formal training, and coaching. The importance of having ongoing feedback from managers during these learning experiences is emphasized. Development centers designed to diagnose potential successors' strengths and development needs more accurately have been piloted, and are proving a useful way of nurturing staff as well as improving the council's reputation as an employer of choice.

As this is primarily an internal resourcing scheme, we have initially conducted evaluation at an internal level. As outlined above, this assessment has revealed that 50 percent of the participants who began the program in 2003 have gone on to more-senior posts within the council.

Anecdotal feedback from staff has been positive, with great appreciation for the career development opportunities, strengthened appraisal system, and emphasis on fairness.

Resources

Since the scheme's launch in 2003, officer time has been the major expense, although the council has provided corporate funding to participants to attend development centers.

All the recruitment processes for the new leadership team have been effective, partly because of the good supply of good internal candidates.

The project is resourced on a day-to-day basis by Marian Mair and the directors and assistant directors involved in the selection and development processes. The development centers account for a significant cost of the scheme.

Leading the project was Marian Mair, Organizational Development Manager. She was reporting ultimately to the chief executive, the chairman of the Appointments Committee, and the director of HR.

Barriers and How They Were Overcome

As previously mentioned, there were some concerns within the authority that succession planning may not develop in a fair or equitable way (certain candidates might be favored over others, from the outset).

This was more an instinctive reaction by a few to a process that depends on nomination and selection, rather than one that is based on evidence.

By explaining the fair and open way succession planning will be conducted—with the use of strategic-management competencies and the development of a business case for each candidate—the council is striving for demonstrable fairness.

By involving a succession planning committee in the final selection process, the council is also reassuring staff that candidates are endorsed by a wider panel than simply their line manager.

Prior to the introduction of succession planning, trade union representatives were also consulted with. Cambridgeshire's Human Resource team has a good relationship with the trade union representatives, who were positive about the proposed scheme because it would be promoting staff development.

Critical Success Factors

We have made the process of succession planning a formalized one, ensuring fairness and clarity. The director/assistant director assesses nominated staff against strategic management competencies and makes a business case for each succession candidate, using a standard format. This process also provides an opportunity for the nominee to become familiar with these senior competencies, and then with the support of their manager to assess where their strengths and weaknesses lie in relation to these. Nominees are also asked to write a statement supporting their application. The manager's assessment, together with the nominee's supporting statement, is then submitted to the Succession Planning Board for endorsement.

In order to manage expectations and ensure the longevity of the scheme, as our guidance material clarifies, nominees might not achieve the particular job they are aiming for, but by participating in the scheme, they have an opportunity to develop themselves. Nominees can also choose to keep their status as a potential successor confidential, which again is helping to encourage their involvement.

Successors could change year-on-year. In order to prevent people from being dropped off the list of potential successors in an insensitive manner, we do not place a limit on the number of people listed as having succession potential.

By creating a succession planning board consisting of members of the appointments committee, directors, and the head of HR, the range of candidates put forward for succession development is constantly monitored. This ensures that the process continually evolves to meet demands; there is another layer of scrutiny when it comes to agreeing on successors; there is consistency across the organization; and the process is in line with corporate objectives.

Contact Information

This case study was prepared by Marian Mair, Organizational Development Manager for the Cambridgeshire County Council. She can be contacted at this Web address: Marian.Mair@cambridgeshire.gov.uk

SURREY (UK) COUNTY COUNCIL FAST-TRACK PROGRAMME

Case Introduction: This is actually a brief case study from the UK. First published elsewhere, it describes how a local government approached the succession planning challenge.

The first of its kind in Surrey, the council's fast-track scheme aims to identify and develop talent in a local government context where career routes are traditionally ill-defined and many careers are developing haphazardly. The fast-track scheme is designed to offer an accelerated development route to parallel the council's management-development scheme. While places on the latter scheme are invariably secured by external graduate applicants, the fast track is aimed at existing staff at any level up to middle management who have been employed on a permanent contract for at least six months.

Background

Surrey has a population of almost 1.1 million. The annual cost of providing services is almost £1bn. The Conservative-controlled county council is the fifth largest local authority in the country, employing 24,000 staff. Like many organisations in the south-east, it is competing for talent.

The council's succession planning process was in need of improvement to ensure longer-term capacity in key management roles.

In 2002, the Audit Commission rated the council as "good" in its Comprehensive Performance Assessment, commending its efforts to build internal capacity and the importance it placed on developing a motivated and skilled workforce. The council recognised that a more coordinated effort was required to head off future skills gaps and maintain service delivery.

Key Challenges

Local government generally tends to suffer from unclear career routes, with career routes developing on an almost "by chance" basis. In Surrey, this has manifested itself in a lack of capacity at senior levels.

The council already had a management-development programme in place, but had found it hard to allocate existing staff to the programme, instead attracting external graduate applicants. A historic lack of succession planning and long-term capacity building were contributing factors. By creating a fast-track scheme aimed at existing staff, the council was able to offer additional career development support to help "fast trackers" be in a better position to be promoted into management positions.

The aim was to develop core management skills so that the council's talent pool was expanded and more managers could be appointed internally.

The fast-track programme was the idea of the head of HR, who had successfully used a similar scheme in a previous role. As always, there were pressures to demonstrate a good return on investment.

What the Council Has Done

The council used its corporate values framework and research leadership and management skills for the future, to develop fast-track competencies that have become the foundations on which the scheme is built. The competencies are used in selection to the fast-track scheme. A self-assessment tool is available on the intranet so employees can see if the scheme is appropriate for them. They are then invited to submit application forms with structured questions based on the competencies, and line managers are asked to provide supporting statements. Shortlisted applicants are then assessed against the competencies through structured discussions with their heads of service.

For participants, the fast-track scheme starts with 360-degree feedback and a development centre. The development centre involves a number of assessments (e.g. presentation, group exercises, written analytical exercises) based on real-life case studies drawn from across the services. Following the development centre, fast trackers are then given feedback by the assessors on their performance, and tailored learning and development plans are drawn up. Development continues through the year. Each fast tracker's service area provides projects to meet their development needs and broaden their experience. Participants are encouraged to engage in coaching with an internal coach and action learning sets. The results of a learning needs analysis are combined with common themes drawn from the development plans and used to develop a series of seminars. Senior managers are invited to talk to fast trackers about areas that meet fast trackers' development needs, such as negotiating and consulting with customers.

As is often the case across local government, services tend to work in silos. Fast trackers come from a broad range of services, and they really appreciated meeting colleagues from different areas. It was useful for developing "big picture" thinking and for identifying different approaches for developing solutions to problems.

As of December 2005—the end of the second year of the programme—a total of 29 staff have participated in the scheme. Evaluation feedback indicates that most felt that the programme has provided opportunities to develop management skills. Four people have been promoted internally, two were promoted externally, and two have changed careers. There were also secondments and lateral job moves.

Key Outcomes

Increasing the learning and development opportunities for staff has been a major and very much desired outcome of the scheme. By taking part in the development centre and having detailed development plans drawn up as a result, candidates receive a highly tailored learning package.

This benefits both candidates and managers, with candidates feeling they are working toward tangible goals, such as promotion, and managers reassured that the skills and capacity of their team will be strengthened over the longer term.

Services also benefit by having projects delivered that address business needs.

Participant feedback to date indicates that the projects are generally perceived as having a positive impact on individuals and the organisation as a whole.

Anecdotally, participants have praised the scheme for allowing them to build upon existing skills while gaining a broader insight into the workings of the council. Internal support for the scheme is strong, with staff being actively encouraged to develop professional expertise and management skills through the fast-track scheme.

Resources

In the first year, an external consultancy (Robertson Cooper) developed and ran the development centre. In the second year, an occupational psychologist working within Human Resources designed and ran the development centre. This limited development centre costs to hotel expenses (where the development centre was located). Assessors were a mix of HR staff and senior managers, which was valued by the participants and also enabled costs to be kept down. The 360-degree feedback process was managed by an external consultancy, which incurred only a modest cost.

Who Was Involved?

The head of HR provided direction for the scheme. Diane Lomas, head of the Organisational Development team, led the project in its first year. Karen Hanson, an occupational psychologist and senior organisational development consultant in HR, managed the project the following year.

Participants nominated themselves to the scheme, and came from a variety of services. Development centre assessors were senior managers and HR staff. They underwent a day's training prior to the centre. All reported afterwards that they found it a valuable development activity.

Senior managers were also involved in the selection interviews and in identifying projects. Graham White, head of Human Resources, is leading on the scheme overall. He wants to see succession planning embedded as good practice in the council.

Barriers and How They Were Overcome

The vast majority of managers are supportive of members of their team who are on fast track. However there were some initial tensions in back-filling posts while the fast trackers were undertaking challenging projects. Many fast trackers completed their projects on top of their day jobs, which provided an opportunity for them to develop time-management skills as well. Some services were slow in providing projects for their fast trackers. This reinforced the importance of regular communication and promotion of fast track. Managers have a lot of demands placed on their time. Often short-term priorities take precedence over medium and long-term development needs.

Critical Success Factors

All unsuccessful applicants are offered face-to-face feedback and given the opportunity to take up coaching with an internal coach. This ensures that all candidates benefit from the fast-track process, not just those who are taken on.

The tailored learning and development plans, together with the projects, coaching, seminars, and action learning sets provide valuable opportunities for accelerated experiential learning and development. This has been key in attracting participants as well as encouraging managers to support their staff who want to take part.

HR insists from the outset that fast trackers are not handed unpopular projects. All projects offered to candidates should address real business needs and provide opportunities for real development. The council considered creating a board to monitor the fast-track scheme and ensure that high-quality secondments are offered by all services. This hasn't happened to date, but it is still a possibility. Another potential change to the scheme is for services to pay for fast track, but stakeholders haven't been consulted on this yet.

How would you do it better?

The development centre was well received, and a number of changes were introduced in the second year as a result of the learning in the first. Fast trackers really appreciated career discussions with senior managers.

As with all change, communication is paramount. A key learning point was to engage with a wider range of stakeholders throughout the programme. One senior manager suggested that senior managers nominate fast trackers, rather than fast trackers applying themselves. This might have assured more senior manager buy-in, but there was a risk that senior managers would not be aware of any staff who would be suitable for the scheme.

Some people have asked that a similar scheme be offered for middle managers, which we will be looking into.

Contact Information

Karen Hanson: Karen.hanson@surreycc.gov.uk

Graham White, Director of Human Resources:
graham.white@surreycc.gov.uk

Part II

U. S. FEDERAL GOVERNMENT CASE STUDIES

The U.S. federal government is enormous. State and local governments and citizens depend on Washington for funding and oversight of many governmental programs. How do these huge and complex U.S. government agencies approach succession planning?

The cases in this section are meant to provide a sense of how specific federal government agencies plan for personnel shifts and retirements. These cases are:

Permission has been granted by each agency to use the case information for this book.

NATIONAL AERONAUTICS AND SPACE ADMINISTRATION: HUMAN CAPITAL PLANNING

Case Introduction: The information provided here was prepared by NASA. We are including it because some content relates to its human capital management initiative.

NASA's position as one of the world's leading research and development organizations is increasingly at risk. Already stretched to capacity due to staffing cutbacks and other employee losses experienced during the 1990s, NASA faces serious challenges to recruiting and retaining the critical experts needed for the agency to achieve its ambitious goals. Under the direction of Sean O'Keefe, NASA gleaned the best management practices from among its 11 individual centers and is applying those practices agency-wide to identify critical skills gaps and develop the strategies needed to build and maintain a world-class workforce. NASA's efforts are paying off. According to the Office of Personnel Management's Human Capital Survey, NASA ranks first among federal agencies in overall employee satisfaction. In addition, the agency's education, recruiting and other human capital management initiatives are building a ready supply of future talent to satisfy NASA's emerging needs.

To Explore the Universe and Search for Life

Established in 1958, NASA is the world's preeminent organization for space and aeronautics research and development. NASA's creative, innovative and dedicated employees define the success of the agency, whether landing men on the Moon in 1969 or building a permanent international space station in the 21st century. Located in eleven separate centers and laboratories across the United States, NASA is a collection of approximately 19,000 highly skilled employees that includes engineers, researchers, technicians, lawyers, and, of course, rocket scientists. NASA also makes extensive use of approximately 42,000 on-site or near-site contractor personnel.

Within the last decade, NASA's standards of technical and managerial excellence have been threatened by internal and external workforce trends affecting the agency's ability to maintain the scientific, engineering and professional workforce needed to break new ground. Like agencies across the federal government, NASA reduced the overall size of its workforce through buyouts, employee retirements and natural attrition during the 1990s. Predictably, the workforce became older as a result. Today, more than 75 percent of NASA's workforce is over 40 years of age, and only 4 percent of employees are under 30. Approximately 25 percent of NASA employees—including almost 50 percent of agency executives—are eligible to retire in 2007.

At the same time, NASA is disadvantaged in its efforts to recruit and retain even replacement employees, let alone the new employees required for the future. The need is especially acute in the fields of science and engineering. The supply of scientists and engineers graduating from our schools is not increasing, but the demand from the public sector, the private sector and academia is intensifying. In spite of its unparalleled mission and history of excellence, NASA is having difficulty competing with sectors offering higher starting salaries and other financial and non-financial incentives.

Launching Strategic Human Capital Planning

With the same energy NASA brings to solving scientific and technical problems, the agency is tackling its mission critical workforce challenges. NASA administrator Sean O'Keefe—a management expert previously responsible for development of the President's Management Agenda at the Office of Management and Budget (OMB)—created a strategic human capital planning committee of senior managers from across the agency to develop a plan. The committee started by designing a Strategic Human Capital Architecture outlining the key elements of successful human capital management. Based on guidance from OMB and Office of Personnel Management (OPM), the architecture includes five key human capital management pillars essential for NASA's success.

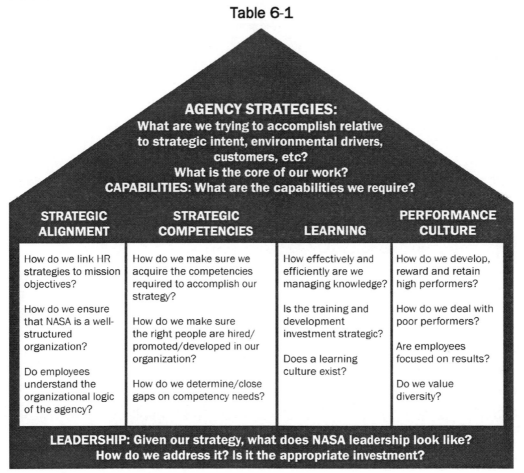

Table 6-1

As a next step, the committee used the architecture to evaluate NASA's current human capital management practices and to develop a set of priority improvement initiatives for the agency. Two initiatives related to NASA's strategic planning and management processes were: Implementing an agency-wide, integrated approach to workforce planning and analysis, and developing a competency management system—defining the key bodies of knowledge NASA must retain through employees, and those that may be accessed through industry, academic, and other relationships.

A "One NASA" Approach to Workforce Planning

Many NASA centers had been engaged in workforce planning efforts in the past. The lack of either a common approach or centralized system, however, prevented the agency from looking across the entire organization for the purposes of integrated planning, budgeting, and staffing decisions. Individual centers acted as "stovepipes."

To create an agency-wide approach to workforce planning, the committee created a structured, four-step process for integrating strategic workforce planning with every other aspect of the agency's overall management agenda. Under the new approach, each of NASA's centers continues to develop workforce plans individually, but does so working from a common framework and set of expectations. Now, when it comes time to build an agency-wide workforce plan, NASA's leaders no longer cobble together a plan from among the centers' submissions. Rather, the centers' plans—though each one is unique—contain a consistent set of elements, which facilitates leaders' efforts to build a strategic workforce plan for all of NASA.

To further support agency-wide planning, a team of employees from across the organization created a Human Capital Management Web site. The Human Capital Management Web site provides leaders and employees from across the agency with one of the most comprehensive workforce planning resources available in either the public or private sectors. NASA's Web site includes a complete workforce planning guide, as well as detailed workforce analysis reports, analytical tools for examining current and past workforce characteristics, and forecasting tools for determining future workforce trends within NASA and across the entire labor market.

At any time, managers and supervisors can access the Web site and use dozens of tools and support materials to help them more effectively formulate workforce plans and manage employees. As a result, agency leaders across the country are managing their employees better, while also working together more effectively as "One NASA" to support the agency's mission and achieve its goals.

The Cornerstone of NASA's Workforce Planning: Competency Management

To ensure that NASA actually has the talent on hand to overcome current and emerging challenges, the agency developed a system for defining the knowledge and skills required for work to be completed safely, assessing current staff capabilities against those requirements, and designing strategies to fill any talent gaps through hiring, reassignments, training or contracting. Called the *Competency Management System* (CMS), it offers leaders and managers a uniform, comprehensive approach for measuring, monitoring and managing employees and external resources. NASA defines competencies as the body of knowledge an employee must possess to perform a given assignment or project. NASA organized an agency-wide team to define a common set of competencies for the entire agency. This was a big challenge: individually, NASA's labs and centers had defined more than 1,000 competencies. Based on interviews and working group sessions with employees from NASA centers all across the country, the team consolidated and validated a set of approximately 140 competencies required of the workforce. The agency's leaders and managers now share a common understanding of the skills and abilities of the NASA workforce.

The team then developed a user-friendly, Web-based tool for managers, supervisors and employees to inventory NASA's competencies. Throughout the agency, managers have inventoried all of the competencies their employees are known to possess. Now a manager at the Johnson Space Center looking for propulsion expertise can simply access the system and find a list of people nationally and across the agency who possess that knowledge. NASA is already using this system, perhaps most noticeably in assembling response teams to the Columbia disaster.

As a next step, NASA will require all employees to complete their own competency profiles. Many of the agency's employees have completed multiple projects during their careers requiring a wide variety of competencies. As critical needs for scarce skills arise, NASA needs to know which employees possess which competencies. Patrick Simpkins, the leader of the competency project, is a great example: while he currently holds a human resources management position, you might not know that his career included lead responsibility for Space Shuttle fluid systems in the Launch Control Center for over 70 Space Shuttle missions.

Kennedy Space Center employees have completed this exercise. The rest of NASA's employees will soon follow suit. Even in this early stage of development, NASA's CMS is paying dividends. NASA is developing its academic outreach, corporate recruiting strategy and training initiatives to ensure that it employs the individuals needed to safely achieve its goals based on information in the CMS. Leaders are also using CMS to identify employees in scarce competency areas to respond to sudden mission requests.

NASA's Human Capital Plans Achieve Lift-Off

NASA's human capital planning has sparked several new agency initiatives and produced measurable results. Already ranked first among federal agencies in measures of overall employee satisfaction on the recent OPM Human Capital Survey, NASA is working to become a leader in federal recruiting, hiring, training, leadership development and retention. The agency's strategic planning efforts—particularly its focus on people—are having an impact after only a few years. Recruiting initiatives offer a concrete example of NASA's efforts to move from planning to action. To replenish an ever-diminishing supply of talent, NASA is educating students from grade school to grad school about the exciting opportunities in the fields of science, technology, engineering and mathematics (STEM). Through the Educator Astronaut Program, NASA is working with experts in K–12 education. NASA's Educator Astronauts will lead the agency's efforts to develop new ways of connecting space exploration to the classroom and inspiring the next generation of explorers. Offering research and fellowship opportunities in partnership with our country's colleges and universities, NASA also seeks to increase the number of students seeking undergraduate and graduate degrees in STEM fields.

NASA works with these students on special projects and is beginning to successfully bring these students into the agency via its aggressive use of student programs and hiring strategies. For example, NASA's new Undergraduate Student Research Program brought in 107 diverse students, from 29 states and 70 institutions, to work with the agency's employees on critical programs. NASA also recently reinstated its Cooperative Education Program, joining other government agencies using OPM's Career Intern Program and Presidential Management Intern Program, as a means of recruiting new talent into the agency. NASA's use of student loan repayments will also undoubtedly attract new employees with critical skills into the agency.

To better build the workforce needed for NASA's safe operations in the future, the agency hopes to build on this success by requesting additional authority from Congress to offer industry exchange programs, improved retention bonuses, more-competitive pay for critical positions, and science and technology scholarships to students for government service, among other changes.

Keys to Success

The focus, passion and creativity of NASA's administrator, leaders, and employees have been critical to the agency's success in overcoming its workforce challenges. NASA points to several factors leading to its success.

Treating Human Capital Like Rocket Science

Although human capital planning may not seem like rocket science, it is to some extent within NASA. To ensure that the agency's planning efforts adequately reflected the diverse, highly technical knowledge and skill areas of its employees, NASA enlisted their support—particularly the support of its scientists and engineers—to build and complete the agency's planning efforts. In fact, NASA relied on its scientists and engineers to build the competency definitions, terms and processes critical to its Competency Management System.

Capitalizing on Internal Resources

NASA did not limit its outreach to scientists and engineers. The agency utilized its internal information technology (IT) experts to develop an agency-wide Human Capital Management Web site. In addition, IT and human resources management experts are collaborating as a virtual team across the agency to develop innovative human capital management applications.

Being Transparent

NASA's Human Capital Management Web site also includes the agency's human capital strategies and implementation plans available for all NASA leaders, employees and stakeholders to view. NASA knew that if its human capital management activities were to be taken seriously by internal and external stakeholders, the agency would need to act in a business-like fashion and communicate broadly. Providing total transparency in its process and results is helping to build a community of support for the changes, investments and flexibilities needed moving forward.

Measuring Progress

NASA did not stop at simply identifying its workforce challenges and generally describing the strategies it intended to pursue. The agency developed an implementation plan, including a detailed list of the strategies and policies it intended to develop to overcome each of its significant workforce challenges, a schedule for completing the work, and the performance metrics NASA would examine to measure progress. NASA is focused on overcoming its human capital challenges to fully realize its mission and goals, and the agency is not afraid to hold itself accountable for doing so.

The Future of NASA's Strategic Human Capital Planning

Consistent with NASA's tradition of innovation and continuous improvement, the agency's leaders will be refining its strategic human capital planning in the years ahead. The first order of business will be expanding NASA's use of the CMS to its entire workforce. However, NASA will not stop there; the agency intends to use its CMS to assess the knowledge and skills of its total workforce, which includes over 40,000 contractors. As NASA continues to improve its strategic human capital management, the agency will ensure that it is the preeminent symbol of American technological achievement and human exploration.

Contact Information

For further information about NASA's strategic human capital and workforce planning, visit NASA's human capital management Web site at http://nasapeople.nasa.gov/hcm/.

TRANSFORMATION DELIVERED AT THE U.S. POSTAL SERVICE

Case Introduction: This case study describes the U.S. Postal Service's efforts to address future talent needs. It originally appeared in the March, 2006 issue of Training and Development.

For generations of leaders at the United States Postal Service, success meant meeting service goals and making budget. That's understandable when—every day—you have to deliver mail to more than 142 million homes, serve seven million customers in 38,000 post offices, and manage 86 million pounds of mail traveling through processing centers.

Four years ago, USPS Postmaster General and CEO John E. "Jack" Potter set his sights beyond the status quo and introduced the USPS Transformation Plan. The plan set new expectations around customer focus, the quality of the work environment, and market competitiveness in addition to ambitious budget and service goals. Significant change, and plenty of it, would reach every corner and every employee in the organization. As a result of the plan, the postal service looks much different than it did just four years ago—and it will look much different four years from now.

Yet change doesn't come easily for a sprawling organization of 700,000 employees scattered across the country. For senior leadership—750 executives—the challenge has been to radically change organizational structures and operations while changing the mindset of hundreds of thousands of people. In many ways, the story of the Postal Service is not unique. Change and uncertainty have become standard in most contemporary organizations. Significant transformation—such as that being undertaken by USPS—involves waves of change. And with change comes transition.

Change Versus Transition

Change and transition represent two distinct aspects of the learning and adaptation process. *Change* is whatever is new or different. *Transition* refers to the psychological and emotional reactions that people experience as a natural human response to living through change. While leaders and employees at all levels may be braced for change and growth, they still struggle to deal with the loss that invariably comes with it.

The higher-order challenge for leaders is to simultaneously pay attention to both change and transition. They must lead the implementation of the change and do so with enough empathetic understanding to bring people through the transition. At USPS, for example, the mail keeps coming in and it has to keep going out. By necessity, the organization is focused on its numerical imperatives. Implementing change requires leaders to be highly skilled in the structural components of leadership. But as Ken McArthur, a USPS district manager responsible for some 45,000 employees, says, "The results are through the people."

Change initiatives typically derail because the ball is dropped on the people side. Perfectly good strategies and change initiatives stall or fail when employees become stuck in some phase of the emotional transition. Leaders who fail to connect around these natural emotions generally struggle to gain sufficient buy-in from employees and thereby undermine their progress toward new goals. Instead of a loyal, productive, and enthusiastic workforce, executives and managers end up leading employees who are insecure, fearful, and skeptical.

Authenticity and Trust

How do leaders address the people side of change without jeopardizing the business of change? How can a leader make tough decisions and address the emotions and needs of employees? The answers lie in being authentic and building trust from the inside out.

Table 7-1

Balancing Paradox

To create and sustain an environment of trust, leaders must be comfortable with the tension of opposites. Imagine a wheel that has trust as its hub. Radiating out of that hub are the spokes, which represent twelve competencies for dealing with change and transition. Six spokes represent structural competencies; the other six represent people-related competencies. The key, paradoxically, is to be skilled at both. They are:

Catalyze change. Champion an initiative or significant change, consistently promote the cause, and encourage others to get on board.

Cope with transition. Recognize and address the personal and emotional elements of change.

Show a sense of urgency. Take action, move fast, and accelerate the pace of change for everyone.

Demonstrate realistic patience. Know when and how to slow the pace down so that people can cope and adapt.

Be tough. Make difficult decisions with little hesitation or second-guessing.

Be empathetic. Take others' perspectives into account; understand the impact of your actions and decisions.

Show optimism. See the positive potential of any challenge and convey that optimism to others.

Be realistic and open. Speak the truth, be candid, and admit personal mistakes and foibles.

Be self-reliant. Tackle new challenges with confidence.

Trust others. Be comfortable with others doing their part; stay open to others for input and support.

Capitalize on strengths. Know your individual and organizational strengths and attributes; confidently apply them to tackle new situations and circumstances.

Go against the grain. Show a willingness to learn and try new things—even when the process is difficult or painful.

Leading with authenticity involves keen self awareness, including one's personal and emotional reactions to change. Authenticity allows a leader to go through change with integrity and honesty, which generates trust from others. And from a position of trust, a leader can more effectively guide others through change and transition.

Sheryl Turner, a postal executive who participated in the program, says she now "thinks more about how I lead, how I'm coming across to people, and how I work." In the past year, Turner has been developing a number of employees who have taken on new roles. She now is more comfortable bringing encouragement and insight, as well as her own experiences doing unfamiliar and unknown tasks, to her role as leader and coach.

The Program

To lead authentically through change and transition, leaders must move from understanding and managing the structure of change to connecting to the emotions and experience of transition. As a starting point for developing the capacity to lead the people side of change, the Center for Creative Leadership (CCL) and USPS developed the Leading People Through Transformation program (LPTT). CCL's work in the area of change, transition, and organizational resiliency was the foundation for the program and, most recently, the book *Leading with Authenticity in Times of Transition.*

LPTT is a five-day program for USPS top executives. The goal of the course is to give the participants an experience that pushes them to rethink their approaches to change leadership within the context of the USPS Transformation Plan. Over the course of three years, 34 sessions have been completed, involving more than 650 postal service executives. Another 100 executives are slated to take the program in the coming year. Potter kicks off every session by spending several hours with the executives. He shares his vision of transformation though stories and examples, offers encouragement, and fields questions from participants.

At the end of the week, a group of five USPS executive officers join the participants. What begins sometimes as an awkward group (the officers sit mixed in with the class) becomes an opportunity for a no-holds-barred dialogue session about what it takes to lead people through this time of transformation. By investing personally in LPTT, Potter and the executive committee demonstrate the open, honest, and direct leadership style that is important for leading authentically in a changing organization.

The Best-Kept Secret

One of the challenges we face in talking about this course is that the most talked about, most significant element of the program cannot be revealed. The element of surprise is crucial to triggering the depth of learning and impact, so program participants are asked not to tell their co-workers about what happens in the session. Also, because this intervention continues to operate with USPS and in variations with other organizations, we cannot describe the details of what has become known as "the experience."

But we can say that this activity is potent enough to bring the emotional component of change to the surface quickly and intensely. People learn the most when they have to experience the lesson. Leaders are more ready to address the human side of transition if they can engage at a personal level—with the impact of change on their own lives. The experience provides a genuine reflective opportunity for the executives to wade in the water of transition and transformation.

During the extensive debrief of the experience, participants realize that their emotional and intense reactions during the program are similar to the way people respond in the face of change at work. As executives, they often believe they are skilled at dealing with change, but most have paid little attention to the emotional and human fallout from that change.

The experience gives them a glimpse into what powerful learning and change feels like—and the barriers it can create—through a lesson that many say will stay with them through their careers. When the executives recognize their classroom experience as a microcosm of their back-home world, the door opens to truthful discussions about how to lead dramatic change.

Participants are able to view plant closings, job relocations, and operational changes in a new light. They can see more clearly their leadership tendencies and the effect they have on others. They become interested in how to better handle the people side of change. They start to consider ways to lead that will help bring people through transition so that they can adapt and contribute in the long term.

Table 7-2

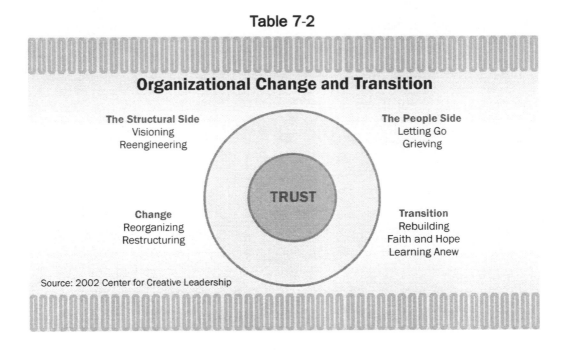

Organizational Change and Transition

The Structural Side
Visioning
Reengineering

The People Side
Letting Go
Grieving

TRUST

Change
Reorganizing
Restructuring

Transition
Rebuilding
Faith and Hope
Learning Anew

Source: 2002 Center for Creative Leadership

Table 7-3

Postmaster General: Change Everything

In 2002, Postmaster General and CEO John E. "Jack" Potter introduced the Transformation Plan to bring organizational changes and modernization to virtually every aspect of the postal service. His leadership enabled the organization to achieve record levels of service and financial stability. The plan has resulted in cumulative cost savings of $8.8 billion. Debt was completely eliminated at the end of fiscal 2005 and productivity has continued to climb to historic levels. New products and services—such as Click 'n Ship, Carrier Pick-Up, and Negotiated Service Agreements—have also been introduced. The innovations were designed to make postal services more accessible and convenient to customers. Today, customer service satisfaction levels are at an all-time high. As a result of service-wide initiatives to improve the workplace environment and to improve relations with the postal unions and management associations, employee satisfaction and safety in the workplace also are at record high levels.

Leadership in Transition

LPTT is an infusion of ideas and energy for postal service executives facing the complex challenges of leadership. The expectation is that they will gain new perspectives and skills for relating to employees in the context of the transformation that is the ongoing work of the organization.

While implementing the USPS Transformation Plan, executives are hitting critical marks. Just as important, the leadership behaviors of executives reflect a new, more balanced perspective on how to lead change and transition.

These shifts generally fall into four areas:

Leadership Is Personal

For a nuts-and-bolts organization like USPS, looking at the personal and emotional aspects of leading through change seemed, at first glance, out of place. Yet, executives have benefited from greater understanding of their style of leadership (both what is working well and what isn't), as well as an awareness of how their approach affects employees. The program ". . . validated that I was on the right track in some areas and gave me a lot of confidence," explains Ken McArthur, district manager from Salt Lake City. "But it also showed things I needed to work on, and things I need to do differently."

Table 7-4

Leading Authentically through Times of Transition

For leaders to effectively harness and maintain the talent and commitment needed to benefit from organizational change, they must:

- *Examine their behaviors and emotions tied to change and transition.* This begins the process of operating from a place of authenticity as a leader.
- *Establish and protect trust.* Without trust and honesty, authenticity and credibility suffer, which undermines solid change initiatives or management decisions.
- *Find a balance between structural leadership and people leadership.* By learning the important competencies for leading in times of change and transition, leaders have a new perspective from which to operate.

Table 7-5

Bill Stefl and Olaf Jaehnigen, the postal service duo behind the LPTT program, offer advice to other workplace learning and performance professionals embarking on new initiatives.

Seek hands-on involvement from senior leadership. Buy-in from the CEO and top executives is essential, but it is even better to have senior leaders participate in the development initiative in some way. The more people they have in the program, the better.

Gain credibility early on. Be sure the participants in your first session of a new program are open-minded and interested in learning. Include some leaders who may be skeptical but are willing give it an honest and fair assessment. A good buzz following the program is essential for credibility and interest.

Don't let up. A dedicated, hands-on program manager should carry the torch, create continuity, and keep the initiative on the front-level radar. You're only as good as your last program. Communication, working behind the scenes, and handling the details all keep the momentum going as a corporate priority.

Relationships and Networks Matter

Given the scope and scale of their work, postal service executives essentially run large companies within the larger organization. Charged with running their own complex businesses, executives across the organization had limited networks and interaction with their peers prior to participating in the program. The shared experience of LPTT has broken up that sense of isolation. Now, executives have stronger connections with their counterparts in other locations and in other functional areas. Sheryl Turner, from Potomac, Maryland, appreciates that aspect. "I know people (from different functional areas). I can pick up the phone and say, *This is what we are working on. Here's what we need. What do you know?* or *How can you help?*"

The Emotional Component of Change Is Real

Through the experience of LPTT, postal service executives felt what it was like to be jolted by change. They also realized that individuals experience the same events quite differently. As a result, the executives are better prepared to lead their people through real-life challenges with greater understanding and authentic empathy. The lessons of the program began to truly take hold for Cliff Rucker when he put into action some of what he learned about how to address the people issues. "I started to see better results from my people," said Rucker, Houston area district manager. "I see the (people side) as another way to manage and as another way to get results from people."

Leaders Need Different Perspectives

USPS has seen a real change in how executives make decisions. They know the value of tapping into the knowledge and expertise of others and are more likely to involve a range of stakeholders in their decision-making process. Prior to LPTT, Rucker operated from the perspective that "I'm the senior executive; I'm paid to make the decisions" and would proceed, for the most part, independently. His process today is about informing people, getting them involved in the process, working to "get buy-in on the front end. I listen to their concerns and then formulate my strategy." Turner adds, "Most of us, as managers, like to think we have all the answers. (The program) helped me to understand that it's okay not to be comfortable. It's okay to ask the right questions and get the information to resolve a problem."

Through the Leading People Through Transformation program, USPS and the Center for Creative Leadership have laid a foundation for more-effective, more-authentic leadership. For the postmaster general, the executive officers, and the hundreds of executives who have been through LPTT, the program's lessons endure as the organization continues its transformation.

One clear example of the power of LPTT: Through 34 runs over three years, the secret of "the experience" has never leaked out, which allows the program to continue to have impact one executive at a time.

Source: Bunker, K., M. Wakefield, O. Jaehnigen, and B. Stefl (2006, March). Transformation delivered. *Training and Development.* Reproduced with permission.

Contact Information

This case study was prepared by the following individuals:

Kerry Bunker, senior faculty member
at the Center for Creative Leadership

E-mail: bunker@leaders.ccl.org

Michael Wakefield, senior faculty member
at the Center for Creative Leadership

E-mail: wakefieldm@leaders.ccl.org

Olaf Jaehnigen, Manager of Human Capital Development,
U.S. Postal Service

E-mail: olaflars.jaehnigen@ups.gov

Bill Stefl, Manager of Employment Development,
U.S. Postal Service

E-mail: william.stefl@ups.gov

SOCIAL SECURITY ADMINISTRATION: PREPARING FOR A RETIREMENT BOOM

> *Case Introduction:* This case study consists of the Social Security Administration's description of its efforts to prepare for pending waves of retirement.

As the "baby boom" of the 1940s and 1950s becomes the "retirement boom" of the 21st century, the Social Security Administration (SSA) has predicted a retirement boom among its own workforce beginning in 1998. Faced with the prospect of losing more than half of the agency's employees by the end of 2010, including a large number of its leaders, SSA developed a strategic human capital plan based on hard data, developed among leaders from across the agency, and linked to specific deadlines and deliverables. As a result, SSA is now recruiting, developing and retaining the high-performing employees they need to ensure that our nation's elderly, disabled and survivors of deceased workers receive needed financial support.

1. **Is the program still in place?**

   The Social Security Administration (SSA) continues to conduct the Retirement Wave Analysis, which is the cornerstone of its human capital planning efforts. The latest report was published in March 2004. The 2004 Report projects that 41.3% of the current workforce will retire by 2013. The new report shows that the "wave" will peak between 2008 and 2010, when approximately 2,800 employees will retire each year.

2. **What adjustments have you made to the program?**

   The 2004 Report featured several enhancements in the model used to project retirements.

They included:

- Basing projections on SSA's mission-critical occupations, in order to better align the Retirement Wave with other planning activities.
- Reducing the projection period from 20 years to 10 years, to provide more accurate projections.
- Providing low, median, and high projections to help Agency leaders visualize, and plan for, various retirement scenarios.
- Including early and disability retirements, as well as regular retirements, in the projections.

These enhancements serve to provide managers with a more comprehensive "retirement picture," helping them to make more informed decisions. The Retirement Wave projections drive many human capital activities at SSA, including leadership development, recruitment and retention, and other workforce development activities.

3. **How has the program prompted other changes or adapted to organizational changes?**

The Retirement Wave Analysis is the cornerstone of SSA's "data-driven" approach to strategic human capital planning. In 2003, SSA was awarded an Honorable Mention in the President's Quality Awards for their strategic human capital management. SSA was recognized for its data-driven approach, by forecasting workforce needs and then implementing strategies to meet those needs.

In December 2003, SSA published an Agency-wide Human Capital (HC) Plan to help track our success in all areas of Human Capital Planning. The HC Plan identifies activities in five key areas:

- Strategic Alignment
- Workforce Planning
- Workforce Development and Knowledge Management
- Performance Culture
- Leadership

The HC Plan associates performance measures with each activity, allowing SSA to measure our success in each area, and therefore make informed decisions about our human capital strategies. The Future Workforce Transition Plan (FWTP) was recently revised to align with the Human Capital Plan. The FWTP (which is updated quarterly), along with Key Performance Indicators in other agency planning documents, serves to regularly update the measures contained within the plan.

4. **What remains the greatest success of this effort? The greatest challenge?**

SSA's greatest success is its ability to constantly monitor our workforce needs and adapt strategies accordingly.

The Retirement Wave Analysis has been the impetus for many important human capital strategies, including our numerous Leadership Development Programs, our revitalized Recruitment campaign, and improvements in the hiring process. The Retirement Wave Analysis is used to make important resource management decisions that are vital to ensuring that, in a time of great change, SSA continues to provide the best possible service to the American public.

One of SSA's biggest concerns is that retirement losses will occur at the same time that our workloads begin growing with the aging of the baby-boom generation. In order to meet these growing workloads, SSA needs to ensure that it has employees with the knowledge and training needed to serve the public. Since it is estimated that it takes a Claims Representative three years to reach the journeyman level, we cannot wait until our older employees leave to begin filling these positions.

In light of this, SSA has made use of Voluntary Early Retirement Authority (VERA) to help "flatten" the wave and ensure that experienced employees will be ready to handle the increased workloads when they occur. Between 1998 and 2003, 4,628 SSA employees have chosen to take the "early-out" retirement. Currently, approximately 21% of all SSA employees are eligible for regular retirement. If those employees had not chosen early retirement, that percentage would be about 27%. The use of early retirements has helped SSA to manage and control the retirement wave, while providing opportunities to hire and train new employees earlier. This will ensure that fully experienced personnel are in place when retirements begin peaking in a few years. SSA's greatest challenge is trying to account for the many factors that can impact on retirement behavior.

Retirement projections are based on historical trends, which can change rapidly. Economic, legislative, or organizational changes cannot always be predicted, but can have a significant impact on employee retirements. Projections, made in good faith and with sound data, can vary from actual retirements, simply because of other changes that could not be predicted, nor controlled. SSA has tried to address this variability by providing low, median, and high projections, allowing Agency decision-makers to visualize the variability in retirements, and to plan for various contingencies. For example, if retirements approach the high projections for several years, the "wave" may be accelerated, hitting earlier than predicted. If retirements approach the low projections, the wave could be postponed.

5. **How have you measured progress in this area?**

   SSA continues to use the retirement wave analysis to provide quantitative justification for many of our human capital initiatives. SSA will now begin publishing the Retirement Wave projections on an annual basis, thereby ensuring use of the most accurate data to make our decisions. As a result of this analysis, SSA has done the following:

   • Successfully used the Voluntary Early Retirement Authority (VERA) to "flatten" the wave.

   • Hired over 15,000 new employees in the last four years to mitigate the impact of current and future retirements, and have ensured that they receive the training necessary to be highly successful on the job.

   • Implemented recruitment and training programs, the success of which are evidenced by new-hire retention rates of nearly 90 percent for FY 2002 (most recent data available).

   • 392 employees have been selected for our national leadership development programs since 1998, and hundreds of others have completed various regional or component-level programs.

   • Hired 189 Presidential Management Fellows throughout the agency between 1998 and 2003.

6. **What advice do you have for others seeking to undertake similar changes?**

There are many variables that impact an employee's decision to retire. Aging parents, college age students, financial stability, career goals, and work environment all play an important role in an individual's decision to retire. On a more global scale, economic conditions, labor-market conditions, and legislative and organizational changes all impact retirements. Yet none are able to be built into a forecast model. While projecting retirements is an important and necessary activity, agencies also must be flexible enough to adapt to the inherent variability of retirements. SSA has addressed these variables by producing low, median, and high projections.

NATIONAL RECONNAISSANCE OFFICE: SUCCESSION MANAGEMENT SUCCESS

Case Introduction: This case study consists of a report by the U.S. Department of Defense National Reconnaissance Office on its succession management program.

For most organizations, succession planning is about looking to the future—developing bench strength to ensure that the organization is prepared to fill mission-critical positions if and when they vacate for any reason. At the National Reconnaissance Office (NRO), however, turnover in mission-critical positions is not a "what if"—it's a certainty.

As the U.S. government's source for satellite intelligence, NRO is responsible for the design, construction and operation of intelligence-gathering satellites. In addition to its highly specialized mission, NRO is unique in that the agency does not "own" its workforce; all of its employees come to the agency on detail from other defense and intelligence agencies, and may be called back to their home agencies at any time—and on short notice.

NRO faced a special challenge in the aftermath of September 11, when many key members of its multi-agency workforce were recalled to their home agencies. Recognizing that not just their satellites, but also their workforce had to be prepared to make adjustments in the face of suddenly changing circumstances, NRO developed a comprehensive Succession Management Program to tackle not only the agency's short-term replacement planning needs, but also longer-term succession planning. Beyond ensuring continuity of operations in times of crisis, the program fosters greater attention to leadership development within NRO and has garnered support from every level of the organization, from senior leadership down to the front lines.

NRO Overview

The NRO designs, builds and operates satellites that gather information for use by the intelligence and defense communities, providing vital intelligence to the agencies responsible for U.S. national security. With a mission "to develop and operate unique and innovative space reconnaissance systems and conduct intelligence-related activities essential for U.S. national security," the NRO is a fast-paced environment that must respond to rapidly changing mission requirements—requirements that are shaped by world events and national security imperatives. Images captured by NRO satellites are used to detect potential trouble spots around the world. NRO's work is vital to both military operations planning and environmental monitoring.

NRO is an organization of the Department of Defense (DOD), and its existence was classified until 1992. The organization has no employees of its own; its entire workforce comes to NRO on detail from other defense and intelligence agencies: Army, Air Force, Navy, CIA, the Defense Intelligence Agency (DIA), the Defense Logistics Agency (DLA), the National Security Agency (NSA), and the National Geospatial-Intelligence Agency (NGA). The Under Secretary of the Air Force serves as the director of NRO, and its agenda is set by the Director of Central Intelligence (DCI), who establishes collection requirements and priorities for satellite-gathered intelligence. Employees are typically detailed to NRO for a period of two to three years.

Challenge

After September 11, 2001, many NRO employees were called back suddenly to their parent agencies, leaving critical leadership gaps at NRO that needed to be filled quickly. While the multi-agency nature of NRO's workforce has always presented certain management challenges, this series of events highlighted the agency's need to keep tabs on its talent in a more systematic fashion. It became clear that for NRO, succession management is not a "nice to have"—it is a necessity if they are to ensure continuity of operations in times of crisis.

In addition to its need to ensure continuity of operations, NRO has a strategic plan that specifically calls for the organization to create and maintain a world-class workforce—and as part of this, to train and develop future leaders. In order to achieve this, NRO needed a system for assessing the organization's bench strength—the knowledge, skills and abilities required to take on mission-critical positions possessed by its current workforce. It also needed to increase its attention to leadership development.

Although NRO has its own HR function, employees are governed by the personnel systems at their parent agencies. An NRO succession management system, therefore, not only had to meet NRO's needs, but also needed to be embraced by at least eight other HR systems—each of which has a distinct way of tracking its employees, conducting performance management exercises, and managing succession (including leadership development activities).

Solutions

The Succession Management Program: Overview

NRO developed a position-based succession planning model—the Succession Management Program (SMP)—to identify key leadership and other mission-critical positions and to inventory employees' interest in and readiness to assume those positions. Through the SMP, leaders monitor bench strength for both imminent turnover (replacement planning) and projected turnover in the next 1–3 years (succession planning). The SMP, launched in September 2001, relies upon a Web-based platform to track and manage all employee data. At the outset of the program, incumbents in first- and second-tier leadership positions, as well as a handful of other mission-critical positions, defined their roles and experience by inputting into the system the competencies and skills required to be successful in their jobs, as well as the education and professional experience required or desired for the position.

NRO employees then had the opportunity to input their own education, qualifications and experience into the SMP system, generating a standardized résumé for each individual. After completing this step, employees may self-nominate for any position in the system, whether they are ready to assume it immediately, or will require years of development before they will be prepared for the role. Managers can also nominate employees from across the intelligence community into the "pool" for any position.

An Iterative Process

NRO's Succession and Leadership Team (SALT), comprised of parent organization and mission representatives, reviews highly qualified and/or high-potential candidates in the pool on a quarterly basis as part of a continuous cycle. At these quarterly gatherings, SALT members formally review existing plans and immediate replacement needs, profile key positions, engage in position management, and assess the employee pool. From this review, the SALT identifies a replacement pool and a succession pool.

Replacement planning is the first phase in this continuous, quarterly process. The SALT, in consultation with senior managers, identifies candidates in the SMP system who possess proven leadership capabilities and can assume key positions immediately (within one year). Succession planning anticipates key staffing requirements over a 1–3 year window. The SALT and senior managers identify employees who have demonstrated leadership potential from the pool of self- and manager-identified candidates in the SMP system, and uses the information provided there as a basis for charting those individuals' development needs to prepare them to assume key leadership positions down the road.

The SALT-identified replacement and succession pools provide information to support and facilitate the formal selection process; however, the SMP does not violate the principles of fair and open competition. Once a vacancy actually opens, the competitive process for application and selection remains intact for competitively-filled positions, as do the procedures governing direct appointments where appropriate.

Ensuring Ongoing Attention to Leadership Development

Because the NRO workforce is relatively transient, replacement and succession planning conversations must occur on a quarterly basis. An added benefit to regular succession planning is that it has made thinking about developing future leaders a habit for senior managers. The developmental feedback form that results from the SALT's deliberations delineates individual employees' development needs, providing a development blueprint that supervisors then share with their reports. Employees are not informed as to whether or not the SALT has included them in the succession pool for a given position; rather, during developmental conversations, SALT representatives, mentors and managers may advise them as to steps they can take (such as assignments, training, rotations or other developmental activities) to make them more competitive for future positions.

Employees may update their credentials in the SMP system at any time to reflect new experience, training, or accomplishments. They can also examine the requirements—competencies, qualifications, experience—for the leadership positions for which they hope to be considered, and use that information to shape their career goals over the short term.

Critical Success Factors

The creators of the SMP devoted a great deal of energy to selling the program to NRO leaders and employees alike. The program administrators knew that without buy-in from every level of the organization, the SMP could not succeed. Succession management was never presented to the NRO workforce as an HR initiative—rather, it is promoted as a strategic (and national security) imperative, and a vehicle to promote employee development. NRO's succession planning program was born in its Office of Human Resources (OHR), which manages the program, assists and supports senior leaders in their roles, and is responsible for tracking its success. OHR included NRO's Human Resources Steering Team (HRST), comprised of executives from all of the parent organizations, in the creation of the system so that senior leaders feel a sense of ownership.

OHR created a detailed and strategic communications plan to roll out the SMP to all NRO employees over the course of a year. They convened senior-level briefings, conducted training workshops for employees at all levels, facilitated communications from senior leadership to employees, went on "road shows," and held feedback focus sessions—to name just some of OHR's efforts to build support for the SMP.

Responsibility for the program's success is also atomized across the organization. The HRST, who initially vetted the program, now "owns" and champions it across the NRO. This body links NRO's succession plans to its strategic objectives, broadly communicates expectations related to the program, and reports to the NRO Board of Directors. Senior managers within each division own and drive the process within their own units; they are responsible for developing key talent—overseeing the execution of the program and ensuring that development opportunities are available. Finally, "embedded" program managers within each of NRO's program areas who have had extensive training in the SMP serve as local experts across the organization.

Results

The institution of the SMP has awakened NRO employees and leaders alike to the imperatives of talent retention and development. In creating a process that demands the attention of the entire NRO workforce on a quarterly basis, the SMP has not only focused attention on these issues, but is bringing about a cultural shift within the organization such that succession planning becomes a proactive, rather than a reactive, process.

In addition, by clearly delineating the competencies, qualifications and experience required to be successful in key leadership posts, the SMP provides managers and employees with a roadmap to guide employee development. Employees are more involved in their own development, and are better-positioned to seek out specific development opportunities.

The SMP is a new program, launched in September 2001, and its full implementation is still underway. Early feedback is positive, but OHR will conduct formal evaluations to identify issues as they arise so that they can be addressed. Already, the Web-based tool has been upgraded based on feedback from program managers and customers.

Next Steps

Now that the succession planning mechanism is in place, phase two of the program will focus on providing developmental feedback to employees. As part of this effort, OHR will conduct workshops for managers to prepare them to have meaningful developmental conversations with their direct reports. In addition, NRO will work more closely with its parent organizations to build its talent pipelines beyond the existing NRO workforce.

The program will undergo regular review to ensure that it is delivering the benefits it intends. Two key success indicators will be the speed with which the agency is able to fill vacancies, and the viability of the employee pool for consideration for leadership posts. A recent feedback survey indicated that the SMP has succeeded in identifying potential candidates to fill key vacancies.

Contact Information

Mona Benbow, NRO Succession Management Program Manager
703-808-1613 or 703-808-5054.

A TALENT MANAGEMENT SUCCESS STORY: HOW VETERANS ADMINISTRATION HOSPITALS BECAME THE BEST

> *Case Introduction:* This case study written by Jim Graber for this volume describes the talent management program at Veterans Administration hospitals.

Executive Summary

The Veterans Health Administration (VHA), the largest entity within the Department of Veterans Affairs (DVA), is comprised of more than 200,000 employees and almost 1,300 facilities. It serves 6 million patients. With a projected need for 193,000 new hires between FY 2005 and FY 2012, and in heated competition with other health-care providers to hire physicians, nurses, radiology technologists, and other talent where shortages already exist, workforce planning is a vital part of the VHA Strategic Plan.

The VHA began designing elements of its current employee development program in 1997, created a workforce succession steering committee in 2000, and significantly strengthened workforce planning and development between 2001–2006. The program has now developed to the extent that it clearly qualifies as a talent management success story and a model for other public agencies and private organizations.

The VHA workforce strategy is built around seven elements: Recruitment and Retention, Communication Planning, Performance Management, Employee Development, Workplace Improvement and Employee Satisfaction, EEO and Diversity, and Legislative and Policy Issues.

Among the many distinguishing features of the VHA program are the following:

- All levels of the organization and all employees are included in the VHA Workforce Plan, with special resources dedicated to critical leadership and technical positions (many of them front-line). This contrasts with talent management programs that are limited to upper management or a small group of high potentials.

- Priorities and programs are carefully grounded on hard data and research, rather than on faith, unproven assumptions, or the talent-management programs of other organizations.

- Program governance and implementation is spread broadly across a number of levels and groups. This builds understanding, commitment, checks and balances, and participation.

- Sufficient resources are committed to the program.

- The program is constantly being expanded and improved. The program in 2005 advanced far beyond what it looked like in its first full year (2002).

- The VHA builds leaders at all levels of the organization, even among individual contributors. The VA calls this the "Leadership Continuum."

- A core competency model called the High Performance Development Model (HPDM) is used to develop all employees. The core competency model is designed to initially build personal mastery and technical expertise, and help all employees progress eventually to organization stewardship.

- Each year the current plan includes a projection of the needs over the next five years. For example, the 2005 plan addresses the projected needs for 2006 through 2010.

- Strategic objectives, demographic trends among employees (e.g., percent eligible to retire), and projections of how the health-care industry will transition are used to shape the plan.

The VHA has earned accolades for its Workforce Planning Program, and serious students of workforce planning are encouraged to become familiar with it.

This is the same Veterans Administration that was described as "the nation's shame" 15 years earlier. Congress had even considered shutting down the whole system in the early 1990s and giving vouchers to veterans so that they could receive quality care from private facilities (Waller, 2006).

All that has changed now. For the sixth year in a row, VA hospitals have outscored private facilities on customer satisfaction with the quality of care received (most recently 71% to 83%). Meanwhile, while the patient load *doubled* over the past 10 years, the VA has been able to care for these veterans with 10,000 fewer employees! The VA has been able to keep the cost per patient constant during that period, while the cost at private hospitals increased by 40% during that period. The turnaround is all the more remarkable for a very large, bureaucratic government organization.

A variety of innovations account for the turnaround. Improved technology (e.g., computerization of patient records, a bar-code system for prescriptions), a focus on preventive care (elimination of half the hospital beds and investment in 300 new community clinics), and reduction of bureaucracy have all helped. At the same time, the VA has significantly upgraded its talent management system while increasing manager accountability and setting strict performance standards for physicians.

The VA and VHA by the Numbers

The VA is comprised of a Central Office (VACO) in Washington, D.C., and field facilities throughout the nation, administered by its three major line organizations: Veterans Health Administration (VHA), Veterans Benefits Administration (VBA), and the National Cemetery Administration (NCA). Services and benefits are provided through a nationwide network of 156 hospitals, 877 outpatient clinics, 136 nursing homes, 43 residential rehabilitation treatment programs, 207 readjustment counseling centers, 57 veterans benefits regional offices, and 122 national cemeteries (in excess of 1,400 sites).

The Veterans Health Administration (VHA), the largest entity within the VA, with over 200,000 employees, is the third largest civilian employer in the federal government, and one of the largest health-care providers in the world (with in excess of 6 million patients). In addition to its size, VHA has one of the most complex workforces within the federal government, having over 300 job series classifications encompassing professional, technical, administrative, clerical, and blue-collar occupations, as well as almost 1,300 worksites covered by two personnel systems established by Federal Title 38 and Title 5 legislation.

The VHA hires on average more than 25,000 new staff each year. Between FY 2005 and FY 2012, on-board strength is projected to increase by 5,100, and total losses are projected to be 187,800. Therefore, a total of 192,900 new hires will be needed. Among the many professions represented in the vast VHA workforce are physicians, nurses, counselors, statisticians, architects, computer specialists, and attorneys.

VHA Workforce Plan Married to the Strategic Objectives

While many experts *talk* about linking workforce planning to current and future needs, the VA has actually done it. The VA projects future veteran needs (e.g., the size of the population that will need to be served, the age distribution, and the types of services to be needed), as well as the probable changes in the delivery of healthcare. VA planners combine this information with demographic information about their current workforce (e.g., the number of persons they have in each occupation, and their probable retirement dates), and can then project their recruiting, development, and retention needs. Workforce Planning resources are carefully allocated to the areas where they are experiencing the biggest talent challenges. Given the huge talent challenges the VHA faces, effective workforce planning is truly critical to achieving their mission.

The VHA's Workforce Planning Challenge

The Department of Veterans Affairs Veterans Health Administration defines workforce planning simply but powerfully as "Having the right people in the right places at the right times, all the time" Further, the VHA's goal is to "Recruit, develop, and retain a competent, committed, and diverse workforce that provides high quality service to veterans and their families."

Healthcare is primarily a people-based process. With the health-care field changing so rapidly, the importance of ensuring the continuous presence of an effective workforce cannot be overstated.

And yet, the VHA faces significant challenges in making sure that it has the appropriate workforce to meet current and future needs. Most significant among these challenges is that it is an aging workforce.

- The average age of VHA employees is approaching 50 years.
- A large percentage of the workforce is eligible for retirement right *now*.

    42% of its senior executives are eligible for retirement.

    22% of its chiefs of staff are eligible for retirement.

    30% of nurse executives are eligible for retirement.

- The majority of the VHA's workers will be eligible for regular or early retirement by the end of the decade.
- There is increasing competition for scarce occupations and professions.

The average age of a VHA employee in June 2005 was 47.9 years. In 2004, 9.3% of VHA employees were eligible for regular retirement, and by FY 2012, 16.6% will be eligible. Between now and the end of FY 2012, it is projected that 46,000 VHA employees will retire.

Leadership positions are projected to experience an even greater percentage of losses from retirements. For example, 53% of senior executives, 27% of chiefs of staff, and 21% of nurse executives were already eligible for regular retirement at the end of FY 2004.

Recruiting talent in the health-care industry, which faces chronic workforce supply and demand gaps, is also a considerable challenge. The major work-force drivers within healthcare: an increasing demand for health services (driven largely by an aging population that exhibits multiple chronic health conditions); and an aging health-care workforce that is not currently being adequately replaced by younger workers.

Collecting data, analyzing it, and proactively responding to it is the crux of VHA Workforce Planning.

Data-Rich Workforce Planning

Through the extensive use of internal and external studies, the VHA attempts to reduce the uncertainties regarding its employee-development priorities. The VHA has assembled extensive data on:

— The age and retirement eligibility of its current workforce, broken down by organization level and job title, for this year and through the next decade.

— Its mission-critical positions today, and those likely to be most critical in the near future as health-care delivery evolves.

— Positions mostly likely to be difficult to fill, based on industry needs and trends.

— VA employee separation data showing, for example, which groups of employees are most likely to leave, and when in their careers extra attention is needed to increase employee retention. Analysis of VHA separation data shows that 75% of all resignations in the top-priority occupations occur within the first five years of employment.

Table 10-1 shows the projected need for registered nurses over the next eight years. Table 10-2 provides a feel for the methodology for developing these projections. Analyses similar to those in Table 10-2 are completed for the ten top occupations shown in Table 10-3. Leadership and extensive diversity/EEO analyses have also been performed.

In addition to setting program priorities, the VHA also specifically targets positions judged to be mission-critical, as well as recruitment challenges. Ten occupations plus leadership have been identified as national priorities for recruitment and retention.

The VHA also scans external studies to help make workforce projections. For example:

• An American Hospital Association report published in November 2003 predicted rapid growth in 11 selected health-care occupations between 2003 and 2010.

• A U.S. Department of Labor study predicted much faster growth in the need for health-care workers between 2000 and 2010 than the rate of non-health jobs (29% increase for health occupations, and a 14% increase for non-health occupations).

Required data collection and analysis and the development of an in-depth workforce planning system might be an impossible task for all but the largest organizations. Certainly, a considerable effort is required, and yet the system was built piece by piece over sufficient time to make it manageable. The VHA chronology of development is sensible and practical, and is within the reach of many organizations, if sufficient commitment is present.

Table 10-1

VHA Projected Registered Nurse Needs 2004–2012

0610 NURSE (Registered) Projected	2004 actual	2005	2006	2007	2008	2009	2010	2011	2012
Employees (FT, PT, Perm and Temp on board by end of FY)	38,765	39,078	39,491	39,938	40,455	41,010	41,514	41,514	41,514
Employees eligible for regular CSRS and full annuity FERS retirement		3,671	4,152	4,527	5,177	5,748	6,403	6,845	7,160
Regular CSRS and FERS retired	689	727	837	894	1,031	1,140	1,278	1,349	1,396
Resignations	1,734	1,734	1,734	1,734	1,734	1,734	1,734	1,734	1,734
All other separations (1.55% of projected on-board)	601	606	612	619	627	636	643	643	643
Total losses	3,024	3,067	3,183	3,247	3,392	3,510	3,655	3,726	3,773
Gains needed	4,554	3,380	3,596	3,694	3,909	4,065	4,159	3,726	3,773

Table 10-2

VHA Nurse Workforce Projection Methodology

On-board projections:

Projected on-board increases and decreases through FY 2010, based on workload projections (including infrastructure capability to care for workload in-house), veteran migration patterns, market penetration rates, aging veteran population needs, re-design of care delivery models, shifting environments of care, and increased efficiencies. Projections are then straight-lined from 2010 through 2012 in order to calculate the longer-range effect of projected retirements.

Retirement projections:

Retirement-eligible numbers are calculated based on permanent, full-time, and part-time employees, age, years of service, and retirement plan. Retirement projections are derived from a VHA age-based formula.

Resignations:

Resignation rates have increased slightly from 4.2% in FY 03 to 4.4% in FY 04. Prior to 2004, resignation rates had been declining. The VHA implemented the High Performance Development Model for employee development, and improved employee satisfaction during this time frame. Other external factors, such as the economic slowdown after September 11, 2001, may also have contributed to the declining resignations. A continuing trend is difficult to predict; for projection purposes, resignations are straight-lined from the FY 2004 rate.

All other separations:

Between 2000 and 2004, the "all other" separation rate, as a percent of on-board, has fluctuated between 3.88% and 4.36%. The higher rates are attributed to the use of "early out" authority during reorganizations in 1999, 2000, and 2001. The FY 2003 rate of 3.99% (rounded to 4%) represents the current climate and was used as the projection methodology. For the top occupations, "all other separations" are calculated using each occupation's FY 2004 rate.

Turnover rates:

Turnover rates are calculated by losses divided by on-board strength at the end of the specified period, unless otherwise noted.

Table 10-3

Top Ten Occupation Needs of the VHA
Leadership positions (senior executives, chiefs of staff, nurse executives)
Registered nurses
Pharmacists
Physicians
Practical nurses
Diagnostic radiology technologists
Medical technologists
Nursing assistants
Human resource managers
Police officers
Medical records technicians

History of Workforce Planning at the VHA:
Five Years of Accomplishments

In August 2000, the U.S. Under Secretary for Health recognized the workforce succession challenge facing the VHA and established a broad-based workforce succession steering committee to develop a comprehensive strategy to meet this challenge. The committee benchmarked best practices, assessed the current workforce, analyzed drivers of employee satisfaction, and examined statutes, regulations, and policies. As part of this initial workforce planning process, current and projected workforce, diversity, employee morale and satisfaction, leadership succession, and employee development were assessed, and initiatives were developed to meet identified gaps.

As recommended by the original VHA workforce succession committee in June 2001, the VHA established the Succession Planning Deployment Workgroup and gave it the responsibility to oversee and manage the development and implementation of the components of the VHA succession program. The Workgroup was chaired by a senior VHA leader (an individual who had previously served as the top operations officer for VHA). Members represented all levels of VHA management, and included key staff people from the national program offices, who would be directly responsible for developing and administering the VHA succession programs.

It takes time to develop a complete talent management system. Table 10-4 shows some of the key milestones during the years of the VHA program.

Table 10-4

A Brief History of Workforce Planning at the VHA

2000
- VHA Succession Planning Committee formed

2001
- First VHA Succession Plan
- Governance development and implementation
- Framework for integrated succession and workforce development programs

2002
- Succession Planning Web site
- Analysis of All-Employee Survey results and Web-based Data Cube
- Ongoing legislative/policy initiatives
- ECF candidate development program
- National leadership database/PDP
- National Center for Organization Development
- New senior executive orientation program
- Integration of succession and strategic planning
- Integration of succession and strategic planning Web-based tools

2003
- Technical career fields intern program
- ECF performance and recognition program
- VA recruitment Web site improvements
- Senior management conference
- Senior Executive Institute
- ECF CDP Career Tracks and Assessment Center

2004
- New All-Employee Survey and ongoing Employee Satisfaction Assessment
- VISN LEAD

2005
- Facility LEAD
- Coaching and mentoring training certification
- Supervisory training
- Expanded recruitment program

Given the fact that it can take years to build a comprehensive program, how does an organization maintain forward momentum in the face of changing priorities, new leadership, changing political administrations, and a constant supply of new problems? One of the key ingredients is effective program governance and administration.

Governance and Program Administration

The Veterans Health Administration created a governance and administrative structure that can maintain the planning system. In other organizations, the burden of administering such a program too often rests primarily on the shoulders of one or two mid-level managers, and many times these individuals have additional responsibilities. Contrast this with the VHA, where five major groups participate in the process. Some of the most influential executives at the VHA are involved. Through their involvement, they become better informed and more committed. Lack of executive sponsorship has frequently been identified as the Achilles heel of other Workforce Planning programs.

The roles of each group are carefully defined, ensuring continuity and efficiency of the process. Responsibility is broken down into **governance** (goal setting, program design, policy making, and evaluation) and **program administration** (budgeting, financial disbursements, consulting, coaching, education, etc.). This division of labor mirrors the typical leadership structure of most organizations. It makes efficient use of executive time, it builds broad commitment, and it lets specialists handle day-to-day implementation.

Governance and Oversight is the responsibility of:

- The National Leadership Board (NLB), which provides final approval for succession planning proposals
- The Human Resources Committee (HRC), which reviews and approves proposals of the SWDMS
- The Succession and Workforce Development Management Subcommittee (SWDMS) and ad-hoc workgroups, which propose and develop the various components of VHA's workforce succession program.

The NLB has six major committees, one of which is the Human Resources Committee. The SWDMS is a standing subcommittee of the HR Committee of the NLB. Having a permanent, accountable organization that is hierarchically linked directly to the top VHA leadership structure to oversee, manage, and drive the program has proven to be a key element in the success of VHA's succession and workforce development efforts. Without this type of structural accountability, a long-term, sustained effort is quite unlikely.

The SWDMS subcommittee meets monthly via teleconference, and holds quarterly face-to-face meetings. The various components of VHA's workforce succession program are developed under the auspices of the SWDMS, usually by chartering an ad-hoc work group to develop a proposal for the program, as well as its implementation strategy, schedule, and budget requirements. The proposal is then reviewed and approved by the SWDMS, the Human Resources Committee, and finally by the full VHA NLB.

Program Administration and Operations is the responsibility of:

- Office of Management Support (responsible for overall program administration and budgeting, along with the disbursal of funds for organizational expenses and organization consulting, assessments, and executive coaching functions)

- Employee Education Service (responsible for the formal educational components of succession planning)

Once approved, workforce succession program funds for each component are provided to the Management Support Office. Funds are then disbursed by Management Support for program expenses. Recurring fund requirements then become part of the annual budget allocation. Since the Management Support Office is the initial budget office for all VHA workforce succession programs, top management can easily identify and control program expenditures.

Workforce succession program evaluation is part of the annual strategic planning process. Programs are reviewed within the context of the overall workforce analyses and specific plans and needs that have been identified by each Veteran Integrated Service Network (VISN). Recommendations for program changes are then included in the update process for the national plan.

To this point, we have completed an overview of VHA, its workforce challenges, workforce planning history, and program governance and administration. We now will finish up with a detailed look at some of the programs that make up the VHA Workforce Planning System.

The Seven Elements of
VHA's Comprehensive Workforce Strategy

The VHA has identified seven elements in its comprehensive workforce succession strategy.

- Recruitment and retention
- Communication planning
- Performance management
- Employee development
- Workplace improvement and employee satisfaction
- EEO and diversity
- Legislative and policy issues

Each year, based on the analysis of VHA workforce needs (described above) and current workforce succession and development programs, leaders make programmatic recommendations for the following year.

We will now look at some examples of programs and priorities associated with the different workforce elements. While some programs are clearly linked to one or another of the seven elemental needs, other programs address the needs of two or more elements.

Recruitment and Retention

As previously noted, the VHA looks at needs and how they are met by existing programs. Effective and relevant programs are maintained and new programs are created where needed, as shown in Table 10-5.

Note the variety of VHA recruitment and retention initiatives. Comprehensiveness is a hallmark of VHA workforce planning. Also, there is openness to trying different types of programs, and an acceptance that not all initiatives will succeed. In other words, the culture doesn't suppress innovation. Annual evaluation serves to separate the wheat from the chaff.

Table 10-5

VHA 2005 Recommendations for Recruitment and Retention

- Promote a system-wide comprehensive program for recruiting personnel in scarce professions and career fields.

- Improve the VA's ability to recruit trainees into the permanent workforce following training.

- Continue efforts to project a consistent "brand" and improve/link recruitment Web sites and develop national recruitment tools (CDs, brochures, posters, etc.) to support local efforts.

- Continue efforts to establish a Web site for recruiters to improve knowledge of and communication within the recruiter community and to provide a forum to coordinate activities and share best practices.

- Establish a national database of recruitment sources and a national calendar of recruitment activities.

- Provide national support for student cadet/intern programs and in-house development programs for scarce/hard-to-fill occupations, and expand the use of recruitment and relocation incentives to draw employees from across the system into VHA facilities in difficult labor markets.

- Analyze instances of failed recruitment across the VHA system, and develop programs and tracking systems to reduce the number of failed recruitments.

Employee Development

Based on VHA benchmarking studies, developing the next generation of leaders seems to be one of the top priorities for high-performing organizations. In response, the VHA developed its "Leadership Continuum," which reflects two things: a philosophy that it is important to develop leaders at all levels of the organization; and an organizing principle for targeting training for all employees. The VHA has divided the Leadership Continuum into four levels: Level 1 = front-line staff, Level II = first-line supervisors, Level III = middle managers, and Level IV = senior executive leaders.

The High Performance Development Model (HPDM) is the foundation for building leadership. The model came out of a 1997 study of top-leadership succession. Benchmarking the best programs revealed one common theme: *Actions consistently based on core competencies lead to success.* Like VHA

Workforce Succession Planning in general, HPDM at the VHA has steadily evolved. Key milestones include a HPDM summit in 1999, HPDM performance measures and HPDM awards established in 2000, HPDM plans established for all networks and national HPDM staff hired in 2001, and integration with succession planning and the VHA strategic plan in 2002–2003.

The VHA reports that the High Performance Development Model is designed to be:

> a conceptual framework for learning
> a context for succession planning
> a roadmap for leadership development
> an investment in its employees

Five principles guide the development and implementation of HPDM. They are:

1. Develop leadership throughout the organization, rather than for just a small layer at the top.

2. View development as an investment in employees—not as a cost.

3. Recognize mutual responsibility for employee development (the employee and the organization share responsibility).

4. Create leaders who teach, coach, and mentor.

5. Foster a learning organization.

Six "tools" provide the primary avenues for employee development. They are:

> Employee development of core competencies (competencies all employees are expected to develop and exhibit)
> Continuous assessment
> Continuous learning opportunities
> Coaching and mentoring
> Performance management
> Performance-based interviewing

These are the VHA's core competencies:

> Personal mastery
> Technical skills
> Interpersonal effectiveness

Customer service
Flexibility/adaptability
Creative thinking
Systems thinking
Organizational stewardship

Figure 10-1

HPDM Competency Model

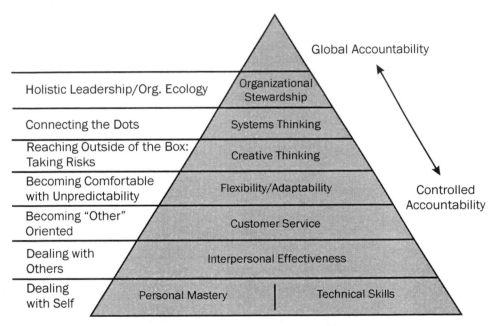

While the same eight core competencies apply to all employees, the definition of the core competencies and exemplary behaviors are customized for each of the four levels of the Leadership Continuum described above. The VHA core competencies are quite unusual in that they are sequential and related to each other. They have been systematically established to cover the continuum, ranging from focus on self as a foundation to developing vision and leadership up through to a high level of organization. They lay out a path of development that could require a career to fully traverse. While standard practice in other organizations is often to use only 3–5 core competencies to increase impact, it is understandable that the VHA has more, given the amount of territory it covers.

VHA has established an HPDM office that facilitates implementation of HPDM, provides administrative management, creates and maintains the workforce development database, provides technical support for national survey and assessment tools, conducts workforce succession planning analyses, and coordinates development of VHA workforce succession plans.

Implementation of HPDM is expected to occur at all levels of the organization so that every employee understands the model's concepts and takes responsibility for continuous growth and learning in order to achieve a high level of competency. Efforts continue at the national level to measure implementation success.

A June 2005 report by Kathryn Young for the Department of Veterans Affairs entitled "HPDM: Acknowledging the Past, Celebrating the Present, Embracing the Future" summarized HPDM deployment. "Our nine years of experience with HPDM provide a rich study of culture change . . . It has reached a critical mass of leaders and changed the way we think about leadership ability in VHA . . . HPDM has moved us significantly toward becoming a true learning organization . . . We need to put more emphasis on flexibility/adaptability, systems thinking, organizational stewardship, and continuous assessment and learning as a way to build resilience and agility."

Using HPDM as a framework, the VHA has integrated its core competencies with FY 2005 Performance Plans, from senior executives through front-line supervisors. Further alignment of the HPDM model includes use of all eight core competencies in the recruitment and selection process of executives.

Other VHA Employee Development Programs

Employee Development is a central element of most workforce planning programs, but the VHA program exceeds others in terms of audiences served and the breadth and depth of its programs. Table 10-6 summarizes succession-related development organized by employee level. Table 10-7 provides a flavor for the richness of the many VHA employee development programs. Note the use of multiple training modalities (classroom training, mentoring and coaching, experiential learning, immersion, etc.); opportunities for prospective employees; the use of individual financial incentives; and in general, the depth of commitment.

Table 10-6

VHA Employee Development Programs, Organized by Level		
Employee Level	**Required**	**Recommended**
All employees	New-employee orientation	
	HPDM awareness and development	
Front-line employees		Technical career field programs
		Graduate Health Administration program
		VAMC Leadership Institute
Supervisory/team leader	Supervisory training	VISN Leadership Institute
	Nurse-Manager development	
Middle management	Service line manager/ service chief	Executive career field candidate
		Development program
		Health Care Leadership Institute
Executive career field		Senior executive orientation
		Senior executive leadership training
		Senior Management Conference

Table 10-7

Details of 4 VHA Workforce Development Programs		
Program	**Description**	**Objectives**
VISN and Facility Leadership Institutes (LEAD)	• Curriculum and selection process is linked to the Workforce Strategic Plan • A variety of learning methodologies • Participants remain in their current position during the training period • Formal mentoring and/or coaching • Personal Development Plan (PDP) • Formal program evaluation process • Senior leadership are involved • Recognition for grads/mentors/faculty	To identify a pool of high potentials from employees at HPDM levels 2 and 3 − Create a cadre of individuals to meet VISN and Facility leadership succession needs. − Provide candidates with learning experiences that prepare them to apply for leadership positions.
Technical Career Fields Training Program	• Two-year internships centrally funded • Recruitment at local colleges and universities • Each intern placed at a VHA facility and trained by someone experienced in the target position • Such "preceptors" receive training • Interns attend annual conference with peers • Program is evaluated at the national level • On an annual basis, target positions and number of intern slots are determined based on current and projected workforce needs and program evaluation data.	To develop employees in fields where full-time training in VHA procedures and regulations is required (e.g., Prosthetics representative, Human Resource specialist, business analyst, etc.)

(continued)

Table 10-7: Details of 4 VHA Workforce Development Programs *(concluded)*

Program	Description	Objectives
Advanced Practice Nurse (APN) Mentoring Toolkit	• Mentoring and Needs Assessment for APNs • APN templates (e.g., scope of practice, peer review, new APN orientation) • Generic resources (VHA Prescriptive Authority Directive, APN Advisory Group Charter, APN Liaison Group Charter) • Resource guides (e.g., certification organizations) • Guide for Community Outreach/ Networking	To help APNs and others explore resources and develop a successful plan of action that facilitates retention and recruitment.
VA High School Outreach Nursing Opportunity Residency (VA HONOR) Program	• Resource guides (e.g., certification organizations) • Targets high school youth 14 years and older • Two-part residency program under guidance of experienced VA RNs. Students have didactic and clinical training, learning very basic nursing support activities and advancing to more-complex nursing support functions. Students will spend approximately 250 hours each year in the clinical setting. • Students may receive VA stipends early in the program, and can eventually be hired into the VA as nursing assistants at age 16.	To recruit and retain the very talented youth of today into nursing careers in the VA. The goal is to have these students select nursing as a career. By age 22–24, these students could have eight years of affiliation with the VHA health-care system.

Knowledge Transfer:
Retaining Organization Wisdom and Memory

Knowledge transfer and retention is another area that has received a lot of coverage in the professional literature on workforce planning, but actual application is still very much in its infancy in most organizations. For the VHA, it is a tool that helps to achieve multiple workforce planning priorities, such as retention, performance management, and employee development. With all the retirements, the VHA realizes that it is not enough to merely replace individuals. Each retiring and/or departing employee may take valuable learning and information with them that their replacements will not have. In recognition of this problem, the VHA is pursuing programs that are intended to partially mitigate this, such as:

- The Mentor Certification Program
- Expanded use of sabbaticals
- Retired-employee consulting contracts
- Rehired annuitant pool
- Temporary SES/T38 positions for transitional leadership assignments

Workplace Improvement and Employee Satisfaction

Workplace Improvement and Employee Satisfaction, one of the seven foundational elements of the VHA Workforce Plan, is a bit broader in scope and less defined than elements such as recruitment or employee development. Many types of programs can improve the workplace. One example of workplace improvement at the VHA is the program that has been designed to reduce violence.

Over half of all assaults in the workplace in the U.S. occur in health-care settings. In the late 1990s, several high-visibility incidents involving violence, including two fatal shootings of VHA physicians, led the Under Secretary to convene a national group that reviewed policies and implementation, identified gaps, and developed appropriate new or modified program elements.

As part of that effort, a national survey was conducted in 2001 that showed that 12% of VHA employees had been assaulted in the prior year (as compared with 6% in the U.S. Postal Service); that the majority of assaulters were patients; and that some occupational groups, nurses, and employees in some specific areas (such as a geriatrics and mental health) represented high risk-areas (Hodgson 2004). The intervention effort to address this significant workplace problem included these activities:

— A half-day seminar for top management at the National Leadership Board.

— Facility reviews and updating of violence-prevention policies.

— A national stand-down on violence prevention education (over 90% of employees participated).

— Training for two violence-prevention staff members at each facility in how to conduct face-to-face training in hands-on skills of deescalation and personal safety, together with other program elements.

— Face-to-face training of all high-risk staff in PMDB.

— Modification of the Computerized Patient Record System to accept a behavioral flag that warns health-care providers of an individual's assaultive potential. Each facility developed a Disruptive Behavior Committee under senior clinical leadership that evaluated each assaultive patient and determined whether and how long those flags would remain active.

— VHA active participation in the national violence-prevention activities sponsored by the Centers for Disease Control, which has identified violence as a major public health problem.

— Establishment of a national VHA campaign on co-worker behavior, under the umbrella of cultural health. A series of pilot projects entitled CREW ("Civility, Respect, and Engagement of the Workforce"), with demonstrated major improvements in civility as measured via VHA's annual survey of employees.

The VHA is also conducting a systematic top-down and bottom-up review of the effectiveness of patient-violence intervention elements. Such sustained program activities require major institutional commitment and resources. They are already helping to protect and help retain the VHA workforce.

Entrance and Exit Interviews:
Tools to Enhance the Workplace and Employee Retention

The VHA pays considerable attention to employee feedback. The VHA has had access to extensive exit and entrance interview data since the year 2000, when the Department of Veterans Affairs implemented the use of an electronic database to capture survey information from employees entering the Department of Veterans Affairs service and employees exiting DVA service.

To get a sense of the scope of this data, we can look at the period from January 2004 to May 2005, when approximately 13,600 responses in the Entrance Survey database and approximately 5,000 responses in the Exit Survey database were collected.

The **Entrance Survey** asks a variety of questions. (Note: Overall results appear in parentheses.)

> *What are the top five reasons for choosing the VHA?* (Finding: benefits, salary, opportunities for advancement, serving veterans, and job security)
>
> *Where do new VHA employees come from?* (54% from the private sector)
>
> *Why do new VHA employees leave their previous jobs?* ("personal reasons" and "advancement")
>
> *How do new VHA employees find out about VHA job opportunities?* (from "VA Employees"—35 percent, followed by "VA Internet Job Opportunities Site"—20 percent)
>
> *What are the most-satisfying things about the VHA hiring process?* ("kindness and professionalism of the staff involved in the process"; "the actual interview process itself"; and "the in-depth orientation new employees receive")
>
> *What are the least-satisfying aspects of the hiring process?* ("length of time the process takes"; "the amount of paperwork involved"; and (ironically) "the extended new-employee orientation")

The **Exit Survey** is equally useful:

> *What are the demographics of the employees who leave?* (24 percent of the employees filling out the survey have worked for VHA for one to three years; 18 percent for only six months to one year, and 15 percent more than 20 years. Approximately 29 percent of the employees leaving fall into the GS 5–8 pay grade range.)
>
> *What are the positions that people are leaving?* (nurses, practical nurses, medical officers, program coordinators, nursing assistants and miscellaneous clerks and assistants)
>
> *Why are employees leaving?* ("Personal," "Advancement," "Early Retirement")

Where are leaving employees going? (Private industry, going into business for themselves, retirement)

What did leaving employees like about working at the VHA? (76 percent agreed or strongly agreed that their job made good use of their skills, and 76 percent agreed or strongly agreed that their work gave them a sense of personal accomplishment.)

Obviously, the data is useful only if appropriate initiatives are developed. For example, only 56 percent agreed or strongly agreed that they were satisfied with the career opportunities they had. This could give pause for reflection, as perceived career opportunities was one of the "highly rated" reasons new employees gave for working for the VHA. Perhaps new programs like the Executive Career Field Program, the Technical Career Field Program, and the VISN LEAD Programs will begin to help address this apparent disconnect.

EEO and Diversity

EEO and Affirmative Employment are among the government-initiated programs that prohibit discrimination and require analysis of gender/race/ethnicity data to identify and eliminate barriers to full participation in the workforce. *Diversity* refers to the VHA's voluntary initiatives undertaken to value people's differences and to use those differences to drive organizational growth and fuel human potential. Equal employment opportunities and diversity are key elements of the Workforce Plan.

Current efforts include continuing to implement MD-715 (a directive providing policy guidance and standards for maintaining effective affirmative employment programs); continuing to analyze leadership programs to identify and eliminate any barriers to full participation; and continuing to implement the "REACH for Diversity" campaign, addressing diversity education and training needs within VHA. (Key principles are respect, education, awareness, collaboration and honesty.)

Overall, the VHA's workforce analysis reflects the national commitment to promoting diversity in the workforce. A review of the percentages of minority employees from FY 2000 through the end of fiscal year 2004 shows that VHA distribution of individuals with targeted disabilities has declined slightly. The distribution of white females, Hispanic/Latino males and females, and American Indian/Alaskan native females is lower than the National Relevant Civilian Labor Force, but in other categories, the VHA minority distribution exceeds the relevant civilian labor force. Table 10-8 provides an example of VHA EEO analyses (distribution for nurses).

Workforce Planning Technology

Given the large numbers of participants and the complexities of their program, technology is critical to the VHA Workforce Planning Program. A few of these technology tools are listed next.

a) VHA Leadership database
   - Contains information on all VHA management officials and positions
   - Tracks all leadership trainees, TCF interns, mentors, preceptors
   - Provides online Personal Development Plan (PDP) for all trainees and interns
   - Tracks ECF Performance System
   - Provides information for program oversight and management, as well as OD research

b) Proclarity Web site—library of Web-based reports; ad-hoc analysis tool

c) KLF—library of Web-based reports

d) Workforce Planning System—automated Web-based system to develop strategic workforce succession plans

e) HPDM, HRRO, and Succession Planning Web sites—reference and general information sources

Table 10-8

610 Nurse—EEO Summary Table								
0610 NURSE **Workforce Distribution** *On board at* *end of Fiscal Year*	FY 2000 %	FY 2001 %	FY 2002 %	FY 2003 %	FY 2004 %	National RCLF %	% Below RCLF %
% White males	10.49	10.59	10.64	10.60	10.73	5.76	0.00
% White females	58.32	57.60	57.17	56.71	56.37	74.66	18.29
% Black or African American males	1.14	1.16	1.17	1.23	1.22	0.64	0.00
% Black or African American females	13.38	13.30	13.36	13.72	13.96	8.19	0.00
% Hispanic or Latino males	1.25	1.34	1.34	1.37	1.40	0.40	0.00
% Hispanic or Latino females	4.63	4.72	4.83	4.88	4.95	2.89	0.00
% Asian males (and Hawaiian/Pacific Islander)	0.77	0.82	0.87	0.91	1.00	0.59	0.00
% Asian females (and Hawaiian/Pacific Islander)	9.44	9.86	9.95	9.91	9.69	5.37	0.00
% American Indian or Alaskan Native males	0.09	0.10	0.13	0.13	0.14	0.07	0.00
% American Indian or Alaskan Native females	0.47	0.49	0.52	0.53	0.52	0.68	0.16
% Non-targeted disability	4.04	4.08	4.16	4.15	4.27	N/A	N/A
% Targeted disability	0.51	0.50	0.50	0.48	0.51	N/A	N/A
% Claiming Veteran preference	9.48	9.41	9.33	8.97	8.72	N/A	N/A

A two-year pilot study of a technology tool was recently completed in the VA Employee Education Service (EES) using a Talent and Performance Management online tool called *focus* (developed by Business Decisions, Inc., of Chicago). An integrated tool, its components are shown in Figure 10-2.

Figure 10-2

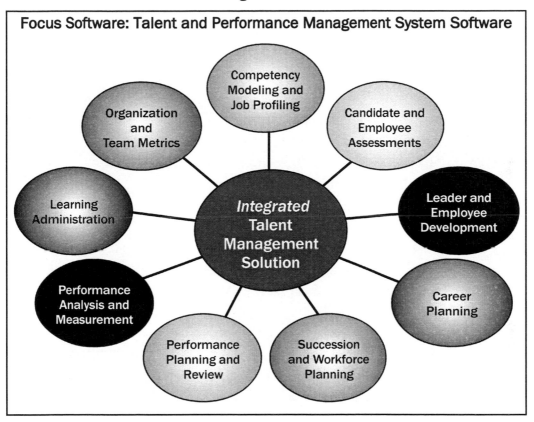

Focus Software: Talent and Performance Management System Software

The Path from Mediocrity to Being #1

In May of 2006, the VHA released the following summary of the steps it took to move from sub-par performance to "#1" over the past 10 years:

- It created a vision for change—an overall strategic direction and plan.
- It reorganized to create an accountable organization based on network management, and clearly delineated line/staff authority and roles.

- It established science-based performance measures linked to overall strategic goals and held accountable and rewarded line senior executives for achievement.
- It established decentralized, distributed, shared leadership and decision making through the National Leadership Board.
- It developed, adopted, and implemented state-of-the-art healthcare and business process practices.
- It developed and implemented the High Performance Development Model and workforce succession programs.

Improvements during this period included:

- Improved patient-centered care
- More patients treated
- Improved access
- Higher quality; better outcomes
- Improved service satisfaction
- Reduced cost per patient
- Achieved recognition as a leader in providing services to special populations.

What does the future look like for the VHA? Certainly, there will be a continued if not increased emphasis on people. Additionally, the priorities are to:

- Continue to improve healthcare and business process improvements.
- Create a "Vision for VHA Cultural Health" (develop a model and strategic plan for workplace and organization improvement)
- Establish a work environment characterized by civility, respect, and engagement, implementing ethical standards previously adopted through all levels of the organization.
- Establish a common framework for performance accountability and recognition at all levels of the organization.
- Improve supervisory skills and team skills for all employees.
- Develop/adopt and implement state-of-the-art employee satisfaction and organization development practices.

- Establish science-based cultural health performance measures.
- Establish a comprehensive program to support knowledge transfer.
- Establish and implement a research program to validate the strategic cultural health model.

The VHA believes that all these accomplishments will help them outdistance the field.

Contact Information

Jim Graber, President
Business Decisions, Inc.
5807 N. Whipple St.
Chicago, Illinois 60659-3708
Phone: 888-452-4BDI
E-mail: jgraber@businessdecisions.com

TWO GOVERNMENT AGENCIES LOOK AT SUCCESSION PLANNING

Case Introduction: This case study written by Grace Endres and James Alexander compares succession planning at the U.S. Postal Service with that of the U.S. Department of Agriculture's Food Safety Inspection Service. It originally appeared in the *Organization Development Journal* in 2006.

Introduction

The first quarter of the 21st century is facing an unprecedented upheaval in the knowledge economy of the United States, with high job turnover, downsizing, and baby-boomer retirements threatening organizations with a brain drain in strategic operational continuity. As more baby boomers near retirement age, the impact of their departure becomes more pronounced within the executive ranks of both private- and public-sector organizations, where the largest percentage of workers age 45 years and older reside. The situation is compounded by the smaller successor pool of workers following the baby-boomers and workers averaging 3.5 years in length of service in the private sector.

This creates a dilemma for organizations as they face a critical mass of knowledge walking out the door, and limited replacement opportunity. The federal government is no exception in the forecasted loss of employees. This paper discusses what two government agencies, the United States Department of Agriculture/Food Safety Inspection Service and the United States Postal Service, are doing to replace the forecasted loss of talent.

What were the drivers or reasons for the Agency's new succession planning process?

The United States Postal Service

A two-year audit conducted by the Office of the Inspector General (OIG) of the U.S. Postal Service on succession planning culminated in 2002 with seven significant findings. The findings primarily focused on the need for process documentation, data management, cost monitoring, tracking of employee development progress, and the assurance of nonadverse impact to minorities. One of the findings revealed labor and paper intensity of the existing process without the benefit of data integrity. The audit report identified the need to leverage technology to manage the development costs and progression of employees identified as future successors to management positions. The recommendation was to ". . . establish a centralized information management system to monitor and analyze potential successor training and associated costs to determine that: (1) potential successor development needs are met; (2) training is proportionately distributed among successors; and (3) overall business goals are achieved."

The USDA Food Safety Inspection Service

The President's Management Agenda (PMA) provides Executive-branch federal agencies with specific guidelines for human capital development and succession planning. The Food Safety and Inspection Service (FSIS) is facing an imminent and increasingly critical crisis: retirement of the majority of its leaders. The agency's Human Resources Department conducted research on the future attrition of its employees. By 2005, 55% of the SESers, 56% of the GS-15s, 59% of the GS-14s, and 62% of the GS-ISs will be eligible to retire. By the year 2007, these figures increase to 70% of the SESers, 77% of the GS-15s, 77% of the GS-14s, and 78% of the GS-13s.

The Agency has established a succession planning system to identify top candidates with managerial and leadership qualities, and to prepare them through select developmental opportunities to assume an executive or managerial position in the future.

What approach did the agency use?

The United States Postal Service

In an effort to address the OIG significant findings and recommendations, the United States Postal Service designed and implemented a corporate-wide, Web-based succession planning process. The new process was grounded on the following design principles:

Fair, equitable
Transparent, non-secretive
Competitive assessment criteria and leadership-competencies-based
Documented process and standard adherence
Technology-enabled
Development-focused
Cost-effective and efficient

These principles were agreed upon by a national cross-functional team established to assess the existing practices in management succession and identify the organization's valid requirements for a new process. The resultant gap analysis served as a blueprint for the new process design features. The United States Postal Service moved forward on the new process by merging its design principles and OIG recommendations with a compilation of best practices in the private sector, which include the following:

- Provide a link to overall business strategy.
- Use technology to facilitate the process.
- Engage in succession-management activities below the executive level.
- Have a structured, formalized approach to managing succession activities, and use a wide array of tools and techniques.
- Evaluate employees using core competencies.
- Ensure that specific and individualized development plans are in place.
- Engage in active learning by placing high potentials across the organization and in special job assignments.

- Use the three main readiness indicators (ready now, ready in one year, and ready in the future) as decision-making guides for assigning development.
- Provide some form of mentoring and/or coaching.
- Employ qualitative and quantitative measures to ensure that the succession management process is on track.

Some of the best practices entailed the use of an automated system. The process design was sensitive to the fact that although technology is highly engrained in Postal Service operations, employees and executives may not be familiar or comfortable with real-time, interactive computer applications or in accessing the Web. This process gently forced those individuals interested in being considered for succession planning to use technology. Thirty-six executives, each from a headquarter's function, and a senior staff employee from each of the nine area offices across the U.S. were appointed by senior executive management under the direction of the Diversity Development organization to assume the responsibility for the new process deployment and administration. These executives were trained in the new process requirements and the computer system interface so they, in turn, could provide guidance to their peers and members on the participation criteria for corporate succession planning and how to access the online application system.

The USDA Food Safety Inspection Service

The Food Safety Service Inspection Service used a competency-based approach to succession planning. The United States Department of Agriculture contracted with Booze, Allen and Hamilton, Inc. to develop a template for individual agencies such as FSIS to use as a guideline for their succession planning efforts. This template, along with the technical support of the department, gave agencies the impetus they needed to develop succession plans that were aligned with the PMA and other federal guidelines, and yet still meet each agency's specific needs. In 2001, a FSIS Succession Planning Leadership Council was established to develop this program. This Council partnered with Linkage, Inc., a leading corporate education and organization development firm, and a model of leadership competencies for the FSIS was developed. The Council recommended the design and implementation of a short- and long-term succession planning program. The short-term phase provided for an online multirater (360 degree) leadership assessment based on specific leadership competencies. The long-term phase focused on selection and development of high-potential candidates for future managerial jobs. In May 2003, the FSIS administrator endorsed a new Leadership Council for Succession Planning. This new Leadership Council initiated a number of succession planning activities that include:

An evaluation of the prior succession planning activity

An extensive workforce analysis and identification of mission-critical occupations and agency-wide skill gaps

A detailed succession planning project plan with deliverables and due dates, as well as a validation study of the agency's competency model

A pilot succession-planning project utilizing assessment center technology to select candidates to address a mission-critical occupation

These activities enabled FSIS to incorporate its succession planning activities with its workforce development projects so that they could be integrated into a comprehensive human-capital-development program. This comprehensive approach to succession planning empowered agency leaders and provided greater flexibility in resource allocation and the ability to align these programs to meet specific agency needs.

How are employees selected for the new Succession Plan?

The United States Postal Service

A four-stage process was designed. The Management Instruction ensured that the United States Postal Service identified, selected, and developed a diverse group of employees who could as future leaders respond to change and maintain performance accountability. The four stages were:

Stage 1: *Application stage.* Eligible employees apply for succession planning online via the Web. This required employees to compose online their leadership experience in relation to the United States Postal Service's eight key leadership competencies. The application process also included taking the Gallup Organization's online Leadership Potential Assessment Survey, called the SRI Index. Another aspect of the first stage required executive managers to review their employees' applications online and make subjective determinations as to whether they support the individual's nominations for each position pool. If the managers did not support the nominations for a particular position pool, the managers were required to justify their nonsupport.

Stage 2:· *Assessment and Selection Stage.* During this phase, functional officers convened their review committees, composed of the officer and the executive managers from their functions, to consider all the complete applications generated from the online application system. The applications include the following information: background information; postal and non-postal experience; education and training; awards; selected position pools for consideration; write-ups for each of the eight leadership competencies; and results of the Gallup SRI Index.

The committees held review sessions to evaluate all applications that pertained to the position pools within their functions, based on the information outlined above. Also, committees were required to record constructive feedback for each non-selected nominee. Selections were made and those nominees who were selected were entered into the system as "pending," meaning awaiting final approval by the Postal Service's Executive Committee.

Step 3: *Final Selection and Approval Stage.* The senior officers, along with their respective reporting officers, presented selections of potential successors to the Postal Service's Executive Committee for final discussion and approval. Based on those discussions, final selection and approvals were made and those "Pending" in the system were changed to "Approved." All others were denominated. At this point, the corporate succession plan was finalized as the official record. Also during this stage, all employees who were not selected for succession planning received feedback from their immediate executive managers, based on the respective functional review committees' comments. This feedback provided an opportunity for both parties to begin discussions on career management for the employee.

Stage 4: *Development Stage.* The final stage of the corporate succession planning process was the career development stage. Those selected for succession planning held discussions with their managers to select activities that best support their career development. At this juncture, the Postal Service required all potential successors to list their development activities, target dates, and estimated costs of training on the Web application.

The USDA Food Safety Inspection Service

FSIS used a two-tier approach for its succession planning efforts. Based on the agency's evaluation of its leadership development and succession planning efforts, additional steps were taken to align all leadership development activities with its leadership competency model. This alignment enabled all managers in FSIS to receive 360-degree feedback and the appropriate resources so they could develop individual development plans. Another aspect of the succession planning process for FSIS was that new programs were developed that targeted key components of the agency's workforce. The entrance requirements for these programs varied, but a common characteristic of these programs is that their recruitment and selection criteria were based on collaboration with senior management and the Center for Learning. This collaboration effort enhanced the profile of succession planning throughout the agency. One of these new pilot programs was developed specifically for district managers. This program utilized assessment center technology to select candidates and address a mission-critical occupation.

What methods of communicating the new Succession Planning process were used?

The United States Postal Service

Communicating the new process was accomplished through messaging on the Postal Service's internal Web page, the Postal Service's daily electronic newsletter, and other internal publications. Other messaging included posters and video messages on the Postal Channel. As mentioned previously, a Management Instruction was posted on the Corporate Succession Planning internal Web site.

The Food Safety Inspection Service

The members of the Leadership Council for Succession Planning are the driving force of the agency's succession plan. They were actively involved in its rollout. This rollout included articles in agency publications such as *The Beacon* and the *FSIS News and Notes*. An e-mail message was sent to all employees from the administrator explaining the new pilot program and how to apply. Senior managers in the agency were given periodic updates on the program's progress as each key milestone in the succession plan was reached. Specific agency personnel were designated by the Leadership Council as contact persons to provide answers to questions and to help with recruitment of program participants.

Who received training on the new Succession Planning process prior to implementation?

The United States Postal Service

Initially, the corporate succession planning team was trained by Gallup Corporation using their Leadership Potential Index and their StrengthsFinder instrument. The Area Manager of Diversity and Human Capital position was a new position, with the primary responsibility in the field being succession planning. An initial orientation was conducted regarding responsibilities, followed by specific training for all four stages of succession planning. Headquarters liaisons received training prior to the commencement of each stage. Their support person performed many of the administrative tasks and received training on stages that applied to him/her.

The USDA Food Safety Inspection Service

FSIS procured the services of vendors to provide a number of succession planning activities. These services included the development of a leadership competency model, an assessment center, and 360-degree feedback for agency leaders. The evaluation of the succession planning activities was conducted by an in-house FSIS unit. The Leadership Council for Succession Planning monitored these activities, and in some cases training was provided by vendors to support agency-wide implementation of these programs. A vendor trained agency employees in how to participate in an assessment center process so that the pilot program could be executed.

Were any innovative online and high-tech approaches used?

The United States Postal Service

The new Corporate Succession Planning System (CSP) has fully automated the succession planning process, with the exception of the committee reviews and managerial discussions regarding development and nonselection. CSP is comprised of five functionalities.

1. Potential successors were able to view and edit their personnel data (e.g., education, work experience, and details).

2. Management was given access to nominations, nominee profile information, and individual development plans.

3. Liaison access was provided to enter nominations, update potential successor records, and create reports.

4. The corporate Succession Planning team was given access, in order to process nominations, update nominee records, create reports, and manage user accounts.

5. The CSP system accommodates changes to the United States Postal Service structure. As organizational changes occur, the CSP team can make the appropriate changes to the reporting structure. CSP offers many advantages to users, as it is a Web-enabled system—it is a central source that eliminates redundant data entry and reduces re-work, interfaces with other postal systems, and is a secure system with user-only access to information for their assigned role.

The USDA Food Safety Inspection Service

FSIS is actively engaged in utilizing the very latest innovative online and high-tech approaches for its succession planning and leadership development programs. Some examples of these techniques are listed below:

- FSIS hired Linkage, Inc. to develop its multi-source assessment of employees. This assessment was placed online so employees in the national and field offices could participate in the process.

- FSIS utilized Quick-Hire, an online recruitment tool, to enlist employees for the new succession plan pilot project.

- Assessment center technology and behavioral-based interviewing, along with a review of the applicant's background, were used to make selections for the pilot District Manager program.

- Blended learning techniques that include online learning and classroom training were incorporated into leadership development programs.

- FSIS utilizes online collaboration for action learning projects to enhance the leadership development of its program participants.

How were internal successors developed?

The United States Postal Service

All those selected for succession planning have discussions with their managers so they can select activities that best support their career development. They then input these activities, target dates, and estimated costs of training into the Web application. Each officer monitors all development activities quarterly via reports generated by the system to ensure that all potential successors are on track. Overall, the Diversity Development Department monitors developmental activities to guard against disparate treatment.

The USDA Food Service Inspection Service

FSIS has developed an executive coaching program for employees who were selected into the pilot succession planning program. These employees receive an initial 15 hours of coaching. Subsequent coaching support is arranged on a case-by-case basis. The coaches participating in this program have been carefully selected by the FSIS and have extensive executive-level coaching expertise, very often in both the public and the private sector.

Based on the agency's evaluation of its prior succession planning activities, there were additional management/leadership development programs designed to develop employees' capabilities. Two of these programs are the New Supervisor Program and the Leadership Assessment Development Program, which address the need to develop internal successors and upgrade the skills of supervisors/managers. The agency has a pilot knowledge-transfer project called the Legacy Program, and is developing a training program based on the competency of Emotional Intelligence for its leaders.

How is the new Succession Planning process being evaluated?

The United States Postal Service

The process is being evaluated through a multitude of reports generated by the new Corporate Succession Planning System. These reports include the diversity of potential successors, and the number of successors selected from the Corporate Succession Plan. The quality of those selected is being evaluated through performance evaluations.

The USDA Food Safety Inspection Service

The Leadership Council for Succession Planning continues to maintain oversight of the evaluation of the succession planning process. The programmatic evaluation of FSIS earlier was conducted with the assistance of the Program Evaluation and Improvement staff of OPEER/FSIS. This evaluation included documentation reviews, one-on-one interviews, and a survey for the program participants. All succession plans for each agency are reviewed and evaluated by USDA at the departmental level. Recently, the Office of Personnel Management conducted a comprehensive review of FSIS human resource activity. This review focused on the strategic management of human capital and on human resource accountability. Some additional areas that this review examined were the key drivers of human capital management: talent, succession planning/leadership development, knowledge management, and a results-oriented performance culture. The findings of this review provided valuable feedback on how well these program areas contributed to mission accomplishment. FSIS is in the process of implementing the recommendations from the Office of Personnel Management.

What are future plans for the Succession Planning process for both the Postal Service and the Food Safety Inspection Service?

Future succession planning activity will be based on the ongoing succession planning assessment and evaluation of current planning activities. The senior leadership of both agencies is firmly committed to the continuous improvement of the succession planning process. As mentioned earlier, the FSIS is in the process of implementing recommendations from internal (in-house) and external (USDA/OPM) assessment.

In addition to its ongoing evaluation and improvement activities, FSIS has taken a number of steps to enhance its succession planning and leadership development programs:

> It procured the services of a vendor to revalidate its existing leadership competency model and conduct a baseline assessment of all supervisory employees.

> It developed a Transitioning Leader Program (TLP) to support leaders during the first 180 days of their new permanent assignment. This program provides intensive one-on-one executive coaching, along with strategic organizational development support by an experienced organization-development consultant during this process.

> It designed and implemented a cross-cutting training program that meets leadership development needs throughout FSIS. Some of the training opportunities included in this program are: conflict resolution, consulting skills, coaching for leaders, high-performance teams, and project management fundamentals.

What are the lessons both agencies learned from implementing a new Succession Planning process?

1. The new succession planning processes at both agencies reinforced the importance of having senior management from across the agency actively involved in the development and implementation of the project. The active involvement of senior management enabled both agencies to develop a consensus on specific succession planning needs, and to develop a program customized to address specific needs. Without the involvement of both agencies' senior management to champion and sponsor the new process, implementation of the program would have been very difficult.

2. The succession planning process needs to reflect the current reality of the agency, so it has to continuously evolve. The evolution of the succession planning process enables both agencies to consider feedback from key stakeholders both inside and outside the agencies. This feedback helps to fine-tune specific programs and contributes to the achievement of both agencies' missions.

Contact Information

James Alexander
710 Roeder Road
Silver Spring, Maryland 20910
Phone: 301-578-1695
E-mail: halex8420874@yahoo.com

Grace Endres
Headquarters, U.S. Postal Service
475 L'Enfant Plaza, Room 9802
Washington, D.C. 20260-9802
Phone: 202-268-4650
E-mail: gendres@email.usps.gov

Source: From Endres, G. and J. Alexander. 2006. Two government agencies look at succession planning. *Organization Development Journal, 24*(2), 23–32.

SUCCESSION PRACTICES AT THE U.S. ENVIRONMENTAL PROTECTION AGENCY

Case Introduction: This case study describes succession practices at the U.S. Environmental Protection Agency. It is presented in the form of an interview conducted by Michele Newhard, who also wrote the brief introduction.

Interviewer: Michele Newhard

Interviewees: Claire Milam, Environmental Protection Agency
Kathryn Parker, Environmental Protection Agency
Carolyn Scott, Environmental Protection Agency
Brian Twillman, Environmental Protection Agency

Having a succession plan tends not to be the standard in public-sector organizations. This case study chronicles the situation at the U.S. Environmental Protection Agency.

To begin, a look at formal succession planning programs is in order. William Rothwell and Henry Sredl assert that the majority of succession plans encompass only the top tiers of an organization's depth chart. A formal succession plan is comprised of the following elements: (1) an evaluation of individual skills; (2) an evaluation of individual experiences; (3) individual development plans; (4) an assessment of individual characteristics; (5) a current job analysis; and (6) a strategic analysis of future needs. A succession plan that includes developmental programs for current employees reflects the importance of organizational memory. Organizational memory consists of the knowledge gained from working in a particular organization, but it is more than just explicit knowledge of the procedures. It is the political, culture-oriented, personality-focused nature of the unit—essentially, how things are done there. As this transcript of a discussion about succession planning shows, the EPA has an effective program for succession planning in place.

The Interview

Michele Newhard: **How does your agency define succession management?**

Claire Milam: That's a good question. It is an evolving definition. Right now, it is to have people prepared to move into critical positions in the agency.

Brian Twillman: We also refer to it as a practice for building leadership bench strength.

Kathryn Parker: I work in one of the program offices. I believe it's also important to identify the process to develop the pool of people ready to step in—not necessarily just one replacement.

Milam: Kathryn just raised a really good point, Michele. I want to clarify a little bit by way of background, because I hope this will help you understand the context. EPA has been working on leadership development with the understanding that leadership occurs at every level of the organization. It's not defined by position per se—it's the responsibility that we share. And through that understanding or philosophy, we have for several years enacted our workforce development strategy, which incorporates leadership competencies. We have worked very hard to develop leadership capability and competencies for every population of the agency in terms of their grade level and where they are in the organization. So, please understand that that's the backdrop for our succession efforts and our philosophy.

By the same token, we have external forces from the president's management agenda. President Bush is saying to us that we need to focus on especially our senior-most leadership—our executives— and being prepared for when they retire, because we have huge anticipated retirements. Lots of people! In the federal sector, up to 90% of the senior executives will be eligible to retire by 2010. Those are the statistics that are being bandied about. For EPA, by the year 2008, close to 60% will be eligible to retire. By the year 2010, we'll have 60% eligible to retire. So, we have our internal sort-of philosophy, if you will, of leadership at all levels. And then we have this external driver that's telling us to pay attention to these particular positions. So, the way that we've married that is exactly what Brian and Kathryn were saying: that we are developing and cultivating leadership—training to create a pool of people who are eligible or who would be qualified to move into these senior executive or senior leadership positions, and then to identify a niche of people, if you will, who are ready to move into what we call "critical positions" at the agency. Specifically mission-critical positions. Make sense?

Newhard: **It makes absolute sense, and it seems to fit in with what the private sector is experiencing, as well, with the onset of the boomers retiring in 2010. It has been estimated that about 61 million Americans will retire over the course of the next three decades, leaving a massive void in the workforce.**

Twillman: According to a note from the Office of Personnel Management, succession planning is a delivered and systematic effort by an agency to ensure continuity of leadership and critical staff skills for mission-critical positions, as well as to encourage individual development. OPM does go on to say that succession planning is largely a subset, as Claire was saying, of workforce planning, and is designed to ensure the continued effective performance of an agency by identifying, developing, and placing key people over time. So, it's one part of an overall human capital planning and implementation effort.

Parker: One other point I wanted to make regarding the impending retirements: The EPA is a fairly young organization, started in the early 1970s, and many people who started with the agency are retiring. That adds another layer of concern in terms of needing to replace those people with knowledge within the agency.

Milam: The whole knowledge-management component is a very significant concern.

Twillman: Unlike some federal agencies, there's a great deal of commitment to the mission of the agency. Therefore, we do have "charter" members—people who've been here the last thirty-five years of the agency's existence. They've perhaps had opportunities to go elsewhere, but have chosen to stay here, so we're now looking at some of these key people going and leaving the agency. So, how we build capacity and how we maintain our momentum as an agency is very important to us.

Newhard: **What is the purpose of your agency's succession management program, and what led to the perceived need for it? That is, is the EPA much like the rest of the government, in recognizing the need to have this topic covered and developed?**

Parker: As Claire mentioned, there is the President's management agenda, and it is key. The human capital component of the EPA's succession management program is one of the key components of the President's program.

Twillman: Carolyn Scott is joining us now from one of our offices. She's going to be just sitting in.

Parker: So the human capital aspect is a key component of the President's management agenda, and as we've mentioned, succession planning is a part of that. Even if the agencies didn't recognize that it was important, they are really paying attention to it now. I should mention, however, that I was involved in doing a benchmarking a couple of years ago of various agencies. The design went across the government, and even though people recognized that it was an issue at least until a couple years ago, very few agencies were actually doing something about it. I don't know if you're familiar with the "scorecard" of the President's management agenda, but most agencies did not have a succession plan in place, and they were in the red on that program. At this point, all agencies are ready to address that very important issue.

Milam: One of the things that I heard you ask is what, if anything, differentiates EPA from other federal agencies. The thought that comes back to me is that it is knowledge management. We have a highly educated workforce, and it takes a lot of time for most people to ascend the learning curve, and that may distinguish us a little bit from some other agencies. Certainly, there are other federal agencies that have similar issues, so I'm not going to say we're unique. I do know that there are many people who will tell you that it's taken them three to five years, if not more, to figure out what they're doing. So that makes our effort a little more complex, I think.

Newhard: **What measurable goals or objectives, if any, helped to provide direction to your agency's succession management program beyond that?**

Milam: Well, as it would happen, I have just literally this past week finished writing what I call a "solid" draft of the agency's succession-management plan, with goals to ensure that we have people ready to move into positions and that they are successful when they move into those positions. So, in terms of measures, we have it broken down into several measures, which include people going through what we call a candidate development program—somewhat of a formal development program to prepare people to become senior executives. So, people going through that program, how many graduate, how many are successfully recruited into our open positions, how many people from outside do we bring in—those kinds of measures. I don't have them in front of me right now, but those are some of the more-detailed measures.

Newhard: **What groups are targeted for participation in the program, and why are they selected? Can anyone in the EPA become involved in your formal development program?**

Milam: Yes, Michele. Let me take a cut at this answer. Have you talked to any other federal agencies? Are you familiar with other federal agencies?

Newhard: **Not so much.**

Milam: One of the things that distinguishes the way those of us in the federal government do our work is that we have a set of Merit Principles. Generally, everything we do from a development perspective needs to be available and open to all employees. Now, there may be a competitive process in which people are selected to participate in a program, but everyone is encouraged to apply and everybody may apply. There may be specific criteria that are used for selecting people, and if there are, those are made known. People know in advance that most if not all of our development programs are structured and formal, and end up with an individual achieving a certain position. In essence, it is like a job-position description, a vacancy announcement. So, an individual might want to go through this candidate-development program, which is a structured formal program for people aspiring to senior-executive service. The individual has to submit a whole application and compete against anybody else who wants to apply. So, that's how we manage that process. Does that make sense?

Newhard: **It does, it does. Building on that, one of you said something about leadership competencies earlier.**

Does your agency use job competencies, defined as characteristics that describe successful performance, as a key foundation for the succession program? If so, explain how. If not, explain what is a key foundation for the program.

Parker: I wanted to follow up on that last question, maybe to bridge to this one. Claire mentioned how people get into formal programs. Besides training, there are other ways in which people learn and develop, and I wanted to just mention a couple of them. Then let other people chime in. We have what are called "details" to other offices; we can basically go on loan to another part of the agency—actually, you can go on loan to a different agency or another organization outside of the federal government for a specified period of time. Learning on the job is another way in which people are developed. We also have a mentoring program—a formal mentoring program, and an informal mentoring program. These are in addition to the formalized training program.

Twillman: Through the years the EPA has had a leadership institute, we have focused on the needs of people at all levels: the administrative support staff, the professional staff, and the senior-level staff, and then the managers themselves, team leaders, advisory team leaders, front-line managers, branch chiefs who are assistant directors, and then the senior-level people. So, we do have a comprehensive approach to developing people. We typically offer courses such as "Stepping Up To Supervision," "Excellence in Supervision," and "Situational Leadership" that are targeted for people from across the agency. We have ten regional offices outside of the Washington D.C. area; they come together and participate in these training programs for typically two or three or four days. We do see that training is just one aspect of development. There are a lot of other challenging assignments: the rotational opportunities or "details"; the opportunity to shadow our senior leaders and other leaders; mentoring; and coaching, for example. We have an executive coaching program where we bring in the coaches from the federal executive institutes coaching pool to work with us. We've given our managers a 360° assessment, which helps them with feedback and developmental feedback, and builds on their strengths and identifies some weaknesses. So, we're doing the things that other federal agencies are doing as well. We did bring in futurists some years ago to talk to our associates and help us look at the skills and competencies needed for the year 2023, twenty-five years out. So, that's helped us to formulate a workforce development strategy and now our human capital plan.

Milam: Michele, you just got a lot of information. Thank you both, Kathryn and Brian. They triggered me to think a little bit more also about the succession plan that I just finished writing. This plan, remember, is targeted to our senior executives, so it's not for the entire agency right now. We did some analysis and looked at what we call "critical positions." In order to succeed in those critical positions, there are competencies; at that level, those are leadership competencies as well as technical competencies. These individuals must also have a solid understanding of the organization—an understanding of the person's home organization, as well as the agency as a whole. So our strategy is not only to do some formal development program training. It's also to build a corporate culture where people actually are thinking about partnering with and leveraging the resources of the agency as a whole—as a corporate entity, not just within their particular area.

Twillman: That's true talent management.

Milam: Right. And so, to that end, we developed a mobility plan where we're actually moving our senior executives across the agency. This is something that the administrator of the EPA (the equivalent of a CEO) has a personal stake and interest in. There is some discussion that this mobility plan will expand, and we will continue to work to integrate that into the culture of the agency so that people do have experience in other parts of the agency and understand the work of the other agencies as well. So that's another key foundation of our current program.

Newhard: **How is individual job performance assessed? Is there a tool or an appraisal every six months or every year?**

Twillman: We have moved in the last year from a pass/fail system of performance appraisal and performance management of a five-tier system. The Office of Personnel Management has required that all federal agencies now move away from a pass/fail or a two-tier system. We had this about five or six years ago, before we moved to the pass/fail. The thought then was that moving to the pass/fail would open up conversations more between managers and employees. Now the requirements of the five-tier system require us to distinguish between the outstanding employees, the exceed-expectation employees, the employees who are fully successful at doing their work exactly as being asked (doing it well, doing it thoroughly, and all of that), the employees who might be minimally successful and will need some support, and then the employees who are unsatisfactory or not satisfactory. So, a five-tier system. We're just putting it into place. We provide a lot of coaching and training support to our managers, and now we're working with our employees to help them see how their job and their work fits in with the strategic goals of the organization that they're a part of. The whole thought is that this gives people a direct line of sight with what the senior executives do, the front-line managers do, and then what the staff at their various levels do so that everybody's in essence on the same page. Not only are we developing people, we're creating opportunities for people to see how their work is meaningful to the overall goals of the agency. And hopefully, doing that in a fair and equitable way.

Parker: To just add a little more to what Brian said, those performance appraisals are based on performance standards that are written on a yearly basis. Every six months, they're evaluated. The standards that you're expected to meet during the year are broken out and have to stay in line with the agency's goals. The various agency goals and how everybody's standards relate to those specifics is all spelled out. That's what you're evaluated on every six months.

Twillman: So that's the new innovation. These goals of the staff person may or may not have been related to the overall agency's strategic goals before, but now they're directly linked.

Newhard: **Kathryn or Brian or Claire, the performance standards that Kathryn mentioned: Who is responsible for reviewing those every year?**

Twillman: Well, ultimately, the chief human resources officer for the agency is, but at all levels of the agency, the managers are—the first-level, second-level, and third-level managers. Each office certifies that they've gone through a process of review and a process of measuring success. They report out the numbers of people who are outstanding, the numbers of people who are exceeds, and so on.

Newhard: **Is the individual's preparedness for promotion assessed in any other way, beyond this five-tier system of appraisal?**

Milam: An individual spends a year "in grade"—the lower-level grade before they receive a promotion. So, the assumption is that they've been doing the work of the next-level down for at least a year before they can be promoted.

Twillman: There are fifteen grades, so someone at a grade thirteen has been performing that work for at least a year before they're eligible for a promotion up to the grade-fourteen position.

Milam: That's a proxy: It doesn't necessarily mean that the person is ready. Certainly, a person could be ready before the year is up, but this is a standard federal practice, and in most agencies, it is a requirement.

Carolyn Scott: Typically, that annual performance or evaluation process occurs when employees are on the career ladder. When they're on a career ladder, they probably come into the agency as maybe a seven or a nine. They automatically are eligible for a promotion at the end of that year, and they go through an evaluation process. When they cap at a twelve or a thirteen, then it becomes more competitive. Whenever an open vacancy is available and they apply for it, they have been in that grade for a year and meet the criteria. Then, there's a whole process of steps for that.

Milam: I've worked in both the federal and the nonfederal sectors. One of the things that may be a little more unique to the federal sector is that if I'm at a grade thirteen and my position only goes up to the thirteen, but I want a grade fourteen, I have to compete with other people for that position. I have to submit my résumé, and I have to go through the whole process. It may be open only to people in the agency, or it could be open to the whole universe or some variation thereof, but I'm going to have to go through a competitive process. That's the way I'm determined to be prepared for that promotion or not.

Twillman: And there can be many candidates for that position.

Milam: Even though it's the next position for my career development and it makes sense for me to be in that position, I still have to compete for it.

Newhard: **So, in other words, there's a possibility you will not receive that promotion.**

Milam: Absolutely.

Newhard: **How is individual developmental planning carried out, if at all? For instance, does your agency use an Individual Development Plan? We've talked about the five-tier appraisal system—does each employee actually have, perhaps, a written, formalized development plan?**

Twillman: Most employees are certainly encouraged to develop an individual development plan. We do call them "individual development plans" or IDPs. We have electronic guidebooks online for everybody in the agency to access, and we have variations of the actual form that people use. Some of our offices actually link up directly to some competencies that they want their employees to develop, short-term (defined as one or two years) or long-term (three to five years).

Ideally, the goal that the employee would develop would be linked to the organizational goals and priorities, but that's not necessarily always the case. So, we've been actually using IDPs since the early 1990s and we require all of our managers to have IDPs on an annual basis, whereas our union agreements with our union organization do not require so much with other employees. But we are strongly encouraged to do so.

Parker: I want to talk a little bit about something that's related to what Brian said—but it is off topic—because it relates to the larger issue. I just want to make sure it's brought out here. Brian talked about IDPs and how they're used in the agency, but there's not really a standard format at this point. People are encouraged to use them, but the issue of whether things are "mandatory" or not is an issue that I think this agency has gone back and forth on over time in terms of what is required, what's not, what is encouraged, and what's not set in a context of how our agency works. We're fairly decentralized and not a top-down agency, so things are done differently in different parts of the agency sometimes, or done differently in different regions. There's kind of an encouragement to do that—more of a bottom-up approach that other agencies such as NASA do not have. NASA's much more top-down, and of course the Department of Defense is, as well. They have very standardized ways of doing things, including training, and they have mandatory requirements for ways of doing things. This agency is not like that, so I think it's important to understand that when you're looking at the way our agency does succession planning, keep in mind that the culture is very different here that at many other agencies.

Twillman: It would follow that the personality of the manager be very focused on development in terms of their own IDP and how that IDP has helped them move to their senior level. They're going to be a champion, or very strongly advocate that all their employees do it. So, if you're an employee under that individual, you obviously want to do an IDP. In other cases, if you do an IDP as an employee and the manager doesn't really give that much thought or attention to it, you might feel like *"What's the point?"*

Newhard: **Obviously you've talked about training, executive coaching, and "details" programs, etc. How are those planned?**

Twillman: Just to say one more thing about the IDP: The training officers across the agency have set priorities for the next year. One of the priorities is to come out with a new approach to individual development plans. We want to increase the level of employee engagement as well as the level of management engagement, because we really want to shift the culture from a results-oriented culture to more of a culture of development and a culture where people are indeed focused on what their skills and talents are, so that they can contribute them to the maximum. We really want to become more of a high-performing organization, where people as a result form more adult-adult relationships in the workplace, and where there's more candor and more openness about how one needs to develop, what one needs to do, and that sort of thing. So, the training officers are actually looking at benchmarking other federal agencies and other organizations to see what they do in the area of individual development. In the midst of that, we hope to modify our process in the next couple of months.

Newhard: **Brian, what do you think is driving the retool of the IDP process for you?**

Twillman: Management planning activities and human capital—the focus on human capital, which is leading managers to think, *Gee, am I getting the best use out of all the employees I have?* And frankly, our budget isn't increasing—it's going down a bit. As a result, managers are recognizing that they need to be smarter about the use of their resources and need to engage their employees differently. We're seeing that leaders are different than managers: Leaders engage employees in ways that managers may or may not. Managers are focused on the task, whereas leaders also focus on people and how they can get their best work done. While you engage them, you provide them with the things that they need to develop themselves more fully.

Newhard: **That's good to know. It's happening at my organization as well, so thank you for sharing that. Back to your array of activities for helping to develop some of these folks. How are these planned?**

Milam: I would say that they're mostly planned at the individual level, in conjunction with the employee's manager through an IDP process. There are maybe some exceptions. Brian and Carolyn, you have direct experience with this.

Scott: I think this is how it occurs, but there are some formal programs that were mentioned earlier that I guess within individual program offices employees can sort of nominate themselves to. They're self-initiated, in many instances. In other instances, a manager might encourage employees to take advantage of specific programs, depending on how driven the employee is toward development.

Twillman: We are actually moving more toward a more centralized approach, where we have learning standards in different parts of the country which we'll be able to deliver to the people out in the regions. Here at the headquarters in Washington, the various main courses we're talking about are "Situational Leadership," "Excellence in Supervision," and "Supervision." We have many other courses for mid-level employees and administrative staff. So, we recognize that we need to get on the same page. The training officers just spent three days in San Francisco a couple of months ago, looking at how best to get on the same page when it comes to leadership development and employment. So, we do have executive coaching support that we're looking to provide, mentoring programs across the agency, and also a number of training classes per se, but we are also encouraging our local offices to come up with plans, come up with activities, come up with events and experiences that people can learn and grow from. We're asking people who have gone to the federal Executive Institute for four weeks or to the two-week OPM training in Colorado and Shepherdstown, West Virginia to come back and report on what they've learned—to make the learning real and to transfer the learning back to the job.

Parker: One of the other things I wanted to mention when Brian said we're working toward a more centralized process of training is that we have had a system that's been, I would say, more ad hoc. One of the things that we're doing is putting out electronic announcements of "details" at various offices. This is also becoming more centralized as a daily Web page for everybody called a "page system" that allows anybody in the agency to go in and see what "details" are being offered by the various parts of the agencies, the time commitments, and so on.

Milam: What's interesting, Michele, is that we are experiencing a culture change. It used to be that being sent on a "detail" assignment was somewhat of a negative thing—people were either poor performers or their managers wanted to get them out or reward them for something. So, with this page, what's happening is that people are seeing all the different opportunities. People are posting opportunities now, and it's being used more developmentally in a whole different way. So, that's an interesting evolution that's happening not only with "details," but with several other developmental opportunities.

Just so you know, some people have alluded to the way the agency is structured. We have the office of Human Resources centrally, and then each region has its own Human Resources office and each program area has its own Human Resources function. So, that gives us, in essence, 24 Human Resources functions. When you're talking about budgets, you're talking about 24 different budgets, if you will, and I honestly don't know that any of us are prepared to speak to that. In terms of the evaluation of the succession program, I think I mentioned that we wanted to know that we had people ready to go into what we consider to be critical positions. What I didn't mention is that we have a target to get a "pool" of two people or a bench of two people for each critical position where there is somebody eligible to retire. In the analysis that I did, I found that we meet or exceed that pool.

Twillman: I just want to move quickly back to a previous question to say that senior human resources officers usually meet twice a year, and they're the ones who need to come up with mandatory training requirements for managers. They've been very involved. In addition, in our executive development program maybe three/four years ago, we had 75 people. We talked about doing executive development for years and years and years, and we did something about it. I think we finally have senior-level focus in a way that we hadn't had before. This is driving some of our training, executive coaching, and other activities as well.

Newhard: **And it sounds like, perhaps, driving the culture change?**

Twillman: Correct.

Parker: I'd just like to follow up on what Brian said—just a larger comment. When I was involved a couple of years ago in looking at the various agencies and what they were doing with succession plans, I realized that it's very important that the organizational culture is really linked to succession planning, and that what takes place is recognized within the agency as being relevant and important and is supported and spearheaded by the highest management within the organization. If you don't have leadership at the top, then it's not going to happen within your organization.

Twillman: At EPA, we have a career manager who is now the political lead of the organization: Steve Johnson, who had been here for a number of years.

Milam: He started as an intern at EPA.

Twillman: Now, for the first time ever, we have the head of the agency who is also a career employee. He's unique. He knows the culture, he knows what's needed to develop the culture, and he's doing what he can.

Milam: We now have interest and attention that's really focused on development, because obviously, the head of the agency knows from his personal experience how important that is. The EPA is now actively engaged in succession planning.

Newhard: **I just want to thank all four of you for participating. It's been a very enlightening discussion.**

Contact Information

Interviewer: Michele Newhard, Special Programs Training Coordinator
Penn State Auxiliary Services
Pennsylvania State University
E-mail: mln4@psu.edu

Interviewees: Claire Milam, Human Capital Planning and Policy Group
United States Environmental Protection Agency
Phone: 202-564-7582

Kathryn Parker, Senior Environmental Protection Specialist
United States Environmental Protection Agency
Phone: 703-603-9065

Carolyn Scott, Environmental Protection Agency
Office of Executive Services

Brian Twillman: AO Training Officer and
Organization Development Specialist
U.S. EPA Office of Executive Services
Office of the Administrator
MC1104-A
1200 Pennsylvania Ave., N.W.
Washington, D.C. 20460

U.S. STATE GOVERNMENT CASE STUDIES

What are state governments in the U.S. doing about workplace succession and related topics? The cases in Part III address that question.

These cases were chosen to present a range of state government succession practices. Case 13 tells a story about how one political official tried to manage transition from elective office. Case 14 looks at a statewide effort to do workforce planning. Cases 15 and 16 examine individual state government agencies that are addressing workforce planning issues. Case 17 explores the need to preserve institutional memory—that is, to ensure that the next generation of government officials is given information about the agency's work learned from past experience.

Note: At the state government level, the term "workforce planning" is often preferred over such terms as "succession planning," "succession management," or "human capital management."

The cases in Part III are:

GUBERNATORIAL SUCCESSION: MANAGING TRANSITION

> *Case Introduction:* How are political succession issues handled? The narrative provided by Utah governor Olene S. Walker, while not exactly workforce planning, offers some clues and ideas for similar but non-political circumstances.

Having served as lieutenant governor for more than 10 years, I witnessed and participated in administration and policy changes, legislative sessions, budget processes and local, national and international events. I had no idea, however, that this experience would become great training for the day I became Utah's 15th and first woman governor. Our governor was younger than I and though I knew it could become my role, I never suspected it would happen.

Nearing the end of his third term, then Gov. Mike Leavitt was appointed by President George W. Bush to serve as administrator of the Environmental Protection Agency. The news surrounding the appointment and the apparent transition of governors became overwhelming and exciting. The buzz included whether or not I would be governor or "acting" governor and the legal authority I had to appoint a lieutenant governor, all of which eventually was solved by our attorney general.

Once we believed Leavitt would be confirmed, we began working on establishing a transition team. We created a shadow governor's office and prepared to step in at the precise moment that Leavitt left office. We shadowed everything from press relations to policy directors.

Have a staffing plan in place.

Even if as lieutenant governor you cannot foresee any reason you would be placed into office as governor, you should have a staffing plan in place. A transition would most likely happen quickly and unexpectedly, and it is best to already have a plan—just in case. I believe the most critical positions in my administration were the chief of staff, the press secretary, and the administrative assistant/scheduler. It is important they are appointed immediately. Once in place, these employees can assist you with your staffing plan.

I also selected a person to assist with the transition events. These events included the farewell speech and party for Leavitt, his resignation and my inauguration, the inaugural gala, archiving, etc. It was also helpful to have a person managing the move into the governor's residence and office.

Investigate and implement the Lieutenant Governor selection process.

Once the attorney general gave his final interpretation of the state constitution, it was determined I could appoint my lieutenant governor.

I kept my selection very private, telling no one, until the day before the announcement. I selected my lieutenant governor based on our past relationship (we served together in the Legislature), his ability to work as part of a team, competency, and skill sets that differed but were complementary to my own and those of my staff.

Immediately communicate with cabinet members.

Communication with the press, employees, and the public was essential during the transition. It was imperative that I be proactive and honest with everyone in order to eliminate rumors and bad press.

I met with department heads and key staff before the transition to express my intentions. I asked specific people to stay, and also asked for their loyalty. We discussed critical policy and budget issues and the method for developing future plans. If you are making changes, my advice is to make the changes immediately. Don't wait!

Handle the media.

At first, most of the media attention was directed to the outgoing governor, and our policy was for me to remain as quiet and in the shadows as possible. But questions soon arose regarding the actual description of my title, my authority, and my future plans for the state.

Although I couldn't formally appoint a press secretary, I had asked for a select few communication professionals to volunteer their time during the transition. I later appointed my press secretary from this pool.

I was surprised at the amount of local and national media attention I received. Not only were reporters interested in me, they wanted to know everything about my family. We prepared extensive biographies, had formal photos taken, and prepared a Web site. I also spent a lot of time briefing my press secretary so she could do many of the initial interviews for me. We also prepared for unusual or controversial stories, which was very helpful.

Start scheduling yourself as soon as possible.

With staff help, we developed a list of important events and began prioritizing them. Once they were on the calendar, we could build a more comprehensive schedule.

It was also critical to develop a procedure to handle the thousands of scheduling requests that came through. Many people wanted five minutes with a new governor. We were able to filter those requests and use staff and department heads as surrogates.

Understand the budget.

I took office one month prior to the governor's budget recommendations being due. Fortunately, I had been present during many of the preliminary budget hearings and was aware of many issues. I also worked on becoming familiar with the budget for the Office of the Governor.

State agencies also supplied critical budget briefings and we were able to present a comprehensive budget.

Understand and develop policy positions.

During the transition, I asked every department, senior staffer, and the budget office to supply briefing papers. They were compiled into binders for me and the new lieutenant governor, as well as for my new staff.

I also scheduled briefings on state/federal issues with our Washington, D.C. office, the National Governors Association, and our congressional delegation.

Plan the inaugural events.

It was incredibly helpful to have a point person for the inaugural events. The most pressing dilemma was payment responsibilities. This should be determined immediately, preferably before any planning takes place.

I began working on my inaugural speech as soon as I learned there was a significant likelihood I would take office. It took much longer to finalize than I thought. Additionally, many lieutenant governors do not have the experience with teleprompters that our governors have, and it is important to have several practice sessions with the equipment and the speech itself.

Develop initiatives quickly.

It was important for me not to be seen simply as a caretaker governor. For years as lieutenant governor, I had initiated and created many successful programs and campaigns. I wanted to continue some of the projects close to my heart and also to roll out new initiatives to benefit our state.

During the transition, I asked key people to become the point people on several initiatives. By the time I took office, we had a schedule for press events and most of the background prepared for the launches.

While developing my initiatives, we also created a brand for the new administration. This was a key element to communicate within days of becoming governor.

Be prepared for surprises.

One cannot predict the future or anticipate every hiccup (or train wreck), so it is essential to have quality staff and as much preparation as possible done ahead of time.

One area that created some anxiety was the amount of fundraising needed. This included budgets for the inaugural events, special projects, initiatives, and running for election. It is essential to understand the fundraising process and to have a fundraising mechanism in place as soon as possible.

Have fun.

While the quick pace of change and new responsibilities swarmed about me, it was critical to take time to enjoy the events. This was a moment in history to never be repeated, and I was at the center. I love public service and tackling tough situations—who could ask for a more perfect opportunity to do those things?

My family was supportive and my staff was loyal. I was blessed with a network of friends and experts who all had the best interests of the state at heart. Looking back, I'd say the transition was one of the greatest moments in my life.

SUCCESSION PRACTICES IN NEW YORK STATE GOVERNMENT

> *Case Introduction:* This case study, presented in interview format, describes how the State of New York is going about succession planning at the state level.
>
> **Interviewer:** Diane Spokus
>
> **Interviewees:** Nancy Kiyonaga, Director of Workforce and Occupation Planning for the State of New York.

Diane Spokus: **How does your agency define succession management, workforce planning (if applicable), human capital management (if applicable), and leadership development (if applicable)?**

Nancy Kiyonaga: New York has 70 agencies, and they are all doing it differently. When we first started, we did not really make a distinction between succession management and workforce planning. Now, we do. For succession management, we have not limited ourselves to the top levels of the organization. Actually, different agencies are looking at succession planning differently. I think Dr. Rothwell refers to that as "technical succession planning," and that is how we are defining it.

Since we are in a merit system, we can't just identify a successor to a position for someone who is leaving. We look at succession planning in a very broad way: getting the entire pool of people who might be successful in an examination for a higher-level position ready for that position. It is a very different definition.

"Workforce planning" is defined as the typical right person, in the right place, with the right skills—the traditional definition.

"Human capital management" is not a phrase we use with capital letters as a defined process.

Leadership development is part of our succession planning—our succession management kind of effort. Looking at the leadership cadre that we have, what the skills are that leaders need in New York State is just about what everyone needs to be a leader. Then trying to provide the opportunities for people to get the skills that they need. Again, this is done not centrally, but on an agency-by-agency basis.

We have a decentralized Workforce Planning program, and our Civil Service office provides tools and resources. We provide tools for the agencies to use, but we don't mandate that they use those tools. Therefore, we have agencies doing quite a bit, and some agencies that are just beginning, and we have 70 different agencies in New York State. That is my problem in answering the questions. I can't answer for New York State.

Spokus: **What is the purpose of your agency's succession management program, and what led to the perceived need for it?**

Kiyonaga: The Department of Civil Service about five years ago joined with the Governor's Office of Employee Relations, and we looked at what the numbers were in the state workforce. Generally, as do most governments, we had an older workforce, and that led us into what we were going to do about this problem. It stemmed from that question.

Spokus: **Do you have a database of retirees to draw upon?**

Kiyonaga: No, but I am thinking about that because different state agencies are hiring back retirees. I don't know how many there are, but we are definitely making use of our retirees—which anecdotally, every other government I talked to is doing unless there is a law that prohibits it. Now we have a law that limits how much money a state retiree can earn if they come back to work for the state. Now, in terms of other peoples' retirees, I don't have a feel for that at all.

Actually, the Department of Civil Service, probably 15 years ago, started to study this problem. We have a very stable workforce. We had a period of time where we hired tremendously, and we haven't been able to hire significant numbers for the past 20 years.

So we had a workforce which was steadily growing older. We are not hiring behind. We essentially missed two generations of workers, and it was really that several people recognized this problem and decided to do something about it. Everything else has stemmed from there. What we did, after identifying the problem, is to pull together all the agency commissioners and explain the issues to them. From their feedback, we decided to produce a *Guide to Workforce Succession Planning.* From there we did a great deal of research on various topics, which all ended up on our Web site. We had over 70 volunteers from inside state government who worked with a very small crew from the Civil Service and the Office of Employee Relations, and we had 70 volunteers who pulled together such information as mentoring, coaching, recruitment—issues that surround the larger issue of workforce planning. The Web site is http://www.cs.state.ny.us/successionplanning/planning/.

Spokus: **What measurable goals or objectives, if any, help to provide direction to your agency's succession management program?**

Kiyonaga: Because we have a decentralized effort, we haven't established measurable goals or objectives. Certainly our goal is to make sure there is a workforce sufficient to carry out the State's mission. In terms of measurable goals and objectives, we haven't set those. You will see on the Web site that there is an annual statistical report that the State does. The last one was for 2005. We will be doing 2006 this summer.

Spokus: **What groups are targeted for participation in the program? Why were they selected?**

Kiyonaga: This is one of those questions that I really can't answer. Each agency has targeted their own. There are certainly groups that I am particularly concerned about—for example, management-level positions—but basically, every agency is looking at its own titles and its own work, and deciding what it is going to concentrate on.

Spokus: **Is there any one particular agency that you could refer to that is a Best Practice?**

Kiyonaga: Our Office of General Services has done a good bit in the leadership arena, as has the Department of Taxation and Finance. These agencies looked at two factors: They looked at the changing nature of work, and they looked at how many people were of an age to retire. They then went ahead and looked at what other people needed to do to succeed in those jobs that so many people would be retiring from.

Tax and Finance has about 300 or so managers, and they developed a program for those managers—a leadership development program. They now require that people in those management jobs complete a training program in the course of a year. They have made it a very flexible program—very much in tune with adult learning and managers who are not having a whole lot of time. They have been very successful with that. They just finished their first year.

It is a pretty similar description for the Office of General Services. It is a realization that you are going to lose most of your managers in a short period of time, and you are going to lose most of the institutional knowledge which will go with them, and that is what those two agencies are concentrating on.

Spokus: **Does your agency use job competencies, defined as character-istics that describe successful performance, as a key foundation for the succession program? If so, explain how. If not, explain what is a key foundation for the program.**

Kiyonaga: We are required under the New York State Civil Service Law to look at knowledge, skills, and abilities as the foundation of our employee examination program. Agencies are bringing in competencies when they do training and development of people, and it is at that point that they talk about the culture of the organization, how they want people to operate, what good behavior is—that type of thing. That comes more in the training program. But I wouldn't call competencies a key factor to our succession planning program.

Spokus: **How is individual job performance assessed?**

Kiyonaga: Well, again, the State has a performance evaluation system and there is an annual evaluation that every person is supposed to have. Some agencies are starting to tie that to succession planning. I don't have any hard proof of that. It certainly could be a valuable addition to any succession plan. It ought to be. A person should know what the job requires, what they are doing, and what would allow them to move to the next step. At the moment, I don't think most of our agencies have made that connection.

Spokus: **How is individual preparedness for promotion assessed?**

Kiyonaga: Well, because we have a merit system, in order to be promoted, a person has to take an examination. The hiring entity has to pick among the top three people on this list. It does lead to situations where a supervisor has identified a person who is a great employee, stellar, but the supervisor cannot promote the person if he or she does not perform well on the test and does not end up on the test among the top three.

On the informal, if you will, because we don't have entry from the outside of Civil Service. Entry is always from the bottom level in any title series. Supervisors do get to know people very well—progress through the ranks, if you will. There is that informal knowing about who you think is capable of working out on a job. That is where the choice from among the top three really comes in—knowing people well, and who from the top three you want to appoint.

Spokus: **They would have had to take the test and pass it?**

Kiyonaga: Yes, that is why in government, succession planning is really different. We can't really appoint someone as our successor and then groom that person for awhile like you hear in the private sector. It is really dependent on the examination process.

Spokus: **How long is the examination good for?**

Kiyonaga: In New York, an eligible list is good for up to four years.

Spokus: **How is Individual Developmental Planning carried out, if at all?**

Kiyonaga: Part of the performance evaluation system is to develop an individual development plan for people, and then to assess performance against that plan. That is to be part of that process.

Spokus: **Could you expand on that a little bit?**

Kiyonaga: New York State has had a performance evaluation system for a long period of time—a lot longer than many organizations that I am aware of. There are two parts: One part is the IDP (what the person needs to develop), and the other is how the person is actually performing. The IDP is about what they need to develop on the job, and because there is a range of duties and job expectancies with each job title, the IDP is to point the way to improving performance.

Spokus: **What activities, such as training, executive coaching, job rotation, and so forth, are used to build individual competence? How are those planned?**

Kiyonaga: Here is where it becomes difficult to answer as one entity, because we have agencies that are doing everything you can imagine along those lines—all kinds of training, all kinds of programs, book clubs—anything that is working for them in terms of leadership training and training for technical duties as well. The Governor's Office of Employee Relations is the central training agency for the State of New York and provides training for all types of job titles—all different levels. Whether those would be tied to succession planning really depends on how the agencies apply to GOER for assistance with that training. We will have that very standard training, and there are agencies who are asking for additional training for succession planning purposes. It runs the gamut, and it is difficult to answer that question.

I'll use the Tax Department as an example. Let's go back to the example that I already used of what they are doing with their leadership development program. I think that that would be a fine example.

The State Education Department is also doing a management development program for their staff, and what they did was go look at the job classifications. They changed some of the classifications so that the titles were keeping up with what the work was. Now they have a management development plan tied to the knowledge, skills, and abilities needed for those jobs.

Spokus: **What is the budget for the succession planning program, if you know it? How is the succession program evaluated? What measures or metrics are used to assess success?**

Kiyonaga: There is no specific budget set aside for succession planning. There is my position in the Department of Civil Service, and in the agencies, succession planning functions are performed by the Human Resource offices.

At this point in time, I don't think the succession planning has been evaluated. Succession planning is a relatively new area. I think people spent the first couple of years trying to get a grip on their numbers and trying to bring this issue to a level of consciousness in their organization so that it could really be paid attention to. And they tried to make program managers aware of what was going on.

Spokus: **What other comments would you like to make about your agency's succession program?**

Kiyonaga: I think probably one of the issues I would like to talk about is the issue of centralized effort versus decentralized effort in a large state government such as New York's. We have 163,000 people in the classified service; that doesn't count our State University system or a few other organizations. That makes us an extremely large employer. We went originally with a decentralized approach to workforce planning, and that is different than other states have chosen to do. I think the jury is still out on what is the best approach in a large, diverse organization. That is an area that warrants further study.

Spokus: **Do you have a percentage of the people who will be at the retirement age within the next five years?**

Kiyonaga: Yes, I do. Eleven percent of employees could retire by 2010 with the correct combination of age and length of service. There are another 24,000 people who are already over the age of 55 who do not have 30 years of service. Clearly, some of them have less than ten, so we refer to them as the wildcard group. I don't think those people are aiming to have the traditional 30-year career. So it is completely unknown as to when they will choose to retire. Twenty-six percent of the workforce could potentially retire within the next few years.

Then we have a very large group behind that who are now between 45 and 55—a very large group. So, I look at that potentially as another wave, if you will, by 2015. Our average age right now is 48. We do have people who work beyond 55.

Spokus: **Do you offer incentives for retirement?**

Kiyonaga: Yes, the State has, at times in the past. The incentives were offered, basically, because of financial considerations. I know the federal government has offered incentives to even out their workforce so that they don't have a huge bubble of people retiring at the same time. We have not done that.

Contact Information

Interviewer: Diane Spokus, Instructor at Pennsylvania State University and Educator for South Central Pennsylvania Area
Health Education Center
Web site: www.personal.psn.edu/dms201.

Interviewee: Nancy Kiyonaga
Director of Workforce and Occupation Planning
Government of the State of New York
E-mail: Nancy.Kiyonaga@cs.state.ny.us.

SUCCESSION PRACTICES IN THE MINNESOTA DEPARTMENT OF TRANSPORTATION

> *Case Introduction:* This case study describes succession practices in the Department of Transportation in the state of Minnesota. It consists of an interview with Wayne Brede, staffing manager for the Minnesota Department of Transportation, who had 12 years of professional experience in succession management when the discussion took place. The interview was conducted by Mark Bernhard.
>
> **Interviewer:**   Mark Bernhard
>
> **Interviewee:**   Wayne Brede

Mark Bernhard: **How does your agency define succession management?**

Wayne Brede: Well, we still call it succession planning, but it's the same thing. The focus is on our executive leadership group. Succession management focuses on the highest levels of management in the organization, which are the critical leadership jobs. Our succession plan is defined and is focused on senior executive management of this department.

Bernhard: **As a follow-up question, has any thought been given to looking at succession planning throughout the entire organization?**

Brede: Let me answer that, because you have another part to this first question where you ask about workforce planning (which we refer to as *strategic staffing*). Strategic staffing captures everybody else in the organization. Succession planning, like I said earlier, focuses on the senior leadership jobs of the organization—the top management group. Strategic staffing captures everybody else: the other managers, supervisors, professionals, everybody all the way down to the janitor really is part of strategic staffing. So we have both models running concurrently: We've got, like I said, succession planning on the senior executive side, and everybody else captured on the strategic staffing model. We have both models operating so we cover everything.

Bernhard: **There are steps you take for your senior executives. Is a similar process used with the strategic staffing, as well?**

Brede: Yes, the gap analysis concept is used where you have your demand side first. You identify your staffing needs, and contrast that with your supply and determine what your gaps are. Then you create gap strategies to address those gaps. So in that respect, both models are the same: They both use the gap analysis approach.

However, the *strategic staffing model* is much more detailed. It's a scenario-based model that incorporates five specific phases:

1. Data gathering, based on best-case/worst case scenario planning.
2. Input from senior management.
3. Local action planning.
4. Organization-wide data and strategy rollups.
5 Organization-wide action plan roll-out.

The succession plan is more global, more broadly defined. Number one, you've got a lot fewer jobs to deal with. In our case, we've got 35 positions in our succession plan, whereas with the strategic staffing model, we've got literally 4,800 jobs you're going to be looking at and thinking about in terms of how they are going to be used in the future. So it's almost like contrasting a macro model (which would be succession planning) with a micro model (which would be strategic staffing). So there is a whole lot more detail with strategic staffing than there is with succession planning.

One thing we've realized is that the strategic staffing model takes a long time to go through. I mentioned that there is the macromodel—succession planning, which is more of a broad review; and the micromodel—strategic staffing, which takes a lot of detailed review and time. However, the Minnesota Department of Transportation management is totally committed to the use of both models.

Bernhard: **Does your agency define** *human capital management* **and/or** *leadership development*?

Brede: The term "human capital management" is referenced as part of our workforce planning efforts. We do have a Leadership Academy here that is open to other than simply managers. We have supervisors and managers and high-level professionals who can be nominated into the Leadership Development Academy, because they are seen as leaders within their own category or area. We do have a formal Leadership Development Academy that we use to recognize certain people in the organization who have been identified as true leaders.

Bernhard: **Is attending the Leadership Academy wrapped into your strategic staffing process?**

Brede: Yes and no. There is not always a direct link there, but if there are people who have been identified as potential leaders or who have shown leadership potential, it is possible that they could be referred to the academy based on strategic staffing analysis or simply because the employee's supervisor feels it is something the employee would benefit from. It isn't always a direct link, but it could be. It depends—it's situational.

Bernhard: **What is the purpose of your agency's succession management program, and what led to the perceived need for it?**

Brede: The perceived need occurred back in the early 1990's, probably 1990, actually. A couple of our senior managers started to think about doing something more proactive with planning for senior-executive decisions. In addition, one of our top managers in our operations division suffered a massive heart attack and died unexpectedly. Of course, it threw this department into chaos, because there was really nobody in his department ready to step in and take over his job. He was one of the most critical people in the organization, and there had been no plans to groom someone to take over his position. So this situation reinforced the thinking of the senior managers, and further triggered the issue that the department needs to be proactive about protecting its critical positions and having people who are ready to step in. That kind of triggered a certain degree of interest. After that, I was asked to look into this thing called "succession planning." I attended a one-day workshop on it back in 1990 and I became enthralled with it. I thought it was a wonderful concept and something we needed to do, although at that time there wasn't really any public-sector model. It was all private sector. So I thought, *there has got to be a way we can adopt it to the public sector.* I went back and talked to my division director and convinced her that we should do this. She gave me the green light, so I went ahead and put together a proposal and brought it to our senior staff. They said to go ahead and do this. The purpose of our succession planning program is to make sure that all of our key critical positions, our key leadership jobs, are supported by internal talent so that they are there when we need them. So we never get caught in the same situation again, where we lose an employee who is in a critical job and we don't have anybody groomed to step in and take over that position. So, that's really the key feature there—to make sure we have people properly trained and properly groomed, available when we need them to step in when a critical position becomes open.

Bernhard: **What do you see are the primary differences and also challenges that are associated between succession planning in the public sector versus in the private sector?**

Brede: Well, the main one is the issue of pre-selection. We operate in a merit-system environment here, which means that, in theory anyway, every job should be filled competitively—that there shouldn't be any kind of positioning of a particular individual who has a stronger likelihood of getting a job over another. That was the issue for us: dealing with the concept of pre-selection, where you've got someone who is essentially the number-one person to step into the job and take the job, where there is no spirit of competition. That was the biggest concern, and probably still is to some degree. But at the same time, we recognize that, and we still use merit system principles here: When a position becomes open, even if it is part of the succession plan, we post the job for interest. We have an automated applicant tracking system, where people can go online and look at a particular position and can express their interest and submit a résumé for it.

Thus we have not lost track of the fact that we operate under a merit system, but we've been able to adopt or adapt. I should say our "succession plan," so we can still use succession planning and at the same time recognize the importance of using merit systems. Like I said, someone who is outside the succession plan process could apply or be considered, although, more than likely, there has been some type of internal review as part of succession planning and a decision has been made. There are probably one, two, or maybe three people who are the most-likely candidates to get the job. So, even though we have an automated applicant tracking process, the most likely situation will be that one of the people who was in the succession plan process will be the likely candidate. So to answer your question—that was kind of a long-winded answer—the issue for all public agencies when it comes to succession planning is the issue of pre-selection. And so you have to find a way to balance that and at the same time still be able to apply the major principles of succession planning.

Bernhard: **With the gap analysis and gap strategy and everything else you are doing, do you have people in mind, even though you have to use a competitive bidding?**

Brede: Well, we are a heavily unionized environment here—we have unions for everybody. The beauty of succession planning is that you are dealing with positions that are exempted from any kind of representation, so you don't have to do battle with the unions every time you want to fill a position. So, strategic staffing is exactly the opposite—you're dealing with contract language and seniority rules and all this good stuff. It is much more difficult to position people in terms of special assignment, because you have to follow the contract: the most senior employee gets the first shot at anything.

It's much more difficult to set up development planning for people who happen to be least-senior, so it's really tough to do the kinds of things that you'd like to do, because the contracts rule. You can still go through your gap analysis and still identify high-potential people, but then the issue becomes how you will develop them, given the contracts that say that the most-senior employee gets first shot at any kind of training or special assignments. It's really tough to do this effectively, so we do the best we can. We try to sit down with the unions and get a little leeway from them, but the difficult part in a heavily unionized environment is that you have very little flexibility as far as who you want to develop or give opportunities to, because contracts say you can't do that. You have to look at seniority all of the time. It's really a prohibitive situation for organizations that want to do true workforce planning or strategic staffing. It really makes it difficult. We do what we can.

Bernhard: **What measurable goals or objectives, if any, help to provide direction to your agency's succession management program?**

Brede: We have one primary goal, and that's essentially our success rate. We call it the "hit rate": Was the appointment of the individual to the position successful as a result of succession plan assessments? If you put somebody into the HR director's job who was identified in the succession plan as a high-potential person and the person works out, that is considered to be a "successful appointment." Obviously, if the person doesn't work out, then you've failed as an organization—you picked the wrong person, and now you have to live with the consequences. Our primary measure of success, like I said, is what is called the "hit rate." Of the 33 opportunities that we've had over the last probably ten years, 28 of the 33 positions that came open were filled through succession planning decisions. No one has yet to fail as far as making a wrong hiring decision. So far, our success rate is 100% in terms of the effectiveness of the person who was hired into one of the succession plan jobs. Obviously, the other piece is the feedback you get. When we go through our full cycle, we always do a post evaluation: We ask the employees who participated "How did you feel about it? What was the quality of your feedback? Did the feedback get to you in a timely manner?" It's almost like a survey of sorts, to kind of give us a reading as to whether or not the employees feel satisfied with the process, do the senior management feel satisfied with the outcomes—that kind of thing. But really, our bigger measure is that "hit rate."

Bernhard: **You've mentioned some of this, but what groups are targeted for participation in the program, and why were they selected?**

Brede: The eligible group here is the management group. All managers in the department are eligible to participate in the succession plan. Again, because we are talking about senior management jobs and we have a lot more flexibility in terms of filling positions, we decided to limit participation only to the management group. We've talked in the past about expanding that almost into a dual-career ladder situation where we start to identify critical high-level expert technical jobs that we would include in the succession plan. But if we do that, we introduce the dimension of a union, because our engineers are unionized here. So, thus far, the Department of Transportation has decided not to take that on right now. Like I said, we've limited it only to management jobs; that's the only applicant group we use right now. Everybody else, like I said before, falls into the strategic staffing model, but any manager can participate in the succession plan program.

Bernhard: **With these key technical positions and these issues you have with the union, when somebody is coming up in terms of retirement age, is one of your key questions how to preserve the institutional memory, once that person retires? Are there strategies that you employ in terms of trying to have people who are underneath that person be prepared to have that kind of knowledge to take over? How does that work?**

Brede: There are a couple of different ways we deal with this. It's a knowledge transfer issue. We may fill the position—we call it double-filling. If a person is going to be retiring in six months and has given notice, then we may post the job six months earlier than the actual retirement date, and go ahead and fill the position. Then we have some overlap there, like five months, maybe, where the new incumbent is working directly with the retiring incumbent. That's one way we do it. The other possibility would be to create a special-assignment opportunity for someone whom we think would be a strong candidate to succeed the retiree. We'd put that person in there six months to a year prior to the retirement, so that when the individual does retire, this other person will be in a good position to be appointed to the position. So it's either one of two ways: double-filling the job for a certain period of time, or creating a mobility opportunity for someone who can spend, like I said, six months to a year with the retiree and then be in a good position to get appointed to the job. But that really is a big issue. We could do a lot better job on this knowledge-transfer issue, because especially with our technical people, our engineering folks, those are the people who are the heart and soul of this organization: the 35-year techs who know everything there is to know about whatever it is they happen to be involved in—bituminous, concrete, whatever it happens to be. We don't do a very good job of capturing that. There is a lot of knowledge that leaves this department, and we need to do a much better job of trying to figure out how to capture that. A lot of times, the information is in their head and not on paper—tricks of the trade they've picked up over the last thirty-some years. We don't do a very good job of capturing it. We should think about having these guys document it in some kind of diary or manual, so that when they leave, at least it's captured somewhere. I would grade us a C on how we do in terms of capturing all that technical knowledge. We need to do a better job of that.

Bernhard: **Have you studied about or are you aware of other governmental agencies that do a better job of that, where you might be able to employ some of their principles?**

Brede: To me, there are some common-sense things to do, but when you're in HR, and especially when you're in an engineering organization, you don't have a lot of clout in terms of convincing these people to change their ways. I've got some pretty good ideas, and I think my ideas are probably best-practice ideas that other organizations are using, but it's more a matter of getting these people to do it. In a perfect world, they would have figured this out on their own and developed a shadowing program or a situation where you can transfer that knowledge from the departing employee to the successor. It's a matter of getting these people to do it.

Bernhard: **Does your agency use job competencies, defined as characteristics that describe successful performance, as a key foundation for the succession program? If so, explain how. If not, explain what is a key foundation for the program.**

Brede: One of the first things we did when we created the succession plan program was create core competencies. The core competencies became the foundation for succession planning, but eventually it became the foundation for our entire HR function here. We originally created them to support the succession plan effort, but about three or four years after we introduced succession planning, we did an HR reengineering. We incorporated the competencies into all the HR functions, so now our job descriptions are competency-based, our interview questions are competency-based, and everything we do is based on these seven competencies. We've been able to define them to fit into each occupational category. Within those seven competencies, you've got definers that would be used for a manager or a professional or a supervisor, all the way down to a janitor. At every level, we have been able to define behavioral statements that describe or help define each of the seven competencies. We are totally a competency-based organization.

Bernhard: **How is individual job performance assessed?**

Brede: We use a modified 360. In the past, we had a more basic evaluation where we'd have an employee do a self-assessment on scales, based on our organization's seven core competencies. Then we'd have the supervisor do their assessment of the employee, and it would be discussed only on those two avenues. We've allowed the employee to now include more than the supervisor for their assessment: a co-worker, a previous supervisor, a customer—any of those. It enriches the assessment feedback we get. We get more feedback from different sources. It's an optional thing. The employee doesn't have to do this, but the employee does have the option. It has been well received.

The minimal requirement is that the supervisor do the assessment. They have the option of including up to three more people. It has to be on observed behavior, going back for the past year and not something that occurred four years ago. It has to be relevant and no longer than one year ago.

Bernhard: **How is individual preparedness for promotion assessed?**

Brede: It's linked to the individual development plan we use here. Part of the planning process includes preparing the employee for upward movement and promotional opportunities. It would be up to the employee and the supervisor to determine what kinds of skill sets that employee needs in order to either move up within their current career cluster or move into another career cluster. It would be addressed through the development plan.

Bernhard: **How is that individual development plan carried out?**

Brede: It depends on the nature of the plan. Obviously, the employee needs to carry most of the weight of what's in there. There are regular checks to make sure the employee is following the development plan. The employee's supervisor is responsible for making sure that what is in that plan is being carried out. The supervisor has to conduct regular meetings with the employee, like check-in meetings, to make sure that what was agreed to in the development plan is being followed. And if it's not being followed, there needs to be some corrective action so that the employee gets back on track.

Bernhard: **The development plan is done on an annual basis?**

Brede: An annual review with follow-up meetings and progress meetings to make sure the employee is following the development plan.

Bernhard: **What activities, such as training, executive coaching, job rotation, and so forth, are used to build individual competence? How are those planned?**

Brede: Again, it's a product of the development plan. All the things you mentioned here we would use, whether it's on-the-job training or classroom training, executive coaching, job rotation (or what we call "mobility" assignments). We've used them. If you talk about succession planning, it's more a matter of the degree of investment the department wants to put into the employee. Obviously, there are limited resources in terms of sending somebody to an Ivy League school or a management academy or sending somebody off to a one-year mobility assignment with another state or federal agency. There's usually a cost involved. If the Department of Transportation sees a person as deserving of a major investment, it will show through in the development plan. The employee will be given exceptional but very limited opportunities, so the employee will know that he or she is being held in high regard, based on that development plan. If you have a manager who is a marginal performer and the department doesn't see any real potential for this person, there is not going to be too much in that development plan. If there is, it is mostly going to be subject to the *employee* trying to make it happen, as opposed to management. So, like I said, it comes out in the development plan, and it's a product of the employee's potential. If the employee has tremendous potential or is seen as someone the department is going to need in a relatively short time, they are going to be putting a lot of interesting things into that development plan. The flip side, as I said earlier, is that if the employee's value is seen as questionable or marginal, there will be very little in there in terms of exceptional opportunities, if any.

In addition to this, we've added a mobility exchange program. If I'm working in central office and I'm an engineering manager who wants to get experience in a field setting and in road design and I happen to know of a person in one of our field offices who would like to get experience in one of our central offices, what happens is that the two of us work out a swap. We fill each other's jobs for six months. We each get the experience, and no one gets hurt in terms of staffing. We cover for each other; even though I'm in a learning mode, at least I'm there to provide some type of input. We've been doing this only for a couple of years, but so far it's been pretty successful. We've had six exchanges, and all have been successful. Managers have been positive, and it may be expanded. This is another tool we've added to our folder. The employee initiates the request for an exchange; once there is a mutual agreement, then we help to work it out. All the managers need to support the succession plan in some way, shape, or form and participate in this program. There has yet to be any management resistance to this program.

Bernhard: **What is the budget for the succession planning program, if you know it?**

Brede: We've never had a dedicated budget for the succession plan program. I do this as part of my regular job. It's pretty much a pay-as-you-go initiative. From a formal standpoint, the budget is zero. There is a formal cost involved, and I have always gotten someone to pay for it—a division director or whomever. I've never had a real issue with getting funding, whether it be for someone to get some developmental experience or anything that involves succession planning as a whole. Even though there isn't dedicated money there, we are able to allocate money as we need it. We don't have a standing line item for this, but we do have the ability to get the money when we need it.

Bernhard: **How do you go about evaluating your succession plan program? Does it go back to the hit rate, and the fact that you've had 100% percent success?**

Brede: That's the more quantitative measure. Qualitative, of course, as mentioned earlier, is based on feedback. Does the senior management team see this as a useful management tool? And on the other hand, do the employees who participate in this process see it as a fair and equitable process? Do they feel as if they are being assessed properly? That kind of thing. So a lot of this is feedback driven, above and beyond the hit rate. So it's how do people feel about it and is it working for them. As I said, when we first did this thing, there was paranoia about what it would do for employee morale. Everybody was worried about what employees would do if they had a terrible experience with it, but things turned out fine. Another issue that was a concern was litigation: Would we be sued if we used preselection? We've done this for ten years and nothing has happened. We've never had that problem, and we've been very careful about confidentiality. It's all about just being smart and doing it the right way. We've had no problems with it. None. If it is done right and it is done fairly, it's a very effective tool.

Bernhard: **Can you describe just a little bit further the whole concept of a merit system, as it's used within the Minnesota Department of Transportation?**

Brede: It's not just the DOT. The State of Minnesota is a merit-system employer. It's by statute that we will use a competitive process in all positions, except political appointments. That to the extent possible, we will open up positions to the general public, for instance, so they have access to them. The whole idea is the spirit of competition: that there is no prejudice, no bias, and no positioning of people for jobs, and that to the extent possible, everyone has the opportunity to compete for our positions on a level playing field. That's kind of the concept behind the merit system. Civil Service is really the merit system.

Bernhard: **In addition to what you have mentioned, are there any other measures or metrics that are used to assess the success of your program?**

Brede: No, I think I've pretty much covered them.

I think it was successful for us and is a benchmark for other organizations. We were able to show that we could successfully adopt a private-sector staffing model into the public sector without too much consternation. So, I think that's one of the biggest things that I like about it: we were able to make it work here. And yet it makes so much sense to do it. It's not rocket science—anybody can do this! It's just a matter of making sure that you have continued commitment to the process, and that you're doing it fairly equitably and don't lose track of the value. It's a very valuable management tool. It's not an HR tool—it's a *management* tool. All we do is help managers use it. And as I said, it makes so much sense to be proactive when it comes to protecting your critical leadership jobs. That's what we've done; we've been able to protect each and every position. We should never, long after I'm gone, have to worry about the unexpected disruption of a critical position that comes open that no one thought about and that there was no one to step into. That should never happen here; we're always at a high-level of alertness, because of the process. We know when people are retiring and we know when we need to think about new initiatives that may impact succession planning. So we've got all of this stuff going in a proactive light, and I think that's really a good thing. I hope other organizations pick up on it—I think they have. In the last five years, especially, I've been bombarded with questions from people in other states, whether it's federal, state, or city, who've heard about this model and want to learn how to do it. I've talked to them, and they're kind of surprised at how relatively easy it is to do.

Bernhard: **Your intent was to create a model for identifying essential executive-level positions, and then to develop internal candidates or recruit externally to support those positions. When this started in 1990, a critical employee had a heart attack. If something like that were to happen again and you felt within the department that you did not have the internal people in place to take over that position, would you solicit résumés, or find someone from the outside who could take a position like that? How does that work?**

Brede: We usually have at least one person internally, anyway. We have this rule of three: If we were to have an unexpected death or something like that, we do have at least one person who could step in and at least maintain the position. They may not be the strongest person in the world, but they would certainly be equipped to handle the position in a maintenance mode, if nothing else. So if the DOT decided that it was not the long-term answer, we would put this person in the position as long as we need them. In the meantime, we would go out and do some recruitment, depending on the position—most likely regional recruitment. I don't see us doing national recruitment anymore, but probably regional. We use a résumé-based applicant tracking system here called ResuMix. We'd go in there and post the job profile, and see how the résumés match up. Then we would do some fairly quick interviewing, and find somebody who could do the job long-term. But we do have, like I said, at least one person for each and every position, so we would not be caught in a situation where we have nobody. I've always had this dream of sitting down at a huge table with other federal, state, and county people who are involved in this, and talking about what works for us and for them.

Hopefully, someone is going to see a need for that someday, and try to create some kind of forum or coalition where practicing agencies can come together, share information, and help other agencies get started. Some kind of a national forum would be great.

Contact Information

Interviewer: Mark Bernhard
Director of Continuing and Professional Education
Virginia Tech University
Blacksburg, Virginia 24061
Phone: 540-231-4682

Interviewee: Wayne Brede was the staffing manager and workforce planning director for the Minnesota Department of Transportation (Mn/DOT) at the time of this interview, serving as project manager for the initial introduction of formal succession planning at Mn/DOT in the early 1990s. He consults on succession planning and strategic staffing.
Phone: 651-335-0434
E-mail: wayne@laumeyerhr.com

SUCCESSION PRACTICES IN THE PENNSYLVANIA DEPARTMENT OF EDUCATION

Case Introduction: This case study examines in detail the approach the Pennsylvania Department of Education has adopted with respect to succession management. It consists of an interview with Jan Pricer, former chief of the Division of Position Management for the Pennsylvania Department of Education.

Tracy Brundage: **How does the Pennsylvania Department of Education define succession management, workforce planning, human capital management, and leadership development?**

Jan Pricer: Let me first talk about how the Department of Education defines succession management and workforce planning, and I will address leadership development separately. I'll also touch on some aspects of what the Commonwealth has been doing to address these issues.

The Department's leadership was very concerned about ensuring the continuation of essential services, so the Human Resources staff developed a plan for personnel in critical areas so people could pass on critical competencies and institutional and program knowledge to their successors. The plan calls for regular annual meetings between the Human Resources staff and all senior managers, which would be bureau directors and above, to review current and proposed functions and programs. This process includes discussing (1) what programs and staff are presently in place; (2) what personnel might conceivably be retiring; and (3) any new or anticipated program initiatives within the next year.

The intent is to help managers plan how to preserve essential program knowledge when people leave, to ensure that PDE can provide an uninterrupted continuation of services. Part of that planning is to make sure there is a way to capture any specialized knowledge or competencies that might be needed for projected program initiatives over the coming year.

The next important aspect of the Department's succession management-planning focuses on leadership development. The Commonwealth has had a number of leadership development programs in operation. One that I think is the best is what is called the Leadership Development Institute (LDI). This program was set up ten or more years ago. At that time, the Commonwealth had identified the fact that the top management positions tended to be predominantly filled by men. In response to this, the Commonwealth developed a program to target women who demonstrated potential for being senior managers. The Governor's Office of Administration asked each agency to nominate from one to two individuals to participate in the LDI. Selected candidates went through a year-long development program to help them develop or hone management skills and to understand broad program goals. Another objective was to help candidates develop and expand networking skills. It has been very effective, and has resulted in an increasing number of women becoming managers. In Education, we have a number of LDI graduates in management positions. For example, one of the deputies is a graduate of LDI. The director of the Bureau of Human Resources is a graduate. Diana Hershey, my successor as division chief, is a graduate of LDI. So we had a lot of people move into senior management through this LDI. And that same pattern was repeated in other agencies.

One of the best features of the eight-month program is how the graduates of the program serve as mentors for the people who follow them. The graduates also serve as a support network for other LDI graduates. I know a good many people who went through the program and have been impressed with the degree the program has helped them hone their leadership skills. I also like the way LDI graduates meet on a regular basis. They keep in touch with the new people who are going through the program, and they help to mentor those people. If someone new is going through a problem or needs assistance, they know that they can contact someone who has been through the program for help. It is something like what has occurred in the teaching profession, which I'm familiar with since I'm an ex-teacher. When I first started teaching, there was no mentoring program. I was thrown into the classroom and I had to sink or swim. That's no longer the case. A number of years ago, the Department directed that school districts implement specific mentoring programs so that new teachers are now paired with experienced teachers. New teachers have someone to go to to help them develop. The LDI program is a similar kind of program, and it has been very effective.

Brundage: **What is the purpose of PDE's succession management program? What is its scope, and what led to the perceived need for it?**

Pricer: The purpose of the Department's succession management program is to address the concerns of senior leadership, who recognized the need for continuity of services. This was a concern of the staff in the Governor's Office of Administration as well. The Commonwealth HR community recognized that we were looking at a potential exodus of a large number of people, the baby boomers, from Commonwealth employment, starting in the early and mid 2000s. You almost have to look at what happened in the Commonwealth in terms of employment from a historical perspective. The late 1960s and early 1970s saw a tremendous expansion in the role of state government in general and there were a lot of people brought into state government. In fact, there were more people employed by the Commonwealth as a result of this expansion than at any other time. The total number of Commonwealth employees has since been reduced, a trend which began in the 1980s and continued through the 1990s, but you still had a large number of people who came into government in the early 1970s, primarily the baby boomers, who stayed and made careers in Commonwealth service.

The Commonwealth HR staff regularly prepares statistical studies. These reports over the last few years indicate that a large percentage of people are approaching retirement eligibility. As a result of this trend, the Commonwealth started to encourage agencies to do succession planning. Some agencies began doing succession planning earlier. Labor and Industry was one of the agencies that developed a very strong and highly effective succession management program. The Department of Education, however, was not as quick to get on board because the Department during this time was working with a lot of changes that various administrations wanted to make with respect to schools. So the primary focus of the agency was school reform. It was only within the last three or four years that the Department started to address the succession management issues that would result from the large number of people who would be retiring. So we looked at what other agencies had done. We also looked at what was done in some private sector areas, but there were many differences between the private sector and the Commonwealth. A lot of the private-sector programs weren't applicable in a Civil Service environment, so when we eventually did develop a program, we needed to structure it for a Civil Service environment. Those were the parameters we had to work with.

We put together a program similar to Labor and Industry's program, which we streamlined in an effort to make it easier for our management to use. The Department of Education has a substantially smaller overall complement and a smaller number of HR professionals. The staffing and structure of the Department's workforce is also different from it and other agencies, like the Pennsylvania Department of Transportation. What works for the large agencies would not work for an agency as small as Education. We customized a program to fit the more-collegial approach that Education operates under.

Brundage: **What measurable goals or objectives help to provide direction to your succession management program? How do you maintain measurable goals or objectives as administrations change?**

Pricer: In part, the goals and objectives change depending on the administration. But they have also become more clearly defined, with the recent changes in the retirement law and in the collective bargaining agreements. At one point, if you retired, you did not have to pay for health benefits; your health benefits were paid. The employees did not have to contribute anything. The Commonwealth is no different from other entities where there has been a tremendous increase in costs for medical health benefits. So the Commonwealth had to negotiate agreements with the unions to have employees pay a share of health and medical costs, but they structured this agreement so that it would take effect in 2005. This gave people an option: If you retired before July 1, 2005, you did not have to pay for your benefits, but if you retired after that date, you were required to pay toward your benefits.

Of course, when senior management negotiated those contracts, they recognized that the new parameters would probably cause a lot of their essential people to retire before the effective change date. And it was for this reason that the Governors' Office of Administration directed all agencies to start planning how they would replace these people, which was the impetus for big changes across the Commonwealth. Agencies that had not been looking at succession-management planning now began to actually think through what they were going to do, and the Department of Education was among these agencies. The fact that we were facing so many retirements helped our HR staff convince the leadership at the time to put into place the succession planning model that exists today. The Department of Education still uses the model we developed in 2004.

Brundage: **Can you describe in more detail how the succession management model at PDE works, and how the Leadership Development Institute fits into the model? In other words, is the Department focused on preparing folks already on board to take on additional responsibilities through professional development programs like the LDI program, or has there been some focus on trying to recruit from the outside for some of those openings when people retire?**

Pricer: The kind of program the Department's HR people developed was focused on (1) providing managers with data identifying key staffing areas they should look at, and (2) meeting with those managers on a regular basis to discuss these areas. The HR staff did statistical studies to identify areas where retirements were likely to occur and began to target classifications or occupational categories where there were people who were currently eligible or within one, two, three, or four years of retirement. The HR staff then developed charts to show senior managers, bureau directors, and deputies which employees in their organizational areas were of a particular category, how many within that category were eligible to retire, and what percentage would be eligible to retire within one, two, three, or four years. And we prepared this information for each of our managers so that when they were doing their budgetary planning they would know, for example, that they might have two Social Studies advisors on staff who were eligible for retirement within the next two or three years. They could then prepare a budget plan with a potential hiring need in mind.

The HR staff would then meet face to face with each manager at the beginning of the year, before managers start their budgetary planning, to provide managers, bureau directors, and deputies with demographic statistics and then discuss in depth what was potentially likely to occur in their respective areas. The discussions always involved how the HR staff could help with succession management issues. They would take a close look at the occupational class specifications, the occupation standards, Civil Service examination requirements, and anything else that might be relevant for those managers who might need to find people to fill slots.

Brundage: **What groups are targeted for participation in this program, and why?**

Pricer: The groups we targeted were those for whom (1) the likelihood of significant turnover was great; and/or (2) turnover would most affect agency goals and objectives. We also targeted groups where we had the greatest problem with recruitment. The Department of Education is burdened with trying to recruit professional educators at a time when, to be perfectly frank, Department salaries are not necessarily competitive with the salaries those individuals can command in the marketplace. We can't meet those salaries. They got better salaries as teachers, or in the public sector, but not necessarily in the Commonwealth sector. The Department of Education is a relatively small agency, but it has a large statewide mission: It covers 501 school districts, as well as area vocational and technical schools and public and private libraries. It covers private schools. It covers colleges. It covers the gamut of education, private and public. So our advisors have to come into the Department with a full functioning knowledge of education. You can't take someone who just graduated from a teacher preparation and educational program and bring them into the Department, simply because the Department doesn't have enough people to permit those new people to understudy for years. When you have two statewide advisors in language, both those people have to be able to deal with a myriad of issues. They have to be fully functioning, full-professional-level individuals. So in order to attract top people, we had to develop non-salary methods for attraction. Those are some of the issues we were dealing with in our meetings. We focused on areas critical to the Department's mission or areas where there were a small number of professionals whose absence would severely impact the continuity of services.

Brundage: **Some organizations use job competencies, characteristics that describe successful performance, as a key foundation for the succession program. What is the key foundation for the succession management program at PDE?**

Pricer: The Commonwealth requires agencies to have competencies for all positions. In addition, because we function as part of a Civil Service environment, potential new hires must pass a test to determine their capacity to do the job. This means that we are required to have job competencies and a thorough knowledge of specific job skills so we can quantify abilities. This performance-focused structure is the foundation of the testing process. From the onset, the HR staff ties position tasks to knowledge, skills, and abilities and the development of assessment processes for professional positions, which means there is a clear correlation between job competencies, performance standards, and employee selection. In addition, managers are strongly encouraged to develop written performance standards and discuss these with each employee on an annual basis as part of their employee performance review, and also as appropriate throughout the year. When someone is hired, they are given a copy of their position description, as well as a copy of their performance standards if they have been developed for that position. So they know their job duties and how the performance standards are associated with those duties.

Brundage: **You had indicated that the managers are meeting to give regular feedback. Can you explain in more detail how individual job performance is assessed?**

Pricer: Job performance and job competencies are integrally related. Let me go back to the succession planning model the Department put in place. When the HR staff meets with a manager, one of the factors they look at are the existing performance standards. Based on these standards, they determine if there are performance problems. We don't have a systematic approach for problems that arise, but we do work with our managers in coordination with our Labor Relations analyst to develop and refine performance standards and to develop performance improvement plans. Sometimes the performance standards for a particular position will no longer be appropriate because the position has evolved or the job duties have changed, so the performance standards need to be updated. This happens when you have a change in management: A new division chief, a new bureau director, or a new supervisor comes in and changes what needs to be done or what is expected. In an agency where our managers are supervisors (and they are working supervisors, in the majority of cases), they don't have the day-to-day time to focus on strictly management things. They have to be making programmatic decisions, and might not have a chance to look at performance standards that were developed by someone else. They may not have gone over standards every year to make certain the standards are updated. So when the HR Position Management staff provides the senior managers with information on performance standards, they would also identify where performance standards might need to be updated. I should also add that while managers meet with each of their employees for an annual Employee Performance Review, there are instances when it is necessary to meet more than once during the course of a year. New employees, for example, are on probation for the first six months, and must go through a formal performance evaluation before they are granted regular status. Employees involved in new initiatives or projects may also need to meet with their managers on a more regular basis to discuss an evolving set of job expectations. When you are looking at job performance in a Civil Service environment, it is critical to have these kinds of discussions. If an employee is performing poorly, the manager will work with Labor Relations to develop a performance improvement plan. Once that plan is in place, the manager will meet with the employee every three to four months to make sure the employee is making progress.

Brundage: **How does promotion work in a Civil Service system? How do you assess whether or not an individual is a good candidate for promotion? If someone wants to apply for a position, do they need to take a Civil Service test? Do they take the test before, or after they are promoted?**

Pricer: Different agencies have different philosophies with respect to how positions are filled or how they identify likely candidates for promotion. The Department of Education has historically encouraged its employees to take tests. That is the method we use to determine who is ready for a promotion. Our employees understand that if they want to be considered for a new position, they need to take the test for that position. We do recognize, of course, that there are times when you need to look at someone from a non-test perspective, but I'll treat that separately.

When managers conduct an Employee Performance Review, they fill out an annual performance evaluation document, which contains a section for the manager to write down what the employee can do to improve their current level of performance and what the manager can do to help. So each Employee Performance Review contains a plan for the professional growth and development of the employee that clearly defines job performance expectations. The process is the same for every position, every evaluation in the Department. Of course, writing down a plan is only the beginning. There are two different things that can happen with respect to individual growth and development. One way employees can develop professionally is by moving to a vacancy via a promotion. The other occurs when the duties and responsibilities of an individual change. In that case, the position may be reclassified, which is not technically a promotion. In some instances, a manager will ask an employee to learn new skills and acquire new abilities, and once this happens, new duties and responsibilities reflecting the new skill sets are assigned to the position. Since the employee is already in the position, the position is simply upgraded to a higher level.

Sometimes a manager or an employee approaches HR to discuss an employee's growth options. If it is a manager, he or she might say, "I've got some really good people and I've got this work that needs to be done. Can you help us structure a program whereby I can assign additional responsibilities to this person to maximize that person's abilities?" When this happens, the HR staff will sit down with both the manager and the employee to best identify how to expand the position so that it can be reclassified. The Department also encourages employees interested in professional development to seek the advice of the HR staff. The HR staff is committed to working with every employee. We help them develop a growth plan that identifies what tests they need to take and what training avenues they need to pursue in order to get where they want to go. We also ask them if they want to continue working with their manager. If they say yes, we bring the manager in and discuss what he or she can do. Naturally, it is the manager's responsibility to say whether or not they want to assign additional work to an employee. But if they are agreeable, then we work with both the employee and the manager to bring about the necessary changes.

Brundage: **You were talking about instances where a manager identifies potential high performers and encourages them to grow, or where an individual wishes to pursue professional growth. But how is individual development planning carried out in general? In other words, how do you go from developing a plan for professional growth to providing the training that will facilitate this growth?**

Pricer: All agencies are required to complete an annual training plan. Our training officer goes out on an annual basis with a training needs survey for everyone in the agency. He asks program managers and supervisors to identify the training needs of their staff. He also asks employees what kind of professional development training they want. Once our training officer surveys the Department, he submits an annual agency training plan to the Office of Administration. From that point forward, training can occur in one of two ways: The Commonwealth looks at the training plans from all agencies and departments to see if there are any common training needs. Once they determine that there is a general training need, such as inter-personal skills training, they will contract with a training provider to develop the program. In addition to this kind of general training, the HR staff in the Department will develop any specialized agency-specific training that is needed. For example, many people in the Department need to do Internet searches on a variety of topics, including curriculum, special education, current technical education, or the latest developments in educational assessment methodologies. Our training officer worked with the staff of the State Library, who are experts in conducting Internet searches, and identified a continuing need to hone staff's ability to do Internet searches. They then set up training for twice a year on how to conduct effective Internet searches. That is just one example of the kind of specialized professional-development training programs the Department develops for our staff.

Brundage: **What other strategies or methods, such as executive coaching, mentoring, or job rotation, does the Department employ to build individual competence?**

Pricer: The answer to that question is that it varies, depending on the occupation and the agency. It does occur a great deal in the Human Resources area. Let me talk about job rotation first. The Commonwealth has in place an HR management training program for new hires with a bachelor's degree. It is an intensive year-long internship program. Trainees rotate through different agencies and different HR program areas to study the Commonwealth's personnel practices in operation. They may spend three months working in the Department of Education, where they are assigned to work in position management or labor relations. They may then go to the Pennsylvania Department of Transportation and work in personnel services or benefits. And so on. The Commonwealth also has what is called the Pennsylvania Management Associate Program, coordinated through the Governor's Office, for people with a master's degree. These people also rotate through different agencies in various specific training programs in a wide range of management areas, such as HR, budgeting, information systems, and planning analysis. When they complete this program, these people are then placed in management positions. This kind of rotational training is an example of what the Commonwealth is doing with respect to preparing future leaders.

Brundage: **What about executive coaching or mentoring?**

Pricer: It really depends on the agency. In the Department of Education, when senior managers identify individuals who have management potential, they provide mentoring and coaching on an informal yet structured basis. The precise nature of the mentoring depends on the manager. Some managers send key personnel to out-service training. Some develop in-service programs. Most managers will have key staff coordinate new projects or give them team leader responsibilities to help them develop their leadership capabilities. The Department has been doing this kind of executive coaching as long as I have been with the Commonwealth.

Brundage: **What is the budget for the succession planning program? And how is the program evaluated? What measures or metrics are used to determine success?**

Pricer: Budgetary management is a separate process. Within the Department, our budget management director and our HR management director are both part of the Department's Office of Administration. Both of those bureau directors are intimately involved in succession-management planning. Our budget director is aware of critical areas with respect to the budget where succession planning is needed, but the overall budget management is controlled by the Governor's Office. In other words, the Governor's Office determines what monies are in the budget for succession-management planning and what can and cannot be done with respect to those monies. The critical issue here is that succession-management planning involves budgeting for new staff. The Commonwealth is under a tight complement control structure, and it is very difficult to increase this complement. Pennsylvania governors historically have been reluctant to increase the size of the state government's workforce. It is difficult for a politician to run for re-election when they have already greatly increased the complement of state workers under their watch. As a political strategy, that would be like running for President and saying that you are going to increase taxes. You just don't do that. Of course, the HR community as well as agency budget directors present the Governor's Office with proposals to provide for succession-management planning, and these proposals are discussed with the Governor's Budget Secretary, but an agency cannot increase monies for succession planning or for any initiative without approval from the Governor's Office. Most agencies, including the Department of Education, have had to find alternative means to provide for succession-management planning that fall within the Commonwealth's budgetary parameters. These alternative means are not always successful.

Brundage: **Does the Department have any measures or metrics to assess the success of its succession-management planning strategies?**

Pricer: Not really, because the budget drives everything. When a governor takes office, he or she must address a diverse range of state needs within strict fiscal constraints. State resources are limited, and are in fact augmented by a significant amount of federal monies. In the Department of Education, a large number of our positions are driven by and funded by federal funds. The objective of most administrations is to drive as much federal money out into the field as possible in order to provide as many services to taxpayers as possible. We are public stewards; that is our responsibility. If the Department gets several million dollars under a certain federal appropriation, most of it will go to fund programs. The goal is to minimize the amount of money retained by the Department for

administrative purposes. Of course, this overall goal has made it
more difficult to create an effective succession-management process.
But we work within the budget constraints we have to plan effectively for the future.

Contact Information

Interviewer: Tracy Brundage, Managing Director of
Workforce Development and Continuing Education
at Pennsylvania College of Technology

E-mail: tbrundag@pct.edu

Interviewee: Jan Pricer, former Chief of
the Division of Position Management
for the Pennsylvania Department of Education

E-mail: pricers@verizon.net

INTRODUCING TECHNICAL (NOT MANAGERIAL) SUCCESSION PLANNING

Case Introduction: This article introduces technical succession planning, which is intended to preserve institutional memory. Authors William J. Rothwell and Stan Poduch explain necessary considerations relative to technical succession planning and conclude with a case study about the Pennsylvania Department of Transportation's approach.

What will we do if we lose our seat of government? Do we have sufficient bench strength outside the capital to continue government operations? Sad to say, the potential exists to lose entire cities like Washington, D.C. or New York to dirty bombs, nuclear weapons, or other forms of terrorist attack. Cities remote from those well-known locations are not immune, either, as the Oklahoma City bombing illustrated. It is not just the potential for the tragic loss of life that we must face, but also the potential loss of massive amounts of knowledge.

What will happen when the baby boomers start to head out to retirement and a life of leisure? Are we prepared to let all of that know-how and experience in government operations walk out the door? Who will be left to keep operations running smoothly? In either case, the knowledge bucket of government is not very secure. There are leaks.

Say the phrase *succession planning* and most government executives will probably think first of executive replacement planning—that is, planning for senior-level backups. But succession planning actually means far more than mere executive replacement planning. As we have explained elsewhere, succession planning goes beyond simple replacement planning. It is proactive and attempts to ensure the continuity of leadership by cultivating talent from within the organization through planned development activities. It can properly be regarded as one way to slash the time required to fill vacancies with qualified people at any level. That issue is increasingly important, as stressed-out workers in lean-staffed, smart-sized agencies attack more work than they can handle. This concept addresses the question posed earlier: *Who is left and capable to keep operations running smoothly?*

Succession planning is not just about finding replacements. It is also about developing talent and building sufficient bench strength. More than that, it is also about preserving the fruits of the organization's experience—its institutional memory—as embodied in the heads of veteran performers at all levels, who possess specialized knowledge about what needs to be done to make government run efficiently and effectively; how that is done; and what has worked well and not so well in the past. These issues have to do with technical succession planning, which is based on the reality that experienced technical and professional experts in government possess specialized knowledge gained from experience that is essential to the continuity of government operations.

But what is technical succession planning, and how does it differ from managerial succession planning? Why is technical succession planning important? How can technical succession planning be carried out? What additional sources and references will shed light on the issue of technical succession planning? And is there a government agency that has actually done such planning? This article addresses these and related questions.

What is Technical Succession Planning, and how does it differ from Managerial Succession Planning?

> *Succession planning:* Any effort designed to ensure the continued effective performance of an organization, division, department, or work group by making provision for the development, replacement, and strategic application of key people over time.

Of special note in this definition is the word *key.* Who are key people, and what makes them key?

Traditionally, the first thing that occurs to leaders when thinking of key people is the top tier of the organization chart. Those occupying the top of the organization chart are the senior-most people in the command structure. They are key because their positions give them the authority to make decisions, mobilize resources, and direct others to take action.

But in reality, that understanding of "key" refers to those who are key to management action. Planning for the development of such leaders focuses on the vertical hierarchy of the organization as shown on an organization chart. Focusing on developing people for leadership at each successive vertical level of the organization chart thus amounts to managerial succession planning.

But what about *across* the organization chart, rather than *up* the chart? Planning for the development of people who are key to the continued operation of the organization—people with the specialized knowledge to perform—centers on the horizontal continuum of the organization, as shown on its organization chart. Technical succession planning is focusing on developing people to preserve and enhance *specialized knowledge,* learned from experience, across the horizontal level of the organization chart.

Understood in that way, technical succession planning is defined as:

> **Any effort designed to ensure the continued effective perform- ance of an organization, division, department, or work group by making provision for distilling, preserving, maintaining, and communicating the fruits of the organization's institutional memory and unique experiences over time.**

It is about capturing, preserving, and communicating information about what it takes for the organization to achieve success in its operations, and toward its objectives, over time. To this end, technical succession planning is a form of knowledge management, and it requires communication to both the givers and the receivers of valuable experiences. The organization becomes a knowledge community. Knowledge is not some abstraction, and knowledge management is not some vague buzzword in quest of meaning.

> ***Knowledge*** reflects what the organization has learned from experi- ence. ***Knowledge management*** in this context means preserving and passing on to successors what has been learned from experience, to avoid having to reinvent the wheel.

Why is Technical Succession Planning important?

Most observers of the contemporary business world acknowledge that people are more than just agents who carry out the daily work. It is what people know and what they have learned from experience that provides a foundation for the corporate culture, the organization's institutional memory, and efforts to improve the efficiency and effectiveness of governmental operations through innovative applications of creative ability. In short, it is the human capacity to make new discoveries that leads to quantum leaps in productivity improvement. It is also creativity that, in the private sector, leads to the discovery of new products, new markets, new ways to serve customers, and even economic development. It is the creativity of human beings that sets them apart from machines, and this is the real source of competitive advantage for businesses.

Technical succession planning is important, then, because it acknowledges that what people carry around in their heads—their so-called tacit knowledge—is an essential starting point for carrying out any government mission. It is also an essential starting point for applying creativity that will lead to quantum leaps in productivity improvement. Without knowledge of what has been done in the past, it is impossible to know how to deal with present issues or future plans. Without knowledge of the past, people in organizations spin their wheels trying to remember or reinvent routine operations. Like Sisyphus in the ancient Greek legend who was forever doomed to roll a boulder up a mountain only to watch in frustration as it rolled down again, organizational members who do not remember the past are doomed to repeat it.

Many government agencies face the very real threat of losing a high percentage of their most-experienced workers to retirement. (And that ignores the potential for sudden death or disability of individuals, or the threat of terrorist attack.) The problem is growing more severe in some jurisdictions, where hiring freezes prevent the infusion of new blood so there will be people to learn how to carry the torch of government operations into the future. Perhaps as much as half of federal, state, county, and city government workforces are nearing retirement. That poses a very real threat to national security at all levels. After all, if the most-experienced people leave and no concerted effort is made to capture and pass on what they have learned, then who will remember how to run the schools and universities; fix roads and bridges; repair sewer lines and keep water running; collect the taxes; protect the public from diseases; issue government entitlement checks; put out fires; solve the crimes and catch the criminals; and do whatever else government does to promote the general welfare and provide for the national defense?

It is worth noting that outsourcing government operations is no solution to the problem. Outsourcing might help get the work done, but the reality is that some knowledge of work processes must be preserved in agencies so that someone knows how to watchdog the vendors. In other words, somebody in the agency must know enough about past agency operations and present executive initiatives *to ensure that the public is getting value for the money spent on outsourced operations.*

How can Technical Succession Planning be carried out?

Technical succession planning is not carried out in the same way as managerial succession planning, for the simple reason that the focus of attention is different. Managerial succession is about finding and developing the "right" people to place in the "right" positions and in the "right" locations at the "right" times to achieve the right or strategically-important objectives. The emphasis is really on the people. Existing roadmaps for managerial succession planning center attention on clarifying what characteristics and competencies people will need in the future to perform effectively, and how to select or develop people to achieve strategic objectives. The biggest challenges facing decision makers in managerial succession are three-fold: (1) avoiding temptations to clone current job incumbents when future conditions might call for different skills; (2) erroneously assuming that successful performance at one layer of the organization's hierarchy automatically guarantees success at higher levels; and (3) ensuring accountability of individuals and their organizational superiors for developing talent, not just handling daily work or managing daily crises.

In contrast, technical succession planning is about isolating, distilling, and transmitting the right information to people at the right times to ensure the continuity of operations, and to provide a foundation for future improvements. The emphasis is really on the what: the implicit and explicit experiences of running a process or operation. The biggest challenge in technical succession planning is the so-called knowledge-transfer problem, referring to the difficulties of transmitting the fruits of experience to successors. Those setting out to address technical succession planning must isolate relevant knowledge, distill it, preserve it, and find practical ways to transmit it in useful forms to those needing it when they need it. In short, how do you know what is important, and how do you sidestep concerns from the people who possess that knowledge that capturing it will not be used against them to replace them or eliminate your need for them?

To conduct technical succession planning, consider following this roadmap:

Step 1. *Make the commitment.* Decide that there is need to identify and capture specialized knowledge and institutional memory before those people who possess that knowledge are lost to government service through retirement, disability, or death.

Step 2. *Clarify which work processes are key to the agency's mission.* Map key work processes that are essential to achieving the agency's mission. Clarify what results are desired and how they can be achieved.

Step 3. *Clarify who possesses specialized knowledge* about those work processes gained from experience. Examine the workforce assigned to each work process to identify individuals who possess, through experience and performance, the most valuable knowledge about the work. Who are the in-house experts on each critical work process, and how do we know they are experts?

Step 4. *Clarify how those work processes are performed* by those possessing specialized knowledge. Engage in a planned approach to tapping institutional memory and institutional wisdom. Use planned or unplanned approaches. Examples of planned approaches include the *critical incident method* (in which experienced performers are asked to tell stories about the challenges of the past and how they addressed them), *storyboarding* (in which specific events are flowcharted to isolate the root causes of problems), and *DACUM charting* (in which experienced performers are asked to build work profiles that describe what they do on a daily basis, how they do it, and what they have learned about performing it based on experience). Examples of unplanned approaches include mentor programs (in which people are asked to share experiences) and shadowing programs (in which less-experienced people are assigned to watch more-experienced ones). An agency wide, planned on-the-job training process can be used, too.

Step 5. *Capture and distill specialized knowledge* about those work processes. Examine the information collected in Step Four and analyze it by theme or by symptom of a problem.

Step 6. *Consider who needs specialized knowledge and how to maintain and transmit it to ensure the efficient and effective continuity of operations.* Once the institutional memory of the most-experienced performers has been tapped, it must be captured. Formal ways to do that include use of electronic expert systems, which catalog a problem by its symptoms and then provide suggested solutions. Informal ways include sponsoring training programs and setting up brown bag lunches to discuss the past.

Step 7. *Continuously assess knowledge gaps and evaluate the action strategies taken to address them and the results achieved.* Assess individuals against the knowledge requirements for the work processes; periodically examine what steps are being taken to preserve and transmit institutional memory; and evaluate what results have been gained from these efforts.

These steps are depicted in the roadmap illustrated in Figure 17-1. The roadmap is intended to make it easy to conceptualize what key information should be captured, distilled, preserved, and transmitted. It also permits a government executive to think about how well his or her agency is presently conducting technical succession planning. Use the questionnaire in Table 17-1 to rate the efforts in your own agency.

Figure 17-1
A Roadmap to Guide Technical Succession Planning

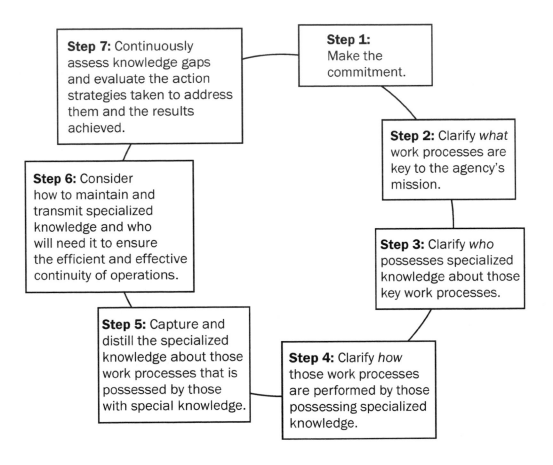

Step 7: Continuously assess knowledge gaps and evaluate the action strategies taken to address them and the results achieved.

Step 1: Make the commitment.

Step 2: Clarify *what* work processes are key to the agency's mission.

Step 6: Consider how to maintain and transmit specialized knowledge and who will need it to ensure the efficient and effective continuity of operations.

Step 3: Clarify *who* possesses specialized knowledge about those key work processes.

Step 5: Capture and distill the specialized knowledge about those work processes that is possessed by those with special knowledge.

Step 4: Clarify *how* those work processes are performed by those possessing specialized knowledge.

Table 17-1

A Checklist for Assessing Agency Technical Succession Planning

Directions: Use this checksheet to assess the status of the agency's technical succession planning. For each issue listed and described in the left column below, assess the current status by marking a number in the right column. Use this scale:

1 = Not at all adequate; 2 = Hardly adequate; 3 = Adequate; 4 = Good; 5 = Excellent

Assessing the Agency's Technical Succession Planning Process

	Not at all				Excellent
Decide how well the agency is doing in each area.	1	2	3	4	5
1. *Making the commitment* (Deciding that there is need to identify and capture specialized knowledge and institutional memory before those people who possess that knowledge leave government service because of retirement, disability, or death)	1	2	3	4	5
2. *Clarifying **what** work processes are key to the agency's mission*	1	2	3	4	5
3. *Clarifying **who** possesses specialized knowledge about the work processes*	1	2	3	4	5
4. *Clarifying **how** those work processes are performed by the best and most-experienced performers*	1	2	3	4	5
5. *Capturing and distilling the specialized knowledge about those work processes*	1	2	3	4	5
6. *Considering how to maintain and transmit specialized knowledge and who needs it to ensure the efficient and effective continuity of operations*	1	2	3	4	5
7. *Continuously assessing knowledge gaps and evaluating the action strategies taken to address them and the results achieved*	1	2	3	4	5

Scoring

Add up your scores and place them in the box at right

Interpreting the Score

If your score is 35–25: Congratulations. Your effort is pretty good.
If your score is 24–19: The agency needs to devote some time and attention to the issue.
If your score is 18–0 : Stop. Do not pass "go" and do not collect $200. Focus attention on the issue immediately!

What additional sources and references are there that can shed light on Technical Succession Planning?

A short article like this cannot do complete justice to an effort as far-reaching as technical succession planning. If you would like to pursue the topic, you will no doubt want to know where to go next to discover more about succession planning. See the Recommended Resources section in the book for an annotated list of sources that will take you through a chronological journey of how tacit and explicit workplace knowledge evolved into today's current understandings of workplace knowledge and its uses.

Pennsylvania Department of Transportation: A Case Study in Technical Succession Planning

"Capturing and transmitting the knowledge from the heads of veteran performers to less-experienced workers may sound like an abstract issue," says Irene Fulk, "but I assure you it is a practical problem for PennDOT." The Pennsylvania Department of Transportation (PennDOT) is the third-largest state agency, employing about 12,000 people. Irene Fulk is a human resource analyst (training) who works in PennDOT's Center for Performance Excellence. She is responsible for the agency's Position Analysis Workbook process. Used for on-the-job training, these position analysis workbooks are also helpful in capturing tacit knowledge from best-in-class performers and transmitting it to others through formal training courses, on-the-job training, and cross training. (Exhibit 3 describes the process.)

Fulk was asked several questions in June of 2004 to help clarify the case situation at PennDOT. What follows are the questions and her answers.

When was the problem first noticed, and how was it noticed?

The problem was noticed about four years ago. A workforce analysis revealed how many retirements were expected. That is a common problem that many organizations will face as baby boomers retire. But a change in the employee benefit package has also encouraged state workers to retire early, and so the biggest wave of retirements began in June 2003. Another wave is expected by the end of June 2004. But because of the aging of baby boomers, the agency is likely to feel the problem for about 10 years. Between July 2004 and June 2009, 21 percent of the PennDOT workforce will be eligible to retire, and when that is extrapolated, it means some 2,484 employees will be eligible to retire.

To make matters worse, the retirements affect not just PennDOT, but all state agencies, which impacts the entire employee lifecycle. That means that the process from recruitment through retirement is impacted as the State Civil Service Commission (which recruits and tests potential employees) and the State Employees Retirement System (which counsels retirees and processes their separation) lose veteran workers. Even senior-level officials are affected, as they scramble to recruit and orient replacements and then deal with the domino effect that is caused when someone is promoted (which in turn opens up the former position as a vacancy to be filled).

How many and what kinds of people are eligible to retire, and how soon is that likely to begin?

A unique issue facing PennDOT is that the agency experienced a big downsizing in the 1970s that reduced the workforce from about 24,000 workers to its current staffing level of about 12,000. The agency grows bigger in the winter season when temporary workers are brought in to aid the statewide snow removal effort. That means that the agency is not only about to experience a large number of retirements, but that it also has a workforce where one group has many years of experience and then there is a gap of people who were affected by the downsizing. And then there is a large group with about 15 years of experience.

Capturing and transmitting specialized knowledge—particularly for civil engineers and other technical specialists who are key to the agency's mission—is no academic problem. It is a very real, practical problem that affects agency productivity. When those employees retire, the agency faces a big problem because they know how to deal with the unique problems and issues in their areas of the state. And replacing engineers in particular is not easy.

What has the agency done about the problem? What steps have been taken to explore the knowledge that must be retained, and what methods have been used to identify, document, retain, and transmit that knowledge?

While I cannot speak to the whole range of methods that PennDOT has used to address this problem, I can speak to the Position Analysis Workbook process. Simply stated, the PAW relies on veteran performers in all areas to explain what they do on a daily basis, how they do it, what they must know to do it, and how they learned it. The workers are called together and, in an organized brain-storming process, provide this information. That information is then organized in a chart—you could call it a job map—that provides detailed descriptions of actual work activities and the knowledge, skills and competencies essential to carry them out. That information can, in turn, be used to cross-train other workers as backups or replacements for incumbent workers, or used as a basis for organized, structured, and planned on-the-job training to prepare newcomers.

How successful has the effort been? What side benefits, if any, have been realized from the effort?

I would say that the effort has been very successful. PAWs are a valuable tool for capturing and transmitting practical knowledge about how to do the work. That is exactly what is needed to solve the technical succession-planning problem. I would also note that a side benefit is that PAWs help to uncover areas in which the work process itself can be improved or even redesigned. Additionally, it slashes that unproductive breaking-in period of newcomers, because this approach provides an organized, efficient, and effective way to teach newcomers what to do.

What advice would you give other agencies facing a similar problem?

My first piece of advice is to avoid taking your experienced workers for granted. They have the know-how to get the work done. Without them, the agency faces a slow-down as less-experienced workers struggle to figure out what to do, how to do it, when to do it, and who has necessary information to make decisions and take action.

I would also advise agency officials to brainstorm ways to establish a culture where information sharing is rewarded. For example, workers should know that having a trained backup increases their ability to be promoted.

Note: Irene Fulk has agreed to speak to other government officials about the information in this case study. She can be reached at irenefulk@state.pa.us.

Conclusion

Technical succession planning recognizes that experienced technical workers and professionals in government are carrying around valuable knowledge in their heads. As the government workforce ages, there is a need to discover ways to pinpoint what information exists in the institutional memory, and then to distill it, preserve it, and transmit it. The authors defined technical succession planning as **any effort designed to ensure the continued effective performance of an organization, division, department, or workgroup by making provision for distilling, preserving, maintaining, and communicating the fruits of the organization's institutional memory and unique experiences over time.** Without doing that, government leaders might find the infrastructure starting to crumble, as the most basic functions of government must be rediscovered. The time has come to do something about this problem. Perhaps this article can be a starting point for your agency to begin thinking about technical succession planning in government.

Note: The information in Case 17 was originally presented in an article by William J. Rothwell and Stan Poduch that was published in *Public Personnel Management* (*33*; 4, 405–420). Stan Poduch is head of S2 Inc., a workforce learning and performance consulting firm. He can be reached at spp139@psu.edu.

U.S. LOCAL GOVERNMENT CASE STUDIES

The term "local government" often brings to mind city or county governments, but there are other entities in local government, including police, fire, sanitation, public health, and elder care. Part IV looks at how a city government and a county government handle succession planning. The final case examines how to manage the loss of institutional memory (what the author of case 20 calls "brain drain") resulting from large numbers of experienced government workers retiring or otherwise leaving their agency and being replaced with less-experienced people.

The cases in this section are:

SUCCESSION PRACTICES IN JAMES CITY COUNTY, VIRGINIA

> *Case Introduction:* This case study is a description of the succession practices used by James City County, Virginia. It was prepared by Rona J. Vrooman, Training and Quality Performance Coordinator for James City County, Virginia.

How does your agency define succession management; workforce planning; human capital management; and leadership development?

We use the term succession-management planning and define it consistent with the National Academy of Public Administration as "a deliberate and systematic effort to project leadership requirements, identify a pool of high-potential candidates, develop leadership competencies in these candidates through intentional learning experiences, and then select leaders from among the pool of potential leaders." We use the term "leadership development" as one strategy of succession-management planning. We do not use the term "human capital management" at all.

What is the purpose of your agency's succession management program, and what led to the perceived need for it?

The purpose of the succession-management planning program is two-fold. One purpose is to enhance current organizational performance by cross-training individuals in key positions. A second purpose is to develop a pool of candidates who, when a vacancy becomes available, will be competitive applicants.

The initiative grew out of the County Administrator's recognition of federal/state forecasts that described an aging and declining workforce. County Administrator Sanford B. Wanner joked that he had proof of an aging workforce every time he looked into the mirror.

Wanner's review of his own workforce and projected retirement dates of key personnel over the next ten years confirmed a crisis: 90% of executive staff was either eligible to retire or was past their eligibility to retire.

In response, the primary focus was to identify and cultivate a pool of internal and qualified applicants who could successfully compete for anticipated vacancies. A compelling reason to be proactive is that local government tends to be very lean; often positions are one-deep. As a result, there was a need to take steps to ensure continuity of services to citizens.

What measurable goals or objectives, if any, help to provide direction to your agency's succession management program?

We track the number and distribution of employees who participate in succession-management planning assignments, participant evaluation of the experience, and evaluation from the "receiving" department. We made a conscious decision to exclude the number of participants who are promoted, as a measure, for a number of reasons, including the realization that the best opportunity for the individual may, in fact, be outside of our organization.

What groups are targeted for participation in the program? Why were they selected?

Our executive-level positions were targeted due to the inordinate number of projected retirements and the skill level needed to be successful in the position. This includes the two highest level positions: County Administrator and Assistant County Administrator. Targeted groups for participation are currently department heads, assistants, and division or program heads.

Some departments have replicated the succession-management planning assignments within their own areas to address division and program positions. In those instances, the groups targeted for participation include all employees.

Does your agency use job competencies, defined as characteristics that describe successful performance, as a key foundation for the succession program? If so, explain how. If not, explain what is a key foundation for the program.

We have identified general skills that someone needs to demonstrate in order to be successful in an executive-level position, and have designed experiences that will assist participants in strengthening those skills. We do not assess skills to determine eligibility to participate in the program.

How is individual job performance assessed?

A survey is sent to people the individual supervises. The individual receives a semi-annual performance evaluation.

How is individual preparedness for promotion assessed?

Individuals do not receive any special certification or special treatment. They must compete for all promotions.

How is individual developmental planning carried out, if at all? (For instance, does your agency use an Individual Development Plan?)

Employees complete an annual individual development plan that is incorporated into the semi-annual performance cycle.

What activities, such as training, executive coaching, job rotation, and so forth, are used to build individual competence? How are those planned?

The County provides numerous development opportunities, such as tuition assistance and in-house training programs such as "Promoting Yourself within the County" and SELF, a leadership-development program. The County has contracted with coaches to assist individuals. The County sends employees to leadership-development programs sponsored by colleges and universities and the Chamber of Commerce. The County offers individuals the opportunity to participate as an Executive-in-Residence for the local United Way and supports a wide range of volunteer leadership opportunities. The County also implemented a shadow program to provide brief exposure to available positions. With about 750 full-time employees, the County is a relatively small organization. There is no budget allocated for succession-management planning, but the County administrator takes a personal interest in people's career development—he is known for dropping by to chat or leaving a note on your desk encouraging you to attend a workshop sponsored by a professional organization. He addresses new employees during their new-employee orientation tour, and encourages each to take advantage of the opportunities available.

Many authorities worry that pending retirements will lead to the loss of institutional memory as veteran government workers retire. What steps, if any, is your agency taking to identify, capture, distill, and make available important information from the most-experienced technical and professional workers in your agency before they retire, and to make that information available to their replacements?

The County has implemented systems to file, archive and retrieve critical documents. It has a well developed intranet, and liberally approves "overhiring" for those instances in which we want the outgoing employee to orient the incoming employee. Selected departments have also developed desk manuals to capture operating procedures.

Contact Information

Rona J. Vrooman has served as training and quality performance coordinator for James City County, Virginia since 1995. She can be reached at rvrooman@james-city.va.us.

SUCCESSION PLANNING IN HENRICO COUNTY, VIRGINIA

Case Introduction: This case study shows how one county government undertakes succession planning. It consists of two parts: background information, and then an interview describing the effort and its results. Supplementary data follows on pages 245–271.

The Background

The purpose of this case study is to document a best-practice example of succession management in the County of Henrico, Virginia. Henrico County borders the city of Richmond to the west, north, and east. It constitutes approximately one-third of Richmond's metropolitan area and employs more than 3,900 full-time employees working in more than 30 agencies. Department heads are appointed by the county manager, with the exception of the elected constitutional officers.

In 2000, Henrico County Human Resources Department forecast that 29 percent of the county's upper managers would be eligible for retirement by 2005 (see Table 19-1). A review of this data in 2003 revealed a trend: 44 percent of upper managers would be eligible for full retirement by 2008. Because of these and other statistics collected by the U.S. Department of Labor, Henrico County researched and implemented a *Succession Management Program* (see Table 19-2).

This initiative addressed two concerns: (1) loss of intellectual capital in key positions as upper managers become eligible to retire in record numbers; and (2) the decreasing number of younger adults in the workforce who are available to develop the skills necessary to move into higher-level positions. The program consisted of two phases. Phase One taught supervisors how to guide employees through a professional development process using individualized learning plans. Phase Two provided information to upper management on strategies for helping them develop subordinate managers for the purpose of planning for succession.

The County of Henrico's Human Resources Department earned national and local recognition for its outstanding and innovative Succession Management Program. According to George H. Cauble, Jr., Henrico County Director of Human Resources, "Henrico County is working hard to maintain leadership continuity both now and in the future so as to ensure that the knowledge acquired by those in key positions in the County will not leave when these individuals do."

The Interview

Interviewer: Jean A. Pulaski

Interviewee: Sheryn R. Holinsworth, Manager of Employment Development and Training for the Human Resources Department, Henrico County, Virginia

Jean A. Pulaski: **How does your agency define succession management?**

Sheryn R. Holinsworth: We actually use William Rothwell's definition from his book *Effective Succession Planning*: a systematic effort by an organization to ensure continuity in key positions; retain and develop intellectual and knowledge capital for the future; and encourage individual advancement. We started out in 2000 using that definition and we still use it in presentations today when people talk about the components of the program. We explain that there are three components, and they are to ensure leadership continuity, retain and develop intellectual capital, and encourage individual advancement. In fact, we've taken his definition and bullet-pointed them out using those three components.

Pulaski: **What is the purpose of your agency's succession management program, and what led to the perceived need for it?**

Holinsworth: We really wanted to make sure that we had continuity in positions that we considered key for the future success of the County. We were concerned about retaining knowledge for the future, and we wanted to make sure that we were meeting individual needs for development and advancement.

We were concerned about losing the knowledge of upper managers. We knew that they were expected to retire in record numbers, but we also were observing a decrease in the number of younger employees in our workforce. From some of the generational data that we had been doing, we found that providing development opportunities was something that the younger generations in particular were insisting upon, and this program would address that as well.

Pulaski: **What measurable goals or objectives, if any, help to provide direction to your agency's succession management program?**

Holinsworth: One measurable goal we had was to try to increase the number of qualified internal applicants for key position openings. We identified early on that our key position holders were our upper managers. We are a workforce of, at that time, approximately 3,700 employees. Approximately 750 of them were managers, and ten percent of that 750 were considered upper managers.

Our program initially focused on them. Two years prior to the program's implementation, we had seven openings for upper management positions, and we only had two of those openings filled internally (see Table 19-3). So, in five cases, we were forced to go outside for upper management positions because we did not have internal bench strength. In the immediate two years after the program's implementation, we had eight upper-management openings; all eight were able to be filled internally (see Table 19-4). So that is definitely a measurable outcome of the program. Just so you know, we are right now at eighteen upper-management openings since the beginning of the program, and fifteen of the eighteen have been filled internally (see Table 19-5).

We were beginning to push this down through the county beyond those original upper managers. Another measurable objective we had was that we wanted to know that managers throughout the county were involving their employees in development and that they were assisting them with individual learning plans. We did a survey and discovered that ninety-one percent of all managers were working with their employees on development plans (see Table 19-6).

Pulaski: **What groups are targeted for participation in the program? Why were they selected?**

Holinsworth: Originally, only the upper managers—about seventy-five people. They were essentially a pilot group, and we were concerned because of their retirement eligibility (see Table 19-7). However, since that time, we pushed it down to all managers in the County, the entire 750.

Pulaski: **Does your agency use job competencies, defined as characteristics that describe successful performance, as a key foundation for the succession program? If so, explain how. If not, explain what the key foundation is for the program.**

Holinsworth: Yes, we do. We have competencies that are divided into three categories: Competencies for upper managers (see Table 19-8), defined as assistant department heads, department heads, deputy county managers, and the county manager himself; for middle managers and managers who supervise other supervisors; and for first-line supervisors, who supervise line staff (see Table 19-9). Those competencies were developed actually ten years ago, and they provided the foundation for a voluntary Leadership Development Program (see Table 19-10), which is our foundation for succession planning. They are on our Web site.

Pulaski: **How is individual job performance assessed?**

Holinsworth: We have a traditional performance appraisal system where, at least once a year, individuals are assessed by their supervisor, based on documentation of performance.

Pulaski: **How is individual preparedness for promotion assessed?**

Holinsworth: Through developmental conversations that employees have with their supervisors. Supervisors report this information upward to their managers, and eventually that information is recorded on the evaluation form. This is a requirement of the program; all department heads must complete and turn in the form to the county manager (see Table 19-11).

This is a document that all upper managers complete to identify their essential job functions (i.e., knowledge competencies, skills, and abilities) that would be lost when they retire. They are required to distribute this completed form to all their subordinate managers. Those subordinate managers then use this form to identify any skill gaps they have, which helps in their own development upward.

One of the things that I think is unique about our program is the emphasis on the relationship between supervisors and their respective staffs. And so this individual preparedness for promotion is assessed through ongoing conversations that supervisors have with their employees.

Pulaski: **How is individual developmental planning carried out, if at all? For instance, does your agency use an Individual Development Plan?**

Holinsworth: Yes, we call it an Individual Learning Plan (see Table 19-12). That document is one that we include in a lot of our training around development. In fact, for the first time this year, the Individual Learning Plan is going to be included in our annual training catalog. Employees will be able to work directly with the plan form and have the list of classes and other programs that are coming up that year. Classes are not all that we do and provide. They could include that additional information on their plan.

Pulaski: **What activities, such as training, executive coaching, job rotation, and so forth, are used to build individual competence? How are those planned?**

Holinsworth: We have a variety of activities, such as the ones that you've mentioned. We do have cross-functional work teams, we have cross-training, we have internships, we have job rotations, and we also have leadership development programs where the participants of that program receive coaching.

We also have telephone coaching that is done after a class we call *"The Role of the Supervisor in Henrico County."* This is a required class for newly promoted and newly hired supervisors. Once they complete that program, which includes two days of classroom training prior to the program, they must also complete eight hours of online just-in-time training when they first get promoted. They also get phone coaching from an executive coach afterwards.

One of the things that I think is unique about our program is our emphasis on the relationship between the supervisor and the employee, as well as the experiential activities such as job rotation and cross-training planned by the employee and the supervisor. These are not managed by HR.

Sometimes the leadership development coach will assist in setting that up, but it is really a contract, so to speak, between the employee and the supervisor to set that up. There are some exceptions: A few departments in our public safety area, such as fire and police, have cross-training that actually is set up as part of how they do business. For example, you might have a fire department captain who is required to ride along with the Fire Battalion chief once a month. That's something that they've set up within their own department.

Pulaski: **What is the budget for the succession planning program, if you know it? How is the succession program evaluated and what measures or metrics are used to assess success?**

Holinsworth: Well, believe it or not, we have no budget at all for the succession planning program itself. The reason for that is that the leadership development program that was developed ten years ago was such a strong foundation for the succession planning initiative that we really did not need additional funding for this program. We really had all the resources that we needed to implement it successfully here at the County. I think organizations that don't have leadership training in place and don't have leadership coaches and the resources that we have would struggle, but we did not have to have a budget.

One of the measures that we use to assess the success is that we keep track of upper managers when they leave and how strong the internal candidates are. We're keeping track of those statistics.

We also set up as part of our accountability in the program a requirement that all department heads have to complete a document every six months and turn it in to the county manager. That document explains what development activities are going on among managers who report to them, what development activities are still planned in order to meet their developmental goals, and what openings they have had for management positions and who applied. Eventually, the document was required only once each year.

The other thing is that if there is an internal upper-management opening and you have internal candidates who could have applied but chose not to, we ask them to explain. Tell us why that candidate did not compete and did not choose to compete (see Table 19-17).

As I mentioned, the focus on the relationship is so key. I've talked to a lot of organizations that have called us over the years—local governments, state agencies, and so on—and they are intimidated by what they think is a complex or expensive program. We have seen our program be successful because leaders understand that their role is to transfer knowledge and that their responsibility is to develop their employees.

I really think that our county leaders, the majority of them, have embraced that concept and incorporated that into so much of what they do during the day. We have seen a huge increase in upper managers bringing other managers within their department along with them for meetings, presentations, board meetings, and things like that. Those lower-level managers are able to get exposure to upper-management activities and responsibilities, and that's just such a great way to transfer knowledge. In other words, it doesn't have to be too formalized and complicated. Sometimes it is as simple as, "Hey, I'm getting ready to go to this important meeting. Would you like to come along with me and sit in, and then afterwards we could talk about it?" That's one thing.

Secondly, I don't think that our program would have been as successful as it was if it hadn't been for the Leadership Development Program. We had a wonderful local board of supervisors who supported that program ten years ago. Our county manager pushed for it and got the funding for that program, and it has been such a great foundation to have in terms of the training that we offer and the executive coaching that we offer.

Next is the support from our county manager. He has been such a champion of this program, and speaks of it frequently in public forums. He talks about the importance of transferring knowledge and explaining your decision making, developing your people, and having difficult conversations with people around their opportunities and development. He has been key to the success of our program.

Another component that I think has really made our program successful is the incorporation of employee input. We have given employees the opportunity to participate in their development and make the decisions around their development. We have not mandated or dictated how an employee develops or what resources they use. What we have mandated is that *development is not an option.*

Early on, we were aware that one of the barriers that we might encounter is the reality that there are people who simply don't want to move up—people who are next in line for a position but were publicly stating that they did not want their boss's job when their boss retired or their boss left. So early on, we made the decision. And by "we," I mean the county manager and those of us on the team who worked on this. We made the decision that vertical development is optional. You don't have to move up, but development is not optional. You must continue to grow, and so we have definitely seen that.

We did emphasize accountability. Early on, we got some grumblings about the "form" the people had to complete every six months and turn in to the county manager, but now, we're seeing that it is just such a part of the culture. We don't hear those grumblings anymore and we now require that form only once a year, on the last business day in September.

One thing that was unique about our program in the late 1990s is that we were emphasizing a develop-then-select structure. A lot of private industry was using a select-then-develop program, which for us would not have been fair. We did not want to identify high potentials by name in any form in any way. We wanted to develop our *entire* workforce and have them all growing and learning and being better prepared for future opportunities. Then we would go through our normal legal selection process.

Another thing I've seen in other organizations that we found important as well is to link the succession management initiatives to other initiatives. We changed our performance dimension to include a dimension that is called "leadership and employee development." Now all supervisors are held accountable for the development that they do with their employees.

We also have a program that began in 1992 called a "Career Enrichment Program," where we actually have a career counselor on staff who can provide assistance to people who want to grow and develop and maybe change jobs within the County. That ends up being a good support system to this program. I think that's it. I know I did have a long list of things to tell you about our succession planning program.

Table 19-1

Demographic and Employment Statistics

Henrico County 2004 statistics used for succession planning

- By 2005, 29% of department heads, assistants, and key officials were eligible for full retirement.

- Seventy-eight percent were eligible for reduced benefits by 2005.

- In 1983, 41–60+ year-olds represented 34% of Henrico County's workforce.

- In 2000, 41–60+ year-olds represented 56% of Henrico County's workforce·.

- Retirements totaled 21 in 1983; in 2000 76 employees retired.

- In June 2001, 18% of all employees were eligible to retire.

- By July 2005, it is expected that 38% of all employees will be eligible to retire.

(Provided by Henrico Country Department of Human Resources, Benefits Division)

National statistics used for succession planning in 2004:

- U.S. population figures by age for years 1965–2025

- Number of 35–45-year-olds projected to decline by 2015

- Executive turnover at 33% in Fortune 500 companies in next five years

- U.S. Department of Health and Human Services
  One-third of permanent employees were eligible for retirement
  Varies, by division, from 23–72%

- Thirty percent of the federal workforce are eligible to retire in next five years

- Fifty percent are eligible to retire in next five years, including those taking early retirement

Table 19-2

Steps in Henrico County, Virginia's Succession-Management Plan

Step One: Identify key positions for succession management.

These positions have already been identified. They are: County manager, deputy County managers, department heads, and all County middle managers (managers who supervise other supervisors). Each of these employees listed above will complete a succession-management plan form.

Step Two: Identify competencies needed.

Core competencies have already been developed and are listed in the Leadership Development Program manuals and Web page. Additional sources for this competency list are: Class specifications, job descriptions, trend data that indicates future skills needed for the position.

Step Three: Employees begin development with assistance of key manager.

Meet with each management employee who directly reports to the above-mentioned key positions to discuss developmental needs and opportunities. Stress that the employee's development does not guarantee promotion, but it is intended to assist them in developing the skills to be a marketable candidate in the event of a vacancy at a higher level of management.

Development responsibilities are as follows: County manager develops deputy County managers and department heads who report directly to him. Deputy County managers develop department heads; department heads develop assistant department heads; assistant department heads develop middle managers or other managers reporting to the assistant department head; and middle managers develop first-line supervisors.

Step Four: Employees assess development with assistance of key manager.

Meet with those employees under your direct supervision during and after developmental activities to assess their progress. Create additional goals and learning plans accordingly. It is important that you provide both positive and constructive feedback to them as they work toward stretch objectives.

Step Five: Evaluate Succession Management Program.

The Succession Management Evaluation Form is to be completed and turned in each year on or before the last business day in September by all County upper managers (deputy county managers, department heads, and assistant department heads). This form provides information on developmental activity and succession management statistics for each department in Henrico County. Middle managers are not required to complete the Evaluation Form, but must participate in steps one through four, as outlined here.

Table 19-3

Upper-Management Appointments		
Two Years Prior to Succession Management Implementation (2000 and 2001)		
Chief Deputy Sheriff	2000	Internal
Assistant Director of Library	2001	External
Assistant Director of Public Utilities	2001	External
Director of Juvenile Detention	2000	Internal
Director of James River Juvenile Detention	2000	External
Director of Public Utilities	2001	External
Fire Chief	2001	External

Note: Two out of seven were internal appointments.

Table 19-4

Upper-Management Appointment		
Two Years After Succession Management Implementation (2002 and 2003)		
Director of Public Information	2002	Internal
Director of Finance	2002	Internal
Director of Social Services	2002	Internal
Assistant Director of Public Information	2002	Internal
Assistant Director of Finance	2002	Internal
Assistant Director of Social Services	2002	Internal
Assistant Director of Community Development	2002	Internal
Director of Information Technology	2003	Internal

Note: Eight out of eight were internal appointments.

Table 19-5

Upper-Management Appointments 2004 and Beyond		
Director of MH/MR	2004	Internal
Director of Community Revitalization	2004	Internal
Director of Planning	2004	Internal
Assistant Director of Planning	2004	Internal
Assistant Director of Planning	2004	Internal
Assistant Director of MH/MR	2004	External*
Director of Community Revitalization	2005	External
Assistant Director of Human Resources	2005	Internal
Director of Social Services	2006	Internal
Assistant Director of Social Services	2006	External
Director of Real Property	2006	Internal
Director of Public Works	2006	Internal
Assistant Director of Real Property	2006	Internal
Assistant Director of Public Works	2006	Internal
Assistant Director of MH/MR	2006	External
Assistant Superintendent of James River Juvenile Detention	2006	Internal
Assistant Director of MH/MR	2007	Internal
Assistant Director of Recreation & Parks	2007	Internal

Note: The first eight upper-management position openings were filled internally (one position hire was a former employee, technically considered an "external" hire). The next two were filled externally.

Table 19-6

2002 Supervisor Survey Statistics

In 2002, a sample of supervisors were surveyed regarding their role in employee professional development. At that time, approximately 750 supervisors were employed by Henrico County. A questionnaire was sent to 206 supervisors. One hundred sixty-two supervisors responded, for a 79% response rate. Of those who responded, 147 (91%) said "Yes" in answer to the question: "Have you had discussions with your employees about their own professional development?"

Table 19-7

Key Positions in Henrico County, Virginia's Succession-Management Plan

County Manager

Deputy County Manager for Community Services

Deputy County Manager for Special Services

Deputy County Manager for Community Development

Deputy County Manager for Administration

Deputy County Manager for Community Operations

Building Official

Deputy Building Official

Director, Capital Area Training Consortium

Deputy Director, Capital Area Training Consortium

Circuit Court Clerk

Chief Deputy Circuit Court Clerk

Director, Community Corrections Program

Director, Community Revitalization Department

County Attorney

Deputy County Attorney

Director, Finance Department

Deputy Director, Finance Department

Fire Chief

Deputy Fire Chief

Director, General Services Department

Deputy Director, General Services Department

Deputy Director, General Services Department (2 positions)

Director, Human Resources Department

Assistant Director, Human Resources Department

Assistant Director, Human Resources Department (2 positions)

Director, Office of Internal Audit

Director of Information Technology

Assistant Director of Information Technology

Superintendent, Juvenile Detention

Assistant Superintendent, Juvenile Detention

Assistant Superintendent, Juvenile Detention (2 positions)

Superintendent, James River Juvenile Detention

Assistant Superintendent for Administration, James River Juvenile Detention

Assistant Superintendent for Operations, James River Juvenile Detention

Director, Mental Health/Retardation Services

Assistant Director for Community Support Services, Mental Health/Retardation Services

Assistant Director for Administrative Services, Mental Health/Retardation Services

Assistant Director for Clinical Services, Mental Health/Retardation Services

Director, Community Development

Assistant Director, Community Development

Director, Planning Department

Assistant Director of Comprehensive Planning and Administration, Planning Department

Assistant Director of Plan Review and Code Support, Planning Department

Chief of Police

(continued)

Table 19-7: Key Positions in Henrico County, Virginia's Succession-Management Plan
(concluded)

Deputy Chief of Police	Director, Public Works
Director, Public Library	Assistant Director, Public Works
Assistant Director, Public Library	Director, Real Property
Director, Public Relations and Media Services	Assistant Director, Real Property
Assistant Director, Public Relations and Media Services	Director, Recreation and Parks
	Assistant Director, Recreation and Parks
Director, Public Utilities	Director, Social Services
Assistant Director, Public Utilities	Assistant Director, Social Services

Other upper managers are invited to attend all succession management initiatives, but they do not report their succession activities to the county manager because they are either elected or appointed, or are state employees and consequently do not report to the county manager or one of the deputy county managers. They include:

Commonwealth Attorney	Director, Health Department
Chief Deputy Commonwealth Attorney	Director, Probation
Executive Director, Economic Development	General Registrar
Administrative Director, Economic Development	Deputy General Registrar
County Agent, Extension Service	Sheriff
	Chief Deputy Sheriff

Table 19-8

Competencies for Upper Managers

1. **Communication:** Provides well-thought-out, concise and timely oral and written information that is tailored to the audience being addressed.

2. **Conflict Resolution/Negotiation/Mediation:** Effectively resolves conflicts and is able to act as a neutral party in the resolution of disputes through use of effective mediation and negotiation principles.

3. **Continuous Improvement:** Consistently takes actions to improve the work process so that quality, service and efficiency improve over time.

4. **Critical Thinking and Decision Making:** Makes decisions that demonstrate a broad and creative range of options and a view toward long-term solutions. Gathers appropriate level of data and analyzes through sound questions and reflection. Makes timely decisions.

5. **Customer Orientation:** Actions reflect a strong commitment to quality, cost-effective internal and external customer service. Anticipates customer needs and expectations. Seeks ongoing customer feedback to improve service.

6. **Employee Development and Coaching:** Promotes the development of staff by providing the direction, support and feedback needed to enable others to reach their full potential. Creates an environment where people can stretch and grow (through delegated assignments and other developmental activities).

7. **Financial and Resource Management:** Takes any steps necessary to maximize the utilization of financial and other County resources. Acts as a trustee of County resources, ensuring that they are neither misused nor squandered.

8. **Individual Learning Skills:** Demonstrates an ability to learn at a pace equal to or greater than the organization's changing needs. Uses whatever strategies work best (e.g. seminars, computer-based courses, audiotapes) to acquire new knowledge/skills.

9. **Interpersonal Relations:** Demonstrates a keen awareness of how his or her behavior impacts relationships with others. Invests in relationships by attentive listening, withholding judgment and anticipating the potential impact of various actions on others.

10. **Organizational Astuteness:** Pays attention to both the formal and informal ways in which the organization operates. Takes into account the needs and preferences of the various players, and uses diverse approaches and strategies to build support and commitment for a particular initiative. Knows when to fight the battles and when to avoid competition and conflict.

(continued)

Table 19-8: Competencies for Upper Managers *(concluded)*

11. **Orientation to the Future:** Articulates a vision for the future and uses it to drive daily decisions, strategies and actions. Helps others to share the vision and stay focused. Strives to develop organizational strengths to further vision. Conducts ongoing assessment to identify what's working and what needs to change to move forward.

12. **Performance Management:** Establishes and communicates goals and standards through a dialogue that ensures understanding and commitment. Stays abreast of individual/team performance, providing feedback and confronting substandard performance as required. Evaluates performance against pre-established expectations.

13. **Personal Accountability:** Accepts responsibility for his/her own actions. Refrains from blaming others or making excuses when errors or breakdowns occur.

14. **Personal Integrity:** Consistently demonstrates trustworthiness. Leaves no doubts about his/her ethics and values. Is both fair and straightforward when interacting with others.

15. **Policy and Procedure Development and Administration:** Recognizes the need for new policies and procedures as well as revisions to existing ones. Develops fair and effective policies and procedures and administers/enforces them with both fairness and consistency.

16. **Strategic Management:** Demonstrates an approach to management that helps others see the big picture. Anticipates events and expectations and stays ahead of emerging issues and trends.

17. **Systems Perspective:** Focuses on the organization as a "system" where changes in one place in the system can have significant ripple effects elsewhere in the system. Uses this perspective to prevent or diagnose problems, as well as to find "leverage" points that will have the maximum positive effects throughout the organization.

18. **Team Leadership and Empowerment:** Supports both teams and individuals to use resources and authority to make and execute decisions. Removes obstacles and barriers to team and to individual authority.

19. **Technological Literacy:** Demonstrates an understanding of technology and ensures that it is incorporated appropriately in service delivery, information sharing, organizational communication and citizen access. Stays current in his/her field.

20. **Versatility:** Shows an ability and willingness to change roles or direction as the needs of the organization change. Can stretch beyond past or current responsibilities, roles, or styles as conditions change.

Table 19-9

Competencies for Middle Managers and First-Line Supervisors

1. **Communication:** Communicates orally and in writing in clear, succinct and understandable ways. Passes information on to customers and staff, as appropriate. Adjusts style to fit the audience.

2. **Conflict Resolution/Negotiation/Mediation:** Addresses and mediates conflict. Encourages expression of different points of view and negotiates to find common ground.

3. **Continuous Improvement:** Consistently focuses on improving outputs and outcomes. Looks for opportunities to make improvements. Sets increasingly higher production and quality standards. Encourages innovation.

4. **Critical Thinking and Decision Making:** Makes timely decisions based on the best information available. Considers alternatives and selects among ones that are cost effective. Is open to new and creative alternatives.

5. **Customer Orientation** (middle managers): Anticipates needs of customers. Provides timely service to customers. Genuinely listens to and considers customers concerns and complaints. Gives employees the freedom and authority to meet customer expectations in a timely manner.

6. **Customer Orientation** (first-line supervisors): Provides timely service to customers. Genuinely listens to and considers customers' concerns and complaints. Gives employees the freedom and authority to meet customer expectations in a timely manner.

7. **Employee Development and Coaching:** Supports employee development through work assignments, training opportunities and coaching feedback sessions. Strengthens employees' confidence in their abilities, while holding employees accountable for results.

8. **Financial and Resource Management:** Identifies fully the resources that will be required to reach a result. Makes good decisions on how employees and dollars are committed. Strives to accomplish the desired result with cost savings.

9. **Individual Learning Skills:** Gives priority to individual learning. Encourages individuals to ask questions about processes and assumptions. Turns mistakes into learning experiences. Learns new things quickly.

10. **Interpersonal Relations:** Interacts in open, objective ways that show respect and interest. Listens attentively to the ideas and concerns of others and gives them genuine consideration. Focuses on issues and not personalities. Is sensitive to impact on others.

(continued)

Table 19-9: Competencies for Middle Managers and First-Line Supervisors *(concluded)*

11. **Organizational Astuteness:** Identifies the organizational units and individuals that need to be included in activities and decisions and includes them appropriately. Earns the respect of individuals throughout the organization and builds a network of positive relationships. Carefully chooses which battle to fight.

12. **Orientation to the Future:** Communicates the County's vision for the future in appropriate ways. Guides short term actions with an eye to the long-term big picture. Helps employees see program strengths and weaknesses in terms of progressing toward the County's vision. Anticipates future needs and works toward meeting them.

13. **Performance Management:** Clearly states what is to be done, why, and with what concerns for priorities, deadlines and quality. Holds others accountable for their actions and results. Provides honest, helpful feedback. Assesses performance against objective standards.

14. **Personal Accountability:** Accepts responsibility for his/her own actions. Meets deadlines and standards for quality and quantity of work. Takes responsibility for the results of decisions made.

15. **Personal Integrity:** Is truthful and honest. Keeps confidences and maintains confidentiality of information. Makes fair decisions based on facts and sound values. Is open and honest when agreeing or disagreeing.

16. **Planning:** Identifies the appropriate level of planning for a program, project, activity or task. Identifies goals, objectives, and strategies. Measures progress periodically. Plans for contingencies. Adjusts and maintains plans as needed.

17. **Policy and Procedure Development and Administration:** Administers County policies and procedures in a fair and consistent manner. Develops procedures needed to guide performance of the work unit. Keeps work unit procedures up-to-date and relevant.

18. **Systems Perspective:** Understands and communicates how the work unit's efforts fit into the organization's goals. In diagnosing problems, considers the interrelationships of departments and functions. Recognizes the ripple effects that can occur from any given change or decision. Assesses actions for their effects within and outside of the work unit.

19. **Team Leadership:** Constructs teams when appropriate. Draws upon the talent of all team members. Recognizes and draws upon the individual differences and talents of team members. Effectively bridges differences in thought and style between and among people. Recognizes team accomplishments.

20. **Technological Literacy:** Keeps up-to-date on information in his/her professional specialty. Bases decisions on up-to-date technical information. Identifies the need for and asks for technical assistance. Personally utilizes technology in cost-effective ways. Encourages uses of cost-effective technology.

21. **Versatility:** Adapts well to changing organizational needs and changing roles. Performs well in ambiguous situations. Reacts quickly and positively to change.

Table 19-10

Leadership Development Program for Henrico County, Virginia (Abstract)

In 1996, the Henrico County Department of Human Resources designed and implemented a competency-based **Leadership Development Program** to promote continuous employee learning and development. This program offers managerial and supervisory employees of this 3,900-employee organization a broad range of choices for assessing personal learning needs and creating custom learning plans with a format for recognition of achievement. It also has become an important foundation to the County of Henrico's Succession Management initiative—an initiative that has enhanced the leadership abilities of employees and maintained leadership continuity as a way of preparing for the future.

At the request of the County Manager, the Department of Human Resources studied private-sector practices in management and leadership development. As a result of this study, Henrico County decided to direct its leadership development efforts toward strengthening specific leadership competencies. County managers identified the top competencies for upper level managers, middle managers, and first-line supervisors that contribute to the success of progressive organizations and that are most relevant to Henrico County. All managers and supervisors were invited to attend an inaugural conference. The county manager, Department of Human Resources' staff, and outside speakers introduced the program and highlighted the crucial importance of leadership and individual professional growth. Each participant received a reference binder outlining this important and multi-faceted learning program.

The objective of the Leadership Development Program is to: (1) identify the top competencies essential to the successful management of Henrico County, and (2) to encourage the professional growth of current and future leaders by offering a framework and resources for the achievement of employee-designed, competency-based learning goals. A variety of assessment instruments, experiential learning options, and competency-based seminars provide managers and supervisors with tools to take charge of their professional development.

The Leadership Development Program is designed to help managers from the highest management levels to first-line supervisors grow professionally and decide what they want to learn, how they want to learn, and when they want to achieve their goals.

Because adults develop most effectively when they "learn by doing" and can develop their own goals, this program includes numerous choices for both traditional classroom and experiential "hands-on" learning. It supports employee learning with a format to design individual learning programs, encourages participants to actively apply learning in service of citizens, and provides recognition for these achievements.

(continued)

Table 19-10: Leadership Development Program for Henrico County, Virginia (Abstract)
(concluded)

The main features of this program include:

Voluntary participation

Self-initiation and direction within a framework for adult learning

Target groups that include upper and middle managers and first-line supervisors

Competency-based focus

Assessments, both self and multi-rater, for identifying leadership and learning styles

Professional development plans customized with assistance from the Department of Human Resources

Workshops, seminars, forums, and conferences of various lengths and topics, based on identified competencies

Experiential learning opportunities that include cross-functional work teams, cross training, internships, job exchange, job rotation, mentoring, practicums, and external experiences to encourage learning by doing and practical application

Equivalency provisions for prior experience and/or training

Recognition by certificate to be earned by the supervisor and awarded by a county manager-appointed committee, based on completion of a personal Professional Development Plan and portfolio material demonstrating that relevant competencies were learned and applied in work situations.

The Employee Development and Training Division of the Department of Human Resources sponsors this program. Three Leadership Development Program advisors from this team meet periodically with individual participants to assist with goal clarification, interpret the results of assessments (both individual and multi-rater), provide guidance with experiential learning ideas, and monitor progress toward goals. This team has designed and presented competency-based seminars targeted for first-line supervisors, middle managers, and upper managers. To provide specific expertise for additional training, staff trainers contract with outside consultants who bring relevant experience from private, public, military, and university settings.

The County's Leadership Development Program has been a very successful initiative, and has added to the reputation of Henrico County. Five hundred thirty-eight awards have been achieved, and nearly 350 supervisors are active participants in this voluntary program. The award-winning program has contributed to the culture of the organization and has become a beacon of learning. The LDP won the 1997 International Personnel Management Association (IPMA) **Virginia Chapter Achievement Award,** the American Society of Training and Development (ASTD) **"Excellent in Practice" Innovative Practice Award,** and the 1998 National Association of Counties (NACo) **Achievement Award.**

Table 19-11

Succession-Management Plan: Accountability Form

Instructions: The manager currently occupying the key position (County Manager, Deputy County Manager, Department Head, Assistant Department Head, or Middle Manager) completes Steps One and Two on this form and distributes to all staff reporting directly to him or her.

Each of these staff members then works with their manager to complete an Individualized Learning Plan (Steps Three and Four).

Evaluation of the program (Step Five) is reported on the Succession Management Evaluation Form by any upper manager occupying a key position.

These completed Evaluation forms shall be submitted through the chain of command and ultimately packaged for the County Manager's review.

Step One: Identify a key position for succession. _____

Step Two: Identify competencies, responsibilities, duties, tasks, and essential job functions of this position. Then list specific examples of how these competencies, functions, etc. are exhibited in this job. (Use additional pages as necessary.)

Competency, Responsibility, Duty, Task, Essential Job Function	Behavioral Examples

_____   _____
Signature of key position manager   Date

(continued)

Table 19-11: Succession-Management Plan: Accountability Form *(concluded)*

Step Three: Employee completes an Individualized Learning Plan with the assistance of key manager.

Step Four: Employee assesses ability by verifying that he/she has closed developmental gaps with assistance of key manager. This information is also recorded on the Individualized Learning Plan.

Step Five: Evaluate program by monitoring developmental activity in your areas of influence, meeting with your manager to discuss internally filled positions and the success of the employees working in those positions.

Table 19-12

Individual Learning Plan for Leadership Positions (page 1)

Directions: Use this Individual Learning Plan to help develop the skills for higher-level leadership positions. Work with your manager to reach agreement on objectives, strategies, etc.

Employee's Name _____   Job Title _____

Department _____   Years in Position _____

Manager's Name _____   Job Title _____

Department _____   Years in Position _____

Today's Date _____   Plan Covering _____ to _____

                                                                       Date   Date

In the space below, list the competencies, activities, responsibilities, duties, tasks, and essential job functions of a higher-level leadership position in which you have developmental needs and to which you aspire.

_____

_____

_____

_____

_____

_____

(continued)

Table 19-12 *(concluded)*

Individual Learning Plan for Leadership Positions (page 2)					
Learning Objective	Methods and Strategies to meet the Objectives	Resources Needed to Achieve Objective (Information, Money, Training, Equipment, Time, etc.)	Deadline or Benchmark Dates	How success of each learning objective will be measured	Verified? Yes ( ) No ( )

Table 19-13

Activities to Support Succession Management

1. **Information Session and Initial Communication** (all upper managers)

   County manager opened this session. He explained the importance of the initiative, gave his "charge" for implementing, and then turned it over to Human Resources for specifics.

2. **Celebration** (all upper managers)

   Acting county manager (county manager was out on medical leave) congratulated upper managers on the successes of the initiative. HR reviewed awards that had been won and articles that had been written about the county and shared the accolades.

3. **Information Sessions** (all middle managers)

   Initiative was pushed down to middle managers. All middle managers are now required to work with first-line supervisors, reporting to them and partnering with them on their development.

4. **Focus on Leadership** (5-day class)

   This course was designed for middle managers to teach them higher-level leadership skills.

5. **Intellectual Capital Series** (all upper managers)

   In this quarterly series, the county manager shared knowledge with the upper management staff about his experiences as county manager. An HR staff person interviewed him and asked open-ended questions that had the chief executive reminiscing about his early days in his role, as well as describing difficult decisions he had made over the years.

6. **Leadership Conference** (half of all County managers attended)

   The county manager was the keynote speaker. His speech focused on his years as county manager. He used stories as a way of sharing knowledge.

7. **Conversations with the County Manager**

   This course took the same format as the Intellectual Capital series, but was open to County middle managers.

(continued)

Table 19-13: Activities to Support Succession Management *(concluded)*

---

8. **Individualized Learning Plan Information Sessions**

These sessions were held several months prior to the implementation of the Succession Management initiative. They covered development planning as a key function of a supervisor's job.

Other courses offered that support the Succession Management Initiative:

- Developing Your Employees
- Retaining Your Star Employees
- Developing Leaders
- Learning and Developing Supervisory Skills
- Knowledge Management
- Leadership Book Club: Lessons Learned

Table 19-14

Experiential Strategies Equivalency Review Form
for Leadership Development Program

The purpose of the Equivalency Review Form is to provide a consistent format for all certification participants who submit Experiential Strategies or course work for review. It will be the only document used by the Review Committee to determine equivalency toward a certificate. It is extremely important that all sections are completed fully.

Name: _____ Department: _____

Equivalency Review for a Certificate in _____

Number of hours for consideration: _____

NOTE: A maximum of 24 hours can be credited for an experiential activity. A maximum of 32 hours can be credited for the completion of a course.

I. Describe in detail the Experiential Strategy or course you want reviewed. List such things as goals, purpose, outcomes, and length of time involved, and any other information that will help the Committee in the evaluation process. (Attach additional pages as needed.)

_____

_____

II. Discuss what you consider to be the most significant learning aspects of the Experiential Strategy or course.

_____

_____

III. How have you used the course content? What contributions have you been able to make to the County of Henrico as a result of the Experiential Strategy or course? Explain.

_____

_____

(continued)

Table 19-14: **Experiential Strategies Equivalency Review Form for Leadership Development Program** *(concluded)*

IV. Other Guidelines:

For a specific course, you will need to fill out this form describing what you learned, how you applied it, and the relevance of the course content to the County of Henrico. Attach supporting material (such as a transcript and work products that show how you applied the course content) that would help the LDP Committee assess your submittal.

For experiential activities, including job rotations, volunteer activities, and professional association activities, complete this form describing the nature and duration of the experience, what was learned, and the relevance of the experience to the County of Henrico. Attach any supporting material (such as letters or a brief narrative from others associated with the experience) so that the LDP Committee can assess your submittal. Attach additional pages for any item, if necessary.

If you are requesting review of courses that were sponsored by the County of Henrico's Department of Human Resources, submit only a copy of your training record or course certificate.

Employee's signature _____ Date _____

Table 19-15

Experiential Learning Contract for Leadership Development Program

Name: _____   Department: _____

Phone: _____   Number of hours for consideration: _____

NOTE: A maximum of 24 hours can be credited for an experiential activity. A maximum of 32 hours can be credited for the completion of a course.

I. **Type of learning experience:**
   (For example: Cross training, job exchange, or job rotation)

   _____

   _____

II. **Learning goals:**
   (What do you hope to learn?)

   _____

   _____

III. **Strategies:**
   (What steps will you take to meet these goals?)

   _____

   _____

IV. **Time frames:**
   (Total length of experiential period and hours per day or week.)

   _____

   _____

(continued)

Table 19-15: **Experiential Learning Contract for Leadership Development Program**
(concluded)

V. **Evaluation criteria:**

_____

_____

_____	_____
Employee's signature	Date
_____	_____
Supervisor's signature	Date
_____	_____
Approval of Department head	Date

Table 19-16

Examples of Developmental Strategies for Leaders		
Any managerial activity contains the potential for learning and development. It might be totally new learning, confirming learning previously acquired, or adjusting previous learning (e.g., "This technique worked with these people in this situation, but it didn't work when I tried it with someone else."). The list of managerial activities from which people could learn would be endless, and would apply to some people in some circumstances and not in others, depending on the relevance of any learning activity to the particular job or project of the managers. With that proviso, following is a list of possible strategies and the ways they can be used to develop leadership skills:		
Strategy	**Gap Addressed**	**Example**
Degree or credential program	Education	Department head completing master's in Public Administration
Intact training for management team	More than one employee has gap in specific area	Management team receives training in Performance Appraisal process
Special project, team assignment	Teamwork skills; Analysis; Visibility; Exposure to new people; Diversity awareness	Critical Issues Team Member
Assignments in new location	Exposure to special location or culture	Sheriff Captain in Jail East working at Jail West
Cross training	Exposure to management skills and knowledge of lateral manager in different division	Recreation Center supervisor training with History and Special Program supervisor
Leadership internships	In depth how-to's of leadership position outside regular area of influence	Department head working as deputy county manager for specified length of time

(continued)

Table 19-16: Examples of Developmental Strategies for Leaders *(concluded)*

Strategy	Gap Addressed	Example
Informal mentoring	Specific developmental areas	Feedback immediately following public meeting on employee's handling of public's questions
Individual short-term assignments	Specific developmental areas	Employee takes over budget-review process
External leadership experience	Exposure to outside groups for competency in higher level position	Police major being involved in state police function(s) and/or training
Human Resources-sponsored training	When specific competencies need to be developed	Employee meets with manager, discusses gaps, and reviews training catalog courses in this area. After training, they meet again to discuss how to apply learning in specific job setting
Formal mentoring	Special skill; management style	Employee paired with another manager for job shadowing to learn team-building skills from manager with style worth emulating.

Table 19-17

Succession Management Evaluation Form

Reporting Period: _____ Due Date: _____

Completed by: (name) _____ Title: _____

Section A: List all managers directly reporting to you. Then for each employee, indicate the *developmental activities that have been completed during the reporting period.* Copy and use additional pages as necessary.

Employee/ Position	Skill being developed	Developmental activity	Result of development

Section B: List your *goals for the next year* regarding development of managers directly reporting to you.

Employee	Developmental goal	Developmental strategy

(continued)

Table 19-17: Succession Management Evaluation Form *(concluded)*

Section C: *(To be completed only by Department Heads or above)*

Has a vacancy of a key position (County Manager, Deputy County Manager, Department Head, Assistant Department Head, or Middle Manager) in your area(s) of responsibility occurred during this report period?   Yes _____   No _____

Title of vacant position(s):   _____   _____   _____

Name of selected candidate: _____   _____   _____

The selected candidate was: Internal _____   External _____

List all internal candidates:

Name:	Title:	Vacant position:
_____	_____	_____
_____	_____	_____
_____	_____	_____

List potential internal candidates who did not apply:

Name:	Title:	Vacant position:	Comments:
_____	_____	_____	_____
_____	_____	_____	_____
_____	_____	_____	_____

Contact Information

Interviewer: Jean A. Pulaski
Pennsylvania State University
Milton S. Hershey Medical Center

E-mail: jap418@psu.edu

Interviewee: Sheryn R. Holinsworth
Manager of Employment Development and Training
Human Resources Department of Henrico County, Virginia

E-mail: HOL17@co.henrico.va.us

MANAGING THE COMING BRAIN DRAIN

> *Case Introduction:* This case study describes an effort to preserve institutional and operational knowledge in local government. It was written by Myron Olstein and published in the American Water Works Association Journal in 2005.

In 2003, the Research Advisory Council of the American Waterworks Association (AWWA) Research Foundation (AwwaRF) recognized that the baby boomers were starting to reach retirement age and that this generation would be followed by a generation only about half its size. In addition, the council was concerned about the increasing shortage of engineers. As a result of these observations, AwwaRF decided to fund a study of these and related issues titled "Succession Planning for a Vital Workforce in the Information Age." Shortly after funding was awarded, the Water Environment Research Foundation (WERF), noting that wastewater utilities shared these concerns, elected to co-fund the study.

A survey conducted as part of the succession planning study confirmed the Research Advisory Council's concerns. Findings indicated that 35% of current utility employees will be eligible to retire in 10 years. Attrition rates, currently at 7%, are expected to rise to 8%. Because the people retiring are the most senior employees in the utility, these retirements will result in a serious brain drain and an accompanying loss of institutional knowledge. A study of a similar situation in the electric utility industry estimated that as much as 80% of the useful operating knowledge was "tacit," such as knowledge that is known by users but not documented (EPRI, 2004). In addition to these problems, the survey also identified related concerns. Utilities are becoming more complex, but competent new hires are hard to find. Human resource (HR) managers complain that they are at a disadvantage and are forced to hire from the bottom of the labor pool. Not all the news is bad, however. In every period of major generational changes, opportunities are present. A reduction in staffing because of retirements can allow utilities to "right size" and to rationalize positions and organizational structures. Properly handled, this transition period will be a time when new, improved ideas can be implemented with less resistance from the old guard.

National Demographics Spotlight Future Labor Concerns

A review of national demographic data highlighted some of the trends that will affect every sector of U.S. industry in the coming years. Many of these trends will have significant consequences, especially for water and wastewater providers. Organizations that fail to start planning today for anticipated changes in technology, economy, and society will be hard pressed to meet their strategic goals.

Average age of the workforce is on the rise. In the coming years, a massive retirement wave will have industries scrambling for capable workers. According to the U.S. Department of Labor's Bureau of Labor Statistics (BLS), the average age of the civilian labor force in the United States has been rising steadily since 1990, increasing from an average of just under 38 years of age in 1990 to 40 currently and to more than 41 projected for the year 2020 (BLS, 2002a). The fastest-growing segment of the U.S. workforce consists of individuals over 55, who are expected to represent 20% of the workforce in 2020.

Water and wastewater utility workers tend to be even older than the national average. The survey conducted for the succession planning study indicated that the average age of water utility workers is 44 and that of wastewater utility workers is 45.

The number of available workers is declining. Not only is the average age of the workforce increasing, but the number of workers available to replace retirees is low. The baby boomers (people born from 1946 to 1964) number about 76 million, whereas Generation X (those born between 1965 and 1980) numbers only about 46 million. National demographic data indicate that the labor gap between replacement needs and workers is increasing. The HR field and its executives are understandably concerned about how the work now performed by a large workforce can be accomplished by a smaller labor pool.

Minorities, females, and immigrants in the U.S. workforce are increasing. Minorities (defined by the BLS as Black, Hispanic, and Asian) are forecast to become a larger component of the national workforce, approaching 50% by 2050. The representation of minorities in the utility workforce is slightly higher than in the U.S. workforce as a whole. However, females represent approximately 47% of the U.S. workforce and are estimated to be only 19% of the utility workforce. According to data from other sources, the U.S.-born workforce is declining year to year, and a high level of work-age immigration is resulting in an overall increase in the national workforce.

In summary, the U.S. workforce is getting older and more diverse. Although the utility workforce is both older and slightly more diverse than the U.S. workforce, it is significantly underrepresented in terms of gender diversity.

Water and wastewater utilities will need more workers. According to BLS data, the water supply and sanitary industries (including wastewater, irrigation, and sanitary services) will experience the greatest amount of employment growth. This growth rate is projected to be 45% within the public utilities industry between 2000 and 2010. A number of factors are driving the need for more water and wastewater utility workers.

- Stricter regulatory standards will force water supply and sanitation services to acquire more equipment and people in order to meet higher measures of environmental compliance.

- As noted at the 2003 AWWA Water Security Congress, securing water sources and treatment facilities from bioterrorism and sabotage has emerged as a new responsibility for water providers.

- Population growth, especially as it relates to areas experiencing increasing numbers of new housing developments, requires the expansion of both water and wastewater services.

- At the same time, national data trends indicate that many of the needed skills for the water and wastewater industry will be in short supply. Engineers will be increasingly difficult to attract because of short supply and competition from private technology firms. In general, skilled labor shortages will continue (BES, 2002b).

Water and Wastewater Utilities Surveyed

Additional data spotlighting workforce trends in the utility sector were obtained from two surveys conducted in conjunction with the succession planning study. The first survey questioned more than 400 individuals who had recently retired from positions at water or wastewater utilities. The second survey focused on retirement trends from the utility perspective. Many utility workers retire as soon as they are eligible. The survey of recent retirees confirmed anecdotal information that had surfaced during discussions with utility HR personnel. They had reported that most utility employees tend to retire soon after reaching eligibility. Most utility retirement plans allow for retirement at age 55 with an appropriate number of years of service. The average age of the recent retirees is slightly more than 56 years of age. Another important survey finding was that the number of years of service with the same utility was more than 24. The utility survey included mostly medium and large utilities. An advisory group composed of utility executives helped frame and review the utility survey. The survey was sent to the 400 largest utilities in the Water\Stats database, the 160 WERF members, and 10 additional organizations. Of these 570 utilities, 126 responded. This sample was somewhat biased toward medium and large utilities. Aside from the relative absence of small utilities, however, the survey pool was fairly representative in terms of geography, scope of service, and governance.

Survey results included the following findings:

- Utility baseline attrition rates, which have been running at 7% per year, are expected to climb to 8%.
- Potential retirements in five years (weighted) are expected to total 22% of the current utility workforce.
- Potential retirements in 10 years (weighted) are forecast at 35%.
- Nearly three quarters of responding utilities (74%) reported having no plan for dealing with retirements (although 9% of respondents claimed to be working on such a plan).
- For those utilities that did have a plan for dealing with retirements, the most common approach involved training.
- Median training hours per full-time equivalent employee per year were fewer than 20.

- Some positions, e.g., operators, field maintenance workers, and first/front-line supervisors, were being vacated at twice the rate of other positions.
- Utilities reported that the positions most difficult to replace were managers, operators, and first/frontline supervisors. Some of these are the same positions being vacated at high rates.
- The survey also tackled a number of topics, including early retirement programs, merit pay, reasons for difficulties in replacing employees, barriers to succession, and leadership planning. In addition, when utilities were asked to rate their level of technology, only a third of respondents ranked their level of technology as "high."

Workforce Planning Can Help Utilities Manage Transition

The advisory group of utility executives met twice to discuss the issues confronting the industry. Also in attendance at these sessions were representatives from George Mason University (Va.); the University of Kansas; the National Center for Construction Education and Research (Fla.); and the American Federation of State, County, and Municipal Employees (Washington, D.C.).

Members of the advisory group discussed the various aspects of succession planning from their own perspectives. Local governments owned all of the utilities in the advisory group, and members felt that government rules made certain aspects of succession planning difficult. To help address these concerns, the advisory group advocated an integrated approach to workforce planning specifically designed for utilities.

Workforce Planning Defined

According to the International Personnel Management Association (IPMA), "Workforce planning is the strategic alignment of an organization's human capital with its business direction. It is a methodical process of analyzing the current workforce, identifying future workforce needs, establishing the gap between the present and future, and implementing solutions so the organization can accomplish its mission, goals, and objectives." (IPMA, 2002)

Workforce planning offers a process that integrates long-term strategic planning with a review of an organization's work and human capital. It gives employers the tools they need to anticipate demographic changes and prepare accordingly to continue to meet strategic goals. A workforce plan can help an organization inventory its current knowledge, skills, and abilities; determine how these elements fit into its long-term work plan; and identify gaps in its ability to meet future obligations and conditions.

A comprehensive workforce plan outlines resources needed, such as training or acquiring personnel with the specific skills that the organization currently lacks. The aspect of workforce planning of greatest importance to both management and HR personnel is the ability to maintain a predictable or manageable flow of talent despite the challenges created by external and internal forces.

External and internal forces will always influence an organization's strategic direction and the human resources needed to achieve goals. Through the workforce planning process, an organization periodically evaluates the effect of these forces on its strategic goals and develops a plan of how to proceed under different potential conditions. Ultimately, the workforce planning process should lead to an action plan to secure the appropriate human resources to meet anticipated changes in technology, economy, and society.

Workforce planning involves three approaches. Workforce planning is not a static process. A workforce plan is a model for future decisions and should be reviewed periodically to ensure that it still fits with the organization's environment and strategic goals. Because strategic planning greatly influences the development of a workforce plan, the workforce planning process should be integrated with the organization's strategic planning process whenever possible.

There are three approaches to workforce planning: workforce, workload, and competency. Usually a combination of the approaches is used to develop a comprehensive workforce planning model for an organization.

Under the workforce approach, the organization examines its current workforce and occupations and projects the number and characteristics of jobs and the number of employees needed to fill them at a specific point in the future. To determine workload needs, the organization defines the amount and type of work it anticipates handling at a specific point in the future and uses this information to project the number of resources (people and skills) needed to perform that work. Under the competency approach, the organization identifies sets of competencies aligned with its mission, vision, and strategic goals. The competency approach assumes that the organization has already considered workforce and workload and can focus not only on the number of people but also on the competencies employees must master for organizational success.

Each of these approaches involves different types of data that can help determine the preferred approach for a given utility.

Workforce planning responsibilities are shared. Although the HR department plays a major role in workforce planning, personnel throughout the organization must participate and help guide the process if it is to succeed. A model to guide the process is divided into four areas.

Step 1: *Scan.* In this first step, the utility begins by assessing strengths, weaknesses, opportunities, and threats. For utilities, a common strength is that they tend to be good places to work (e.g., the survey of recent retirees indicated that many had been with their utility for 24 or more years). In addition, utilities have competitive retirement offerings (e.g., three out of four utilities still have defined-benefit retirement plans). For government-owned utilities, one weakness is that government ownership places limits on the competitiveness of starting salaries and succession and leadership planning.

Next, the utility scans the environment to identify external and internal forces that will affect its goals and operations. These forces include increases in retirements and attrition levels over the next 10 years, difficulties in replacing engineers, and the gender diversity gap. The utility may need to revise its strategic plan to accommodate these factors. However, the succession planning survey indicated that most utilities don't have a workforce plan or are relying on training that is at low levels. In reality, half of the utilities train less than 20 hours per full-time equivalent (utility wide), and the median value is 20 hours. Not only is this very little training, but if the rules on safety training are followed, those alone should account for 20 hours per year (bi-weekly sessions are required).

Step 2: *Assess Supply and Demand.* For utilities, the workforce supply picture in the near term is not a rosy one. Most workers are likely to retire shortly after achieving eligibility. An additional 35% can retire in 10 years, and attrition is expected to go up to 8%. As for workload demand, the BLS has forecast a significant increase in demand for utility workers because of growth and increasing levels of regulations.

The next step also entails an assessment of skills and competencies. The competency levels needed in the utility workforce are likely to increase as utilities become more automated. Utility survey results indicated that only one third of utilities currently rank themselves as "high tech."

Step 3: *Optimize.* To meet the challenges of the changing workforce, utilities must "right size"—that is, be as streamlined as possible while maintaining efficient operation. Today's utilities can establish benchmarks based on data and performance measures that are much more readily available than they were previously. With higher levels of retirement and nonretirement attrition in the coming decade, utilities need to identify desired target staffing levels now.

Utilities must also identify staff excesses and deficits. Although setting target staffing levels is useful, the utility must also identify the practices that need to be implemented to support efficient staffing levels. As utilities right size, each position should be analyzed to see if it is needed (50% of utilities report that they conduct regular position assessments), and the organizational structure should be evaluated to ensure that it supports a right sized utility and optimized operation.

Step 4: *Act.* Given the workforce environment utilities will face in the coming years, the ability to recruit and retain leadership is even more important. Some 45% of utilities report difficulty in replacing employees, and 25% believe that governmental rules limit succession planning options. Management and training are also key elements in creating a topnotch workforce. Nearly 74% of utilities do not have a succession plan, and only 21% have mandatory training of more than 20 hours per year.

Through effective knowledge management, utilities can help ensure that institutional and operational knowledge is not lost as workers retire or move to other industry sectors. The research institute investigating succession planning in the electric utility industry estimated that more than 80% of useful operating knowledge is tacit—generally understood, but not documented (EPRI, 2004). Utilities also rely heavily on their operations and maintenance (O&M) manuals, with 75% reporting that the manual constitutes their documentation of operating procedures. The following section highlights strategies for successfully managing a utility's institutional and operational knowledge.

Knowledge Capture Safeguards Tacit Knowledge

During the succession planning study, one issue that came up time after time was the loss of tacit knowledge that would accompany the imminent wave of retirements. Tacit knowledge is employee know-how that is not documented and, in most cases, not verbally transferred. Given the length of time that many utility workers work together and utility reliance on O&M manuals as the source of procedures, it is reasonable to estimate that 80% of useful operating know-how is tacit knowledge. In addition to a standardized approach to knowledge management, utilities need a method of knowledge capture—a way to identify and document tacit knowledge within a short time frame. Furthermore, utilities require a methodology unique to their operations and circumstances. Whereas classical knowledge management techniques recommend ignoring infrequent activities when capturing knowledge, utilities face the challenge of infrequent events (such as floods and other natural disasters) that are important but not likely to be well documented.

Utility methodology was pilot tested. A methodology was developed and pilot-tested at the Frederick County Sanitation Authority (FCSA), a water and wastewater utility in northwest Virginia. The first step was identification of all O&M processes. A process was defined according to the classic definition used in re-engineering: a group of tasks that has a beginning and an end, a single owner, and typically, suppliers and customers. Approximately 600 processes in water and wastewater O&M were identified; it was estimated that if all administrative, financial, and customer-related activities were included, the total number of processes for a combined water and wastewater utility would reach 1,000.

Processes were ranked according to risk, using a three-component approach: (1) level of documentation, (2) likelihood of a problem escalating if not corrected early, and (3) effects across processes (i.e., the extent to which a problem in the process affected other operations). The top 10 processes were then mapped by groups of four to six people. The teams were a mixture of owners and customers and of varying ages. The older, more experienced people described how the processes were carried out, and through their participation, the younger people were thereby trained. As the knowledge involved in successful process completion was identified, the level of documentation of that knowledge was noted to create a knowledge process map. Steps were also taken to make some processes more efficient. Important tacit knowledge was targeted for documentation either as standard operating procedure or through other knowledge management techniques.

This pilot effort highlighted why it was important to develop a special methodology for knowledge capture in utilities. One process that scored high on risk was flood conditions. At the time of the pilot program, the last flood that FCSA dealt with had occurred more than 20 years previously—too long ago for classic knowledge management techniques to label it as important. However, because of the high risks associated with flooding, the process was mapped during the pilot project. One month after the pilot exercise, Hurricane Isabel tore through northern Virginia. According to FCSA Director Wendy Jones (2004), having the utility response to flooding fully mapped was invaluable during the crisis. "My expectations were that we would have a method to capture information gained through the experience of retiring employees. What we got was a method to capture employee knowledge gained through experience, criteria for prioritizing processes, and a way to drill down to find the critical areas of the processes to document." Jones cited other benefits of the knowledge-capture process, including:

- identification of problem areas, bottlenecks, and non-value-added work
- increased understanding of critical tasks
- an excellent training tool
- a method to communicate with employees and obtain their feedback
- improvement of FCSA efficiency and effectiveness

For FCSA, the knowledge-capture process proved most beneficial in mapping operations that occurred infrequently; securing knowledge in processes and areas in which information and know-how were held by one individual; understanding what, how, and why others perform their work; and identifying the critical tasks of a process. Since the facilitated pilot program, FCSA has successfully continued conducting knowledge capture on its own.

Summary

A joint study funded by AwwaRF and WERF confirmed that the water and wastewater utility sector will shortly face the loss of experienced workers (and their institutional knowledge) and may have difficulty hiring competent replacement personnel. One way that utilities can properly manage this transition is by implementing workforce planning. This process can aid in planning short- and long-term staffing needs, identifying the external and internal forces that influence an organization's strategic direction, and developing an action plan to ensure that the appropriate human resources are on board to meet anticipated changes. In addition, knowledge capture can play an important role in ensuring that operational and institutional know-how is not lost as employees retire or move to other industries.

Challenges and opportunities go hand-in-hand. Although the coming generational change presents some daunting challenges, it also affords utilities an opportunity to become right-sized, efficient, effective organizations. Utility executives, line managers, and HR personnel must work together to effect this transition and provide the leadership that will enable their organizations to successfully navigate these developments.

The study included other components. The succession planning study group analyzed demographic data to identify trends, surveyed recent retirees and utilities, developed and pilot-tested a workforce planning model designed specifically for water and wastewater utilities, and developed and pilot-tested a knowledge-capture approach tailored to utilities. In addition:

- The study led to an approach to developing training programs, which was demonstrated at two utilities: one for water operators, and one for wastewater operators.

- The study group developed a knowledge management toolkit based on the "circle of knowledge" approach to facilitate incorporation of knowledge management techniques into utility management and operation.
- The study group created additional modules addressing O&M skill sets, merit pay, strategies for becoming an "employer of choice," and other topics.

When published, the project report for the "Succession Planning for a Vital Workforce in the Information Age" study will provide a complete summary of study components and offer HR personnel and utility executives valuable strategies for managing the future brain drain.

Source: Olstein, M. (2005). Managing the coming brain drain. *American Water Works Association Journal, 97*(6), 60–8. Reprinted with permission.

AFTERWORD

Cases in Government Succession Planning has focused on government succession planning at the international, U.S. federal, U.S. state, and U.S. local levels. It is the only volume in print that does so. Some cases were originally published from other sources and some were commissioned especially for this volume. Each shares a common focus: how to recruit, develop, and retain government workers at a time when a tidal wave of retirements in government has already begun.

Succession planning in government is a front-burner issue for many government leaders. In the wake of cost reductions and reductions in force, government leaders are finding it difficult to build a compelling case for investing in the government workforce. It is tough to make the sale for it to citizens. When times are good, citizens would rather focus on ways to cut taxes or hold the line on spending. When times are bad, citizens would rather focus on ways to sustain public services as tax revenues fall. Either way, it is not easy to build enthusiasm and find the funding for succession planning initiatives. Yet without it, there is a very real risk that government services will not be adequately sustained in the future.

What conclusions can be drawn from the cases in this book?

First, those government entities that make an effort to plan for succession and to develop their workforces are better positioned to ride out the wave of retirements than those that do not.

Second, there are a range of effective strategies. There is no such thing as a "cookie cutter" approach. The best strategy is likely to be the one that can be defended in political settings and acted on in cool, rational ways.

Third, elected officials and career professionals in government must have a stake in succession efforts if they are to work. Elected officials control the resources, but career professionals possess the valuable institutional memory of why government does what it does—and what laws, rules, and regulations might be broken if shortcuts are taken.

What does the future hold in store?

At the time this book goes to press, the future for government succession planning looks bleak. Some government entities are reeling from a three-fold onslaught of hiring freezes, reductions in force, and early-retirement offers to save governments money. For some political leaders, the solution is to outsource or privatize government services, and to sometimes do so without retaining the wisdom of oversight within the agencies that are contracting for the outsourcing or privatized work. That approach might be planting the seeds of future scandals: ill-informed contractors hired to do work that isn't done properly and according to law open the door to poor service, accidents, expensive litigation, and other serious consequences. Only if government develops its workers and plans for the future can it avoid such scandals.

APPENDIX

SUCCESSION FACTOR CHECKLIST FOR AGENCY WORKFORCE PLANNING

Introduction

It is easy to get lost in trying to decide what should be in a government workforce planning program. A good place to start is the U.S. government's scorecard used to grade the Human Capital Management programs of U.S. federal government agencies. Use this checklist as a starting point to guide your thinking in what your government agency should have in place. It can also be used as a scorecard to assess the case studies you read in this book.

Directions: For each item listed in the left column below, indicate "yes" or "no" in the middle column. Then, in the right column, make notes about what to do to improve any items rated "no."

	Does the agency:	Yes ✓	No ✓	What should be done to convert any "no" to a "yes"?
1	Approach workforce planning strategically?	❏	❏	
2	Approach workforce planning strategically and in an explicit, documented manner?	❏	❏	
3	Link the workforce plan directly to the agency's strategic and annual performance plans?	❏	❏	
4	Use the workforce plan to make decisions about structuring and deploying the workforce?	❏	❏	

(continued)

Success Factor Checklist for Agency Workforce Planning *(concluded)*

Does the agency:		Yes ✓	No ✓	What should be done to convert any "no" to a "yes"?
5	Identify and document mission-critical occupations and competencies, providing a baseline of information for the agency to develop strategies to recruit, develop, and retain talent needed for program performance?	❑	❑	
6	Does the agency have a documented workforce plan that identifies current and future workforce competencies in order to close identified competency gaps? If yes, which gap reduction strategies are used?	❑	❑	
	Restructuring	❑	❑	
	Recruitment	❑	❑	
	Competitive sourcing	❑	❑	
	Redemployement	❑	❑	
	Retraining	❑	❑	
	Retention	❑	❑	
	Technology solutions	❑	❑	
7	Does the agency implement a business forecasting process that identifies probable workforce changes, enabling agency leadership to anticipate changes to human capital that require action to ensure program performance?	❑	❑	
8	Does the agency appropriately structure its work based on functional analyses, allowing the right mix and distribution of the workforce to best support the agency mission?	❑	❑	
9	Does the agency achieve the right balance of supervisory and non-supervisory positions to support the agency's mission, based on analysis of customer needs and workload distribution?	❑	❑	

Based on the U.S. Office of Personnel Management's Success Criteria
(https://www.opm.gov/hcaaf_resource_center/3-4.asp)

WEB SITES TO SUPPORT GOVERNMENT DECISION MAKERS IN TALENT MANAGEMENT, SUCCESSION PLANNING, AND HUMAN CAPITAL MANAGEMENT

Selected international Web sites

South Australia—Local Government

http://www.lga.sa.gov.au/webdata/resources/Files/Workforce_Planning_for_Local_Government Report___LGA_2002_pdf1.pdf

South Australia Planning Guide

http://www.ope.sa.gov.au/ref_docs/SUPP07.PDF

UK Government—Home Office

http://www.drugs.gov.uk/drug-strategy/workforce-planning/

Scotland—National Health Service

http://www.scotland.gov.uk/News/Releases/2006/12/18133942

Selected U. S. state and federal government agencies

Selected U.S. government links

U.S. Department of the Interior Workforce Planning Manual
http://www.doi.gov/hrm/WFPIMappendix.html#APPENDIX%20A

Building Successful Organizations—Workforce Planning in HHS
http://www.hhs.gov/ohr/workforce/wfpguide.html

Workforce Planning Guide. U.S. Department of Transportation
http://dothr.ost.dot.gov/HR_Programs/Workforce_Planning/workforce_planning
.html

U.S. Office of Personnel Management
https://www.opm.gov/hcaaf_resource_center/3-4.asp

Selected state government links

California
http://onestep.on.ca/whatsnew/successionplanningbiblio.cfm

Colorado
http://www.colorado.gov/dpa/dhr/workforce/docs/workforcereportFY02-03.pdf

Georgia
http://www.gms.state.ga.us/agencyservices/wfplanning/index.asp

Kansas
http://www.da.state.ks.us/ps/

Minnesota
http://www.doer.state.mn.us/wfplanning/relatedlinks.htm

New York
https://www.cs.state.ny.us/successionplanning/index.cfm

Pennsylvania
http://www.hrm.state.pa.us/oahrm/cwp/view.asp?a=135&Q=125177&PM=1

South Carolina

http://www.ohr.sc.gov/OHR/wfplan/wfplan-home2.htm

Texas

http://www.hr.state.tx.us/workforce/workforceplanning.html

Virginia

http://www.dpt.state.va.us/workforceplanning.html

Washington

http://www.wa.gov/dop/workforceplanning/index.htm

Wisconsin

http://workforceplanning.wi.gov/

Note: This list is not intended to be exhaustive. Rather, it is intended to give you a place to continue investigating the topic of succession planning.

TABLE OF CONTENTS FOR THE RESOURCES ON THE CD-ROM

RECOMMENDED RESOURCES

Ackerman, M., V. Pipek, and V. Wulf (eds.). (2003). *Sharing Expertise: Beyond Knowledge Management.* Cambridge, MA: The MIT Press.

Baker, M. (2000). The knowledge people. *The British Journal of Administrative Management* (19), 18.

Bresnen, M., L. Edelman, S. Newell, H. Scarbrough, and J. Swan. (2003). Social practices and the management of knowledge in project environments. *International Journal of Project Management, 21*(3), 157.

Brown, J. S., and P. Duguid. (1998). Organizing knowledge. *California Management Review, 40*(3), 90.

Davenport, T. H., and L. Prusak. (2000). *Working Knowledge: How Organizations Manage What They Know.* Boston: Harvard Business School Press.

Dubois, D., and W. Rothwell. (2000). *The Competency Toolkit.* 2 vols. Amherst, MA: HRD Press.

Dubois, D., and W. Rothwell. (2004). *Competency-Based Human Resource Management.* Palo Alto, CA: Davies-Black Publishing.

George, T. (2003). Educational advantage. *Information Week* (930), 57.

Goldsmith, M., H. Morgan, and A. J. Ogg (eds.). (2004). *Leading Organizational Learning: Harnessing the Power of Knowledge.* San Francisco: Jossey-Bass.

Krogh, G. V., K. Ichijo, and I. Nonaka. (2000). *Enabling Knowledge Creation.* New York: Oxford University Press, Inc.

Lengnick-Hall, M. L., and C. A. Lengnick-Hall. (2003). *Human Resource Management in the Knowledge Economy.* San Francisco: Berrett-Koehler Publishers, Inc.

Nonaka, I., and H. Takeuchi. (1995). *The Knowledge-Creating Company: How Japanese Companies Create the Dynamics of Innovation.* New York: Oxford University Press, Inc.

Norton, R. (1997). *DACUM Handbook.* 2nd ed. Columbus, OH: The National Center for Research in Vocational Education.

Olstein, M. (2004). The coming utility brain drain and what it means to young professionals. *American Water Works Association Journal, 96*(2), 43.

Orr, J. (1996). *Talking About Machines: An Ethnography of the Modern Job.* Ithaca, NY: ILR Press/Cornell University Press.

Polanyi, M. J. (1966). *The Tacit Dimension.* Gloucester, MA: Doubleday & Co. Inc.

Rothwell, W. (ed.). (2000a). *Effective Succession Management: Building Winning Systems for Identifying and Developing Key Talent.* Lexington, MA: The Center for Organizational Research.

Rothwell, W. (2000b). *Effective Succession Planning: Ensuring Leadership Continuity and Building Talent from Within.* 2nd ed. New York: Amacom.

Rothwell, W., and H. Kazanas. (2004). *Improving On-the-Job Training: How to Establish and Operate a Comprehensive OJT Program.* 2nd ed. San Francisco: Pfeiffer.

Schindler, M., and M. J. Eppler. (2003). Harvesting project knowledge: A review of project learning methods and success factors. *International Journal of Project Management, 21*(3), 219–228.

Smeltzer, J. and D. Bonello. (2004). Building the foundation for knowledge management. *Chief Learning Officer, 3*(6), 20–25.

Sveiby, K. E. (1996). Transfer of knowledge and the information processing professions. *European Management Journal, 14*(4), 379–388.

ABOUT THE EDITORS

William J. Rothwell is a professor of Workforce Education and Development in the Department of Learning and Performance Systems at Pennsylvania State University. He holds a Ph.D. in Education/Training and life accreditation as a Senior Professional in Human Resources, and is a Registered Organization Development Consultant with his own private consulting firm. He served as director of human resource development in the public and private sectors before entering academe, managing, planning, designing, and evaluating training, HR, and organization development programs.

A prolific author known for his work on succession planning and talent management, William Rothwell's most recent books include *Instructor Excellence: Mastering the Delivery of Training,* with B. Powers (2nd edition 2007); *What CEOs Expect from Corporate Training,* with J. Lindholm and W. Wallick (2007); and *Competency-Based Human Resource Management,* with D. Dubois (2007).

Contact information: William J. Rothwell
Workforce Education and Development
The Pennsylvania State University
305A Keller Building
University Park, PA 16802
Phone: (814) 863-2581
Fax: (814) 863-7532
E-mail: wjr9@psu.edu

James Alexander has more than 20 years of experience in the fields of change management, strategic planning and implementation, and training in the public and the private sectors. Currently an internal consultant with the U.S. Department of Agriculture's Food Safety Inspection Service, he holds a master's degree in Management of Social and Human Systems and is a graduate of Georgetown University's Organization Development Program. He has most recently been studying the effectiveness of human capital development and knowledge transfer initiatives in the United States and abroad.

Contact information: James Alexander
710 Roeder Road
Silver Spring, MD 20910
Phone: (301) 578-1695
E-mail: halex8420874@yahoo.com

Mark Bernhard is the director of Continuing and Professional Education at Virginia Tech University, supervising faculty collaborations with the university's colleges, centers, and institutes to develop lifelong learning programs. He was formerly a senior conference planner at Penn State, and served as project director for a national economic-development summit. Prior to that, he spent several years working in the trade-association field. His current professional focus and the subject of his Ph.D. dissertation is on factors influencing a college graduate's decision to either stay with or leave an employer—commonly referred to as "brain drain."

Contact information: Mark Bernhard
Director, Continuing and Professional Education
702 University City Boulevard (0364)
Virginia Tech University
Blacksburg, VA 24061
Phone: (540) 231-4682
Fax: (540) 231-9886
E-mail: mcb7@vt.edu